The British Presence in Macau, 1635–1793

Royal Asiatic Society Books

The Royal Asiatic Society was founded in 1823 "for the investigation of subjects connected with, and for the encouragement of science, literature and the arts in relation to, Asia". Informed by these goals, the policy of the Society's Editorial Board is to make available in appropriate formats the results of original research in the humanities and social sciences having to do with Asia, defined in the broadest geographical and cultural sense and up to the present day.

Royal Asiatic Society Books:
Ibrahim Pasha of Egypt Series

The Royal Asiatic Society's Ibrahim Pasha of Egypt Fund, established in 2001 by Princess Fazilé Ibrahim, encourages the growth and development of Ottoman studies internationally by publishing Ottoman documents and manuscripts of historical importance from the classical period up to 1839, with transliteration, full or part translation and scholarly commentaries.

The British Presence in Macau, 1635–1793

Rogério Miguel Puga

Translated by Monica Andrade

ROYAL ASIATIC SOCIETY BOOKS

香港大學出版社
HONG KONG UNIVERSITY PRESS

UNIVERSIDADE DE MACAU
UNIVERSITY OF MACAU

Hong Kong University Press
The University of Hong Kong
Pokfulam Road
Hong Kong
www.hkupress.org

ISBN 978-988-8139-79-8 (*Hardback*)

Originally published in Portuguese in 2009 by Centro de História de Alem-Mar (CHAM), FCSH-New University of Lisbon, and by Centro Cultural e Científico de Macau (Lisbon, Portugal) as *A Presença Inglesa e as Relações Anglo-Portuguesas em Macau (1635–1793)*. This English translation has been generously supported by the University of Macau.

British Library Cataloguing-in-Publication Data
A catalogue record for this book is available from the British Library.

10 9 8 7 6 5 4 3 2 1

Printed and bound by Kings Time Printing Press Ltd. in Hong Kong, China

To
my mum, Maria da Conceição Nunes do Deserto de Puga
and
Professor Maria Leonor Machado de Sousa

Contents

Contents

Acknowledgements

Research work always stems from a convergence of individual and institutional endeavours; I therefore wish to thank all my friends and colleagues who contributed to achieving the aims I had set myself while writing this book, thus enriching its outcome. Firstly, my deepest gratitude goes to Professor João Paulo Oliveira e Costa, who, from 2001 to 2004, supervised a research project I carried out on the theme which I treat in this study. This project was made possible, thanks to a grant from the Fundação Oriente (Oriente Foundation), whom I thank for the opportunity afforded me, over a period of three years, to conduct research at the following institutions: the British Library (*India Office Records*), the School of Oriental and African Studies, the Institute of Historical Research, (University of London), the Wellcome Library, the University of Cambridge, the Public Record Office, and the National Maritime Museum, Greenwich. I am also indebted to the Luso-American Foundation for its financial support, which enabled me to carry out research at the Library of Congress, Washington, DC, at the Massachusetts Historical Society (Boston), and at the New York Historical Society, in 2005.

At a personal level, many individuals contributed towards the making of this book: Jin Guoping; Professor António Martins do Vale, who supplied several references to the British in Portuguese sources regarding Macau during the first stage of my research; Professors Maria Leonor Machado de Sousa, Leonor Carvalhão Buescu, and João Paulo Ascenso Pereira da Silva, whose encouragement and knowledge of travel writing of British and Portuguese travellers have left an indelible mark on my academic career. My thanks also go to Isilda, Francisco, and Gabriel Cunha, whose friendship made me feel most welcome during the many, long weeks I spent sharing their home in London. I also thank Monica Andrade for translating this book into English, and the University of Macau for funding the translation. At Hong Kong University Press, I would like to thank former publisher Colin Day, publisher Michael Duckworth, associate publisher Christopher Munn, and managing editor Clara Ho. At the University of Macau, I would like to thank Professor Rui Martins and Dr Raymond Wong for their continued support.

I also wish to thank the staff and management at the different institutions I consulted frequently, among which: the Macau Historical Archives, the Arquivo Histórico Ultramarino (Portuguese Overseas Historical Archive), the Arquivo Nacional da Torre do Tombo (Portuguese National Archives), the Scientific and Cultural Centre of Macau in Lisbon, the Portuguese National Library, the Lisbon Geographical Society, the British Library, the Wellcome Library, the Public Record Office, the Hong Kong University Library, the School of Oriental and African Studies Library, the Caird Library at the National Maritime Museum, and the libraries of the Universities of Cambridge and of London (Senate House).

Abbreviations and acronyms

ADM   *Admiralty* (Public Record Office, London)

AHG   Arquivo Histórico de Goa (Historical Archive of Goa)

AHM   Arquivo Histórico de Macau, Macau (Macau Historical Archives, Macau)

AHU   Arquivo Histórico Ultramarino, Lisbon (Overseas Historical Archive)

AM   *Arquivos de Macau* (*Macau Archives*)

AN/TT   Arquivo Nacional da Torre do Tombo, Lisbon (Portuguese National Archives)

BA   Biblioteca da Ajuda, Lisbon (Ajuda Library)

BL   British Library, London

BL-IOR   British Library/India Office Records

BNP   Biblioteca Nacional de Portugal (National Library of Portugal)

ch.   chapter

cod.   codex/codices

CSP   *Calendar of State Papers Colonial*

doc./docs.   document/documents

EIC   East India Company

fl./fls.   folio/folios

FO   Foreign Office, London (Public Record Office)

FUP   Filmoteca Ultramarina Portuguesa, Lisbon [Portuguese Overseas Film Library]

Mans.	*Liv. Manuscritos da Livraria* (Portuguese National Library, Lisbon)
PRO	Public Record Office, London
SP	*State Papers* (Public Record Office, London)

Introduction

The Marchandy also of Portugal
By divers lands turne into sale.
Portugalers with us have trouth in hand:
Whose Marchandy commeth much into England.
They ben our friends, with their commodities,
And wee English passen into their countrees.

> "Libel of English policie, exhorting all England to keepe the sea"
> [c.1436], in Richard Hakluyt, *Voyages in Eight Volumes*,
> vol. 1, 1962, p. 178

This study sets out to present a history of the British presence, at first in the Indian Ocean, pursuing the Portuguese route, and later, in the Far East, in Macau, from 1635 to 1793, as also in Japan (Hirado) from 1613 to 1623, from where the English attempted unsuccessfully to set up direct trade links with China. The British presence in Macau stemmed from Elizabethan interest in Portuguese profit-making in the East Indies, and began with the arrival in 1635 of the first English vessel, the *London*, in Macau. I end my study with the year 1793, the date of the first British embassy to China led by Lord Macartney, which constituted Britain's first, albeit diplomatically fruitless, attempt to institutionalise relations between the two countries. I therefore present the most representative episodes of the first two hundred years of the British presence in Macau, a presence which has left its mark, still visible today, on the humanised face of the city, notably in the ancient Protestant cemetery and chapel. In both Portuguese and Anglophone documents, mainly those of the nineteenth century, references were made to other British haunts in the city, notably the English Tavern (Hotel),[1] the British Museum (the first museum to open its doors in China, 1829–1834, as I have recently shown)[2] and the East India Company (EIC) Library.[3] Even before the English started to send trading expeditions to Amoy and to Formosa, travelling to China meant putting in at the port of Macau, so these two latter place-names became synonymous by a synecdochical process. In fact, Thomas Naish's 1731 report to London advises every vessel en route to Amoy to stop off in the enclave, putting in at Taipa for protection against typhoons and to take in supplies,[4] hence testifying to the strategic value of the City of the Holy Name of God of Macau both for travellers and for British interests in the Far East.

References to Macau in the EIC Records (India Office Records-British Library, IOR) are relatively scant, since, as is known, the China Trade took place in Canton, the main destination for traders, who only lived in the Sino-Portuguese enclave because they were banned from living all year round in the Canton factories. References to episodes in the lives of the British and to their experience of Macau which I found in the IOR cover the periods between the trading seasons (March–September), when the supercargoes remained there. In turn, most English-language studies on the Western presence in Southern China study the British presence in Canton, relegating Macau to a secondary place,[5] for the EIC's supercargoes traded mainly in Canton and, as I have already stated, only resided in the enclave between trading seasons, with the city acting as a "means" to attain a commercial "end". My study thus fills in what has hitherto been a historiographical "vacuum". Over the many years of preparing for this study, previously published in Portuguese as *A Presença Inglesa e as Relações Anglo-Portuguesas em Macau (1635–1793)* (Lisbon, 2009), I published portions of the conclusions of this study in *A World of Euphemism: Representations of Macau in the Work of Austin Coates: City of Broken Promises as a Historical Novel and a Female Bildungsroman* (Calouste Gulbenkian Foundation/ Foundation for Science and Technology, Lisbon, 2009) and in several articles in Portuguese and international journals. These have been listed in the bibliography which concludes the present volume.

Of the documents pertaining to the EIC to be found in the British Library, I consulted the India Office Records, collections R/10 and G/12 (China and Japan, some of the documents are duplicated in both collections). Volumes R/10/3–7 fill the vacuum of documentation in series G/12 for the period from

1754 to 1774. Most of the data contained in these volumes cover economic and trade concerns, that is, the arrival and departure of vessels, their cargoes and the transactions carried out in China. Sporadically, I found data pertaining to the British presence in Macau, including the conflicts between the supercargoes and the Portuguese authorities.

By cross-referencing an ample set of British, Portuguese and (translated) Chinese sources in the Overseas Historical Archive (Arquivo Histórico Ultramarino), the Macau Cultural and Scientific Centre, the Portuguese Library, the National Archive Institute/Torre do Tombo, and the Ajuda Library, in Lisbon, the India Office Records, the Public Record Office, the National Maritime Museum, the School of Oriental and African Studies, in London, and the Macau Historical Archive (Macau), a tri-dimensional image emerged of the British presence in that territory during the seventeenth and eighteenth centuries. I cross-referenced data from European historical sources, with a special focus on the British, Portuguese and, although to a lesser extent, Chinese documents summarised and translated into Portuguese, English and French, opting to use present-day spelling with regard to the manuscripts and keeping the spelling used in the British published documents. The archive material I studied thus allow us to reconstitute both the first fruits of the China Trade and the ensuing growth of British influence in Macau—which became the centre of Chinese control over Westerners—and the relations of the EIC's supercargoes with the Portuguese and Chinese authorities in the second half of the eighteenth century. Given that the trading system and *modus vivendi* of Westerners in Canton and in Macau remained relatively unchanged until the first Opium War and the subsequent founding of Hong Kong, I also consulted travel writing and journals of US and European residents produced in the first half of the nineteenth century, with a view to reconstructing certain dimensions of the day-to-day life of the foreign community residing in Macau.

The early voyages of the EIC to China were the first form of contact between the Macau Portuguese and the EIC's supercargoes, a relation that was governed by trading interests, diplomatic measures taken locally and in Europe, and attempts to obtain financial gain. The study of the British presence in the enclave takes on special importance, for, besides Austin Coates's comprehensive survey, *Macau and the British 1637–1842: Prelude to Kongkong* (1966)—whose sub-title points above all to the events leading up to the founding of the British colony—this is the first academic study exclusively devoted to the British presence in Macau and to the importance of the enclave for the EIC's China Trade. Coates's book proves to be a synthesis on the subject, lacking the critical frame that identifies the sources used, and merely presenting a general bibliography.

By comparing Western and Chinese sources and bibliography (the latter in translation), my research contributes to the study of the beginning and development of Anglo-Portuguese relations in the Far East, especially in Macau, up to 1793, the date of the first British embassy to China. The (failed) embassy, and its consequences, signalled a change in British attitudes to China, increasingly viewed as a stagnated nation in need of reform, with such trading pressure culminating in the Opium War. British descriptions and travel writing, such as George Anson's, began to replace the image of China conveyed by the European Jesuits, which was called into question by such Protestant authors as Oliver Goldsmith, Samuel Johnson, Thomas Perch and John Barrow, who visited the imperial court and became familiar with its workings during the embassy.

It is not my aim to present a history of the EIC trade in China or of diplomatic relations between the Cantonese Mandarinate and overseas traders. Rather, I aim to study Anglo-Portuguese relations in Macau from 1635 until the end of the eighteenth century,[6] and, within the scope of the extension to the Far East of the Anglo-Portuguese alliance, to contribute towards altering the situation described, with a strong nationalistic flavour in 1961, by the Macanese historian, J. M. Braga:

> Histories of this period have given little space to the importance and value of the help rendered to so many foreigners by Macau, for writers on this subject have gone exclusively to accounts by writers using British source material. [...] A Portuguese would like to feel that it might not be forgotten that if there had been no Macau or that if the community there had been less accommodating, although admittedly the Portuguese received benefits from the presence of the foreigners, neither John Henry Cox nor any other of the "interlopers" who contributed to breaking the E.I.C. monopoly, on behalf of the free-trade movement in Britain, would ever have had the opportunity of accomplishing what they did.[7]

The founding of Hong Kong after the first Opium War occurred after 141 years of British presence in Canton, and in Macau during the "summer residence",[8] between the trading seasons, when the Chinese authorities did not permit members of the EIC Select Committee[9] to remain in mainland China. From the eighteenth century onward, the Luso-Chinese enclave gradually became the gateway for Western nations into China and also the spring-board for the lucrative trade which numerous European powers endeavoured to develop and maintain there. British social attitudes to the "Gem of the Orient" were expressed in EIC documents and in comments found in different authors' travel writings which I used as sources to study the representation of Macau in Anglophone China Trade narratives written by male and female residents and visitors. In the main, British historical sources also present a Protestant clashing-gaze both of Macau's familiar European 'façade' and exotic and oriental dimension. This being so, the Anglophone accounts differ from the Portuguese (Roman Catholic) view, while the dialogue between Chinese and Western sources, as well as descriptions of Eastern realities, should be interpreted in the light of the concept of ocularcentrism, a term coined by Grimshaw, to refer to "the relationship between vision and knowledge in Western discourse".[10]

The voyages of the Company's vessels to Macau—both the initially sporadic expeditions, decided by the English factories in the East, and the voyages organised in London—as well as the fruits of these expeditions, at first almost nil, testify to initial lack of interest and the succession of forward and backward movements in English trade in Southern China from the late 1630s, results which were also influenced by Portuguese interests and stratagems. As we shall see, business journeys and the continued EIC presence in the Macau-Canton circuit gave way to a degree of cultural exchange of which Chinese Pidgin English (CPE) is a symbol in China, its European "counterpart" being *chinoiserie*, for, after 1717, British trade in tea gradually overtook Portuguese might in the Guangdong province, and the presence of the supercargoes in the territory became essential for its economy due to the profits it generated.

As signalled by the titles of the seven parts of the *Handbook of Urban Studies* (2001) edited by Ronan Paddison, a city can be read in terms of its economy, environment, eclectic multitude, and organised polity, with this variety of dimensions demanding a pluri-disciplinary approach to that human space. If urban studies advocate the need for cities to be interpreted through a multi-disciplinary approach,[11] the origin and history of Macau demand just such an approach and a multinational gaze to fully understand the development and importance of the multicultural territory which is the object of my study and which was enriched over the centuries not only by its Chinese and Portuguese communities, but also by the Japanese, African, Indian, British, North-American, Armenian, French, and Swedish residents, among other nationalities.

1

Anglo-Portuguese conflicts and the founding of the East India Company

We should share with the Portugall in the East.

—Richard Hakluyt, *Voyages*, vol. 5, p. 116

Euro-Asian relations, determined in part by the European response to societies such as the Chinese and the Japanese, developed slowly, and, as stated by Donald Lach, reflect the feeling which those cultures aroused in Western traveller-writers, as well as the latters' preconceived ideas and tastes.[1] From the end of the sixteenth century, when Macau was enjoying its economic apogee, reports reached England about the enclave and Japan, both in the form of translated Portuguese sources and in the writings of travellers and traders such as the Dutch Dirck Gerritszoon Pomp (1544–1608) and Jan Huygen van Linschotten (1563–1611) who established themselves beyond the Cape of Good Hope, in the Portuguese domains that they would later describe.

The English maritime enterprise clashed early on with Iberian interests, and the first frictions of the fifteenth and sixteenth centuries foreshadow later, more serious conflicts. In the aftermath of English buccaneer raids on Portuguese trade in Africa,[2] King Sebastian put in place measures of trade reprisals against England, decreeing that Portuguese ports should be closed to English vessels and products, namely textiles. Negotiations for an Anglo-Portuguese treaty, which Philip II of Castile, as an enemy of England, did not desire, dragged on until 1576, and in October of that year the Portuguese king and Elizabeth I signed a treaty whereby each nation undertook to return vessels and goods seized before that date, and English traders gained freedom to trade in Portugal.[3]

During the dual monarchy of the Phillips, the Anglo-Portuguese alliance remained "dormant",[4] while a number of expeditions to distant Cathay departed from England, without success, however. In 1553, Sir Hugh Willoughby set sail for the East, but never reached it, and in 1591 three English vessels, one of which under the command of Sir James Lancaster, sailed beyond the Cape of Good Hope to avail themselves of Portuguese trade, as did the same sailor again in 1601, when he travelled to Banten (Java), where the Dutch had been since 1596, and which later became an English factory of strategic importance for the pepper trade. In 1596, the first official expedition to China left England, comprising three vessels (the *Bear*, the *Bear's Whelp* and the *Benjamin*) under the command of Benjamin Wood. This fleet did not, however, reach its destination.[5] In 1602–1604, Sir Edward Michelborne obtained leave to travel to the East, notably to China and Japan, although this initiative bore no fruit.[6]

In Elizabethan England, Richard Hakluyt (1552?–1616) collected, translated and published, in *The Principal Navigations, Voyages and Discoveries of the English Nation* (1589–1600),[7] dozens of European sources, including Portuguese,[8] in which Macau is a tenuous presence, functioning as a symbolic space of origin of the riches and the experiences which Portugal had imported from the Far East. Later, all this information was complemented by the collection published by Samuel Purchas (c.1577–1626), *Hakluytus Posthumus or Purchas His Pilgrims* (1625),[9] in part comprising manuscripts inherited from Hakluyt, which encouraged English traders and investors to venture forth in the wake of Portuguese vessels. All these data on the Asian human and trading realities later became crucial in the clashes between the Portuguese and the English in the Eastern seas and were decisive in weakening the former and in the ensuing upset of the "Carreira da Índia", the Portuguese kingdom being unable to defend its Eastern territories effectively.

From the mid-sixteenth century onward, the English sought alternative routes to those used by the Portuguese to reach the East, and several adventurers attempted to discover passages to China via the Northwest and Northeast.[10] If English corsairs had already been taking Portuguese vessels and invading Portuguese territories, the annexation of Portugal by Spain in 1580 meant that the political reasons which had led England—within the context of the oldest political alliance in the Western world[11]—to respect Portugal now waned.

Attacks on Portuguese ships intensified, carried out by Sir Francis Drake (c.1540–1596), Sir Walter Raleigh (1552?–1618), among other "sea dogs", in an attempt to weaken the Catholic Spanish enemy and demonstrate English naval superiority. The circumnavigations undertaken by Drake (1577–1580) and by Thomas Cavendish (1586–1588), as well as the defeat of the Spanish Armada (1588), proved to England that it could compete on the sea with Phillip II. Similarly, the lucrative Portuguese trade in the Far East drew the attention of the English, especially after the capture of the *Madre de Deus* [Mother of God] in 1592, by Sir John Burrough, off the coast of the Azores. The cargo of the Portuguese vessel stimulated the covetousness of Elizabethan traders, who realised what riches would also be theirs should they upset the Iberian trade monopoly in the East Indies.[12] Approximately four years after the capture of the *Madre de Deus*, and forty years before the first English vessel reached Macau, Laurence Keymis Gent[13] concluded that England could become as powerful as the Iberian Peninsula, putting forward the following arguments in favour of the opening up of the *mare clausum*:

(1) Elizabeth I's nation had the same might, rights and capabilities as the Iberian Peninsula to create new trade networks,

(2) although the Papist Spanish enemy ruled Portugal, each Iberian country was a distinct political entity,[14] as shown by the Portuguese colonies' non-recognition of Philip II's might,

(3) the West Indies, under Spanish rule, were divided and badly governed, which meant they could be easily taken by England, as could the Portuguese fleets which enriched Phillip's coffers.

It was in this context that naval battles were fought between the English fleets and Portuguese territories and ships, and in late December 1600, when the first Dutch vessels appeared on the coast of Macau, Elizabeth I authorised the founding of the Company of Merchants of London, Trading into the East Indies,[15] whose aim it was to begin voyages to the East Indies, with a view to importing consumer goods and exporting English textiles; this event signals the beginning of English expeditions to Asia. Northern European expansion, organised through private initiatives based on shareholder capital, differed from Iberian expansion, and the EIC's instructions for the second voyage advised Henry

Middleton of the precautions he should take en route to the Moluccas, given the "malice of the Portingalls toward our discovery of the trade to those parts".[16] Royal assent for the third voyage advised against conflicts with Iberian vessels in the East, while the directors of the EIC suggested that, with a view to maintaining trade in the face of the threat posed by the Portuguese rivals, factors should ascertain whether the governors of Cambay and Surat were subjects of the king of Portugal and which other ports were not in that position.[17] The arrival of English vessels in Surat, which, starting in 1613, would become the Anglo-Dutch base in the western Indian Ocean,[18] gave rise to clashes with the Portuguese, who took several vessels and led the EIC to address complaints to the authorities in London.[19]

Although England only turned towards the East in the seventeenth century, initial activity and clashes between the English and the Portuguese in the East Indies gave the former ever-greater knowledge of the trading space concerned, and this information gradually replaced what England had learnt indirectly from European, especially Iberian, sources during the sixteenth and early seventeenth centuries.

2

The voyage east: The beginning of Anglo-Portuguese relations in the East Indies

From the earliest English trading days in China; under special permission from the Portuguese, both sides had shown remarkable ingenuity in interpreting the laws to their mutual advantage and in accommodations, without which the trade would have very early died.

—W. E. Cheong, *Mandarins and Merchants: Jardine Matheson & Co*, 1978, p. 5

In 1602, two years before England and Spain signed their Peace Treaty, and in the wake of the Dutch,[1] the English, using their increasing naval military might and diplomatic activity, reached the Indian Ocean, gradually moving towards Macau. The English defied Portugal at the very heart of her empire, India and Persia, and took advantage of the desire of certain indigenous authorities to shake off the Portuguese yoke,[2] of the uprising of terrified indigenous slaves,[3] of the experience of countrymen who had already lived in the East for a number of years, and of certain Portuguese who shared vital information with them.[4]

In 1608, the *Hector* was the first English vessel to reach Surat, while, given the defensive strategy of the Portuguese *Estado da Índia* (Eastern Empire), the French trader François Pyrard de Laval (1578–1621) returned to Europe in February 1610, confessing that he had been accompanied by an Englishman. The viceroy of Goa had made all northern Europeans in India return to Europe, "for they had with them no other intent than to spy and gather information about the land".[5] The same measure would be taken again in 1630 on the orders of Count Linhares.[6] The recently arrived "enem[ies] from Europe",[7] faced with the defensive stance of the Portuguese and the indigenous population, fought for the founding of the EIC factory in Surat in 1612,[8] which, as reported by

António Bocarro (1594?–1642) in 1635, caused concern for the Viceroy of Goa, since he knew that

> one of the main things that could finish [in India] for the Portuguese was this trade and commerce which the English were starting in Surat, from which [...] with great loss to his vassals and even greater [losses] to His Majesty's exchequer, the English took from this port the goods with which they were admitted in every part of the South to pay for drugs, pepper, clove, nutmeg, and many other goods to be found here.[9]

In early 1622, the year in which the Dutch and English attempted in vain to take Macau from the Portuguese, and after several Portuguese attacks on English vessels, as well as Anglo-Portuguese naval battles,[10] the English, in alliance with the Shah of Persia, Abbas, took Ormuz, the most profitable customs house in the Portuguese Eastern Empire. The English thus acquired more and more territory, gained greater self-confidence and power in the East, where the Portuguese held the monopoly in trade, and where, since the Defence Treaty (1619) signed by the two Protestant enemies against the Catholics,[11] the combined English and Dutch fleets "seek to master all shipping activity and trade"[12] and attempt to infiltrate China. In 1627, the director of the Batavia factory, in his conclusions on the factors to be considered when attempting to set up trade with China, stated that the Chinese did not allow foreigners to enter their country.[13]

After successive defeats in naval combats against the English off the coast of Surat and the fall of Ormuz, the Portuguese realised they could not keep the EIC away from Eastern markets. A contributing factor was that English military support was essential both in Portuguese Asia, to resist Dutch attacks and blockades, and in Europe, so that post-1640 Portugal could maintain its independence.

Behind the bamboo curtain: The English in Japan and their attempts to trade directly with China

The origin and initial wealth of the city of Macau were intimately linked to trade with Japan. This trading activity took place annually through the voyage of "Portuguese great ship from Amacau",[14] an activity to which the arrival of the northern European rivals helped put an end in 1639.

From their trading centre in the Hirado factory (1613–1623), the English attempted, albeit in vain, to set up direct trade with China, thus evading control by the Macau Portuguese. The latter, in turn, defended their interests in the Far East, where northern European competition made itself felt with increasing vigour. Before the first contacts and clashes between the English and the Portuguese in Macau, conflict between the two nations' interests flared up in Japan, as will be shown below.

The Portuguese presence in Japan until the coming of their northern European rivals

The *nanbanjin*, or "[Portuguese] barbarians from the South", setting out from Ningbo (1542–1545) and Chincheo (1545–1548) settlements in the Chinese province of Fukien, arrived in Tanegashima, Japan, around 1543. It was through Portuguese descriptions that Renaissance Europe became acquainted with the archipelago.[15]

The history of early Portuguese Macau, haven for the Black Ship, is closely linked to trade with and voyages to Japan.[16] The "discovery" of this archipelago was decisive for the Portuguese decision not to leave the China Sea, as trade-derived profit, the emperor's need for both grey amber and Portuguese weapons, coupled with the Portuguese efficiency in combating piracy, led the Canton officials to authorise Portuguese traders to set themselves up in the enclave, thus consummating the settlement of the Portuguese in the Far East. Over the centuries, the latter acknowledged the need to maintain good relations with Canton and Beijing, with a view to the survival of Macau, a strategy in which, later, the more influential Chinese residents would be vital partners.

The first Portuguese traders realised the advantages and profits involved in exchanging Chinese silk for Japanese silver, since trade between the two countries had been banned by the Chinese emperor. The route between Macau and Nagasaki became permanent in 1571, with cordial relations between the new arrivals and the Japanese from the outset, and the latter city grew both with the Luso-Japanese trade and with evangelisation. In 1580 there were 150,000 Christians in Japan, including members of the ruling class, and the Society of Jesus came to have an influential impact on local society. This meeting of civilisations was filtered through the Japanese "gaze" and represented in Namban art, which bears witness to the arrival of Portuguese traders and clergy in Japan.

With the arrival of the Dutch, and later the English, in Japan in the early seventeenth century, the Portuguese trade monopoly came to an end, and with it the so-called "Christian" or "Namban" century in the Land of the Rising Sun,[17] which began, in a systematic way, in 1549 with the voyage of St. Francis Xavier and the permanent settlement of the Jesuits, and ended in 1640, following the expulsion of all Catholics from Japanese soil. From the Portuguese point of view, the multi-faceted phenomenon of Luso-Japanese relations flows from two contrasting states of mind: the quest for profit by influential traders in Macau with Senate seats and the missionaries' quest to sanctify the souls of the indigenous population—both of which parties were centralised in the enclave. As would also happen during the English attempt to settle in the province of Guangdong, Macau defended its trade interests in Japan with every means at its disposal, for the city's survival also depended on these. It should also be pointed out that even when Portuguese royal surveillance over the trade of the Black Ship increased, the Macau traders attempted to sabotage the interests of the Crown for their own individual gain.[18]

The period of the Portuguese apogee in Japan (1570–1587) was followed by a process of decline in Portuguese influence (1587–1639), which began with the anti-Christian edicts of the late sixteenth century and the arrival of the Dutch rivals in 1600. Toyotomi Hideyoshi, who succeeded Oda Nobunaga in 1582 and centralised the Japanese government and administrative apparatus, feared that the network of missionaries, previously used to influence the population, would turn Christians against the central government and decided to weaken the position of the foreigners by publishing an edict in 1587 which expelled the Jesuits. This edict, though not fully enforced, restricted the movement and influence of Japanese Catholics, which did not immediately affect trade, closely linked as it was to Portuguese evangelisation, but worked as a first warning to Portuguese players in the missionising of Japan.[19] In that year, Macau, dependent on the profits of the Black Ship, sent an embassy to Japan, and there was an improvement in the situation of Christians in the archipelago, who witnessed the arrival of the first traders from northern Europe, notably the Dutch who, from 1601, upset the Macau-Nagasaki route, affecting the life and the economy of the Sino-Portuguese enclave.

Tokugawa Ieyasu succeeded Toyotomi, and in 1606 abdicated in favour of his son, Tokugawa Hidetada, but continued to rule the country until his death in 1616, developing anti-Catholic policies[20] and consolidating his power. As is known, in that same year Hidetada restricted the movements of foreigners to Nagasaki and Hirado.

The English attempts to trade directly with China from Hirado, and the final voyage of the Portuguese Black Ship

> The China Captains which labour to get us entrance into China do tell me that your Worships cannot send a more preciouser thing to present to the Emperour of China then a tree of currall [...]. They say the Portingales of Macau gave a white corrall tree to the Emperour of China many yeares past, w'ch he doth esteem one of the richest jewells he hath. And were it not for hope of trade into China, or for procuring som benefit from Syam, Pattania and (it may be) Cochin China, it were noe staying in Japon.
>
> —"Richard Cocks (Hirado) to the EIC (January 1, 1617)", in Anthony Farrington, *The English Factory in Japan, 1613–1623*, vol. 1, 1991, pp. 562, 564

William Adams (1564–1620), the first English sailor on record as having reached Japan, put in at Bungo on the island of Kyushu in 1600, on board the *Liefde*, a stricken Dutch vessel.[21] He immediately faced the rivalry of the Portuguese Jesuits who placed obstacles to the entry of the Protestant heretics;[22] these were arrested on arrival at the instigation of the Jesuits, who described them to the Japanese as being thieves. Nevertheless, Adams, after his arrest and interrogation, became an adviser to Tokugawa Ieyasu and informed him of the religious division between Catholics and Protestants, and of many other matters concerning Europe, as yet little known in Japan, and he also played an important role in setting up the Dutch (1609) and the English (1613) factories in Hirado. The presence of the heretical *kômôjin*,[23] and of Adams in particular, displeased the Jesuits, for a large part of the Company of Jesus' influence and work as interpreters from then on also fell to the Englishman, who quickly learnt Japanese and whom Tokugawa Ieyasu often consulted. The Jesuits and the Franciscans tried in vain to convert the Englishman to Catholicism, spying as much as they could on the movements of the *Liefde*'s crew. Adams eventually married a second time in Japan, where he died in 1620. The English interpreter and adviser to the emperor also worked as a trade mediator between the Verenigde Oostindische Compagnie (VOC), the EIC and the Japanese court, to the detriment of Iberian interests. The Dutch initially concealed the letters which Adams sent to England through them, since they feared that these would attract northern European competition to the archipelago of the Rising Sun. However, in 1611 Adams sent a letter to the English factory at Banten, at the time headed by Augustine Spalding, in which he described the potential for trade with Japan and provided a summary of what he had observed there over the course of eleven years. In April of the following year, the Englishman Peter Floris, sailing on the *Globe*, arrived in Banten, where he was persuaded to visit Japan via Patan. During the EIC's eighth voyage at the end of October 1612, Captain John Saris, sailing on the *Clove*, paid a second visit to Banten. In early 1613, Saris too travelled to Japan, arriving in June. Four months later, and as a result of mediation by William Adams, the EIC was authorised to open a trading post in Hirado, a "Portuguese" port before the removal to Nagasaki. However, unlike the Portuguese, the English did not have a trading centre on the coast of China, nor, as yet, a solid trade route in the Far East. The EIC finally reached the archipelago, which was already known to the English through Richard Eden, Richard Willes and Richard Hakluyt's translations of Portuguese sources on Japan. The profits of the Black Ship's trade were at once perceived by the English factors, who informed the Company of the movements, cargo and transactions of the "great gallion or ship of Portingalls from Amacau in Chyna".[24] They further advised on its absence in some years and on the transporting of goods on smaller vessels as a means of circumventing the Dutch menace.

The presence of two northern European rivals of the Portuguese in Hirado gave Tokugawa Ieyasu and Japanese traders greater power to negotiate, which affected the Catholics (they too divided among themselves)[25] engaged in evangelising the country and who would now be overtaken in trade by the Protestants. Adams became one of the English factors and defended the interests of the EIC in Hirado, then headed by Richard Locks. The *Clove* returned to England in September 1614, and Saris gave the EIC directors an inaccurate view of trade in Japan, which in the long term also contributed to the end of English trading in the archipelago. The cargo of the *Hosiander*, which sailed from Banten and arrived in Hirado in late August 1615, was as a result inappropriate for the Japanese market, as was that of the *Thomas* and of the *Advice* in 1616. The matter of importing goods yielding little or no profit was an issue which troubled the English factory until it closed down, with Locks regarding the Portuguese and the Dutch as sources of valuable information on trade with Japan but from whom English factory plans had to be concealed.[26]

In addition to the competition presented by Chinese traders from Fukien, who arrived in increasing numbers on the coast of Japan, and to the religious and power crisis faced by the Portuguese, the appearance of the Dutch and of the English heightened Portuguese vulnerability, especially from early 1614. This year saw the promulgation of a new anti-Christian edict, which, to the joy of the English, expelled all Catholic priests from Japanese territory. The edict targeted not the Portuguese traders, with whom the Japanese and the English negotiated,[27] but rather the priests and religious orders. This therefore did not affect the Protestants, who were merely required to remove the flag of St. George from the top of their factory; the cross, as a Christian symbol, had become undesirable after the edict.[28] In a letter to Banten, Cocks described the expulsion of the priests and religious orders and the destruction of churches, remarking that "Thay [Portuguese] laid the fault of this alteration one the arrivall of our nation in thease p'tes [...]. Once howsoever I am glad thay ar gon, som of them beinge shipt for Amacau in China [...] the rest are gone for the Phillippinas".[29] Macau is constantly referred to as the destination of the Catholic priests expelled from Japan,[30] where the commercial power and status of the Portuguese community was weakened by the presence of other European traders. The Tokugawa rulers decided to eradicate Catholicism and restrict Japanese Christians to Nagasaki, the port from which vessels set sail for Macau. Native-Japanese Catholics were compelled to renounce their faith. From 1616 onwards any Japanese subject who harboured missionaries was put to death, and in the autumn of 1619 fifty Catholics were burnt alive in Kyoto.

Despite the persecution of the Catholics, in September 1616 the northern European traders saw their privileges renewed by the emperor, thanks to

Adams's influence; they were, however, confined to Hirado.[31] We are thus looking at three "foreign" trading enclaves in Japan and China: Hirado, Nagasaki and Macau. The Portuguese enjoyed a preponderant presence in the latter ports, with the volumes of Dutch or English trade never matching the commerce of the Portuguese, who had direct access to the Chinese market via Macau. Between 1618, when the Thirty Years' War broke out in Europe, and 1620, the English factory in Hirado was badly affected, since besides the paucity of trade, the conflicts between England and the Netherlands eventually made themselves felt in relations between the factors of each country in Japan. In the face of Tokugawa's repression, Macau's Portuguese traders smuggled missionaries into the archipelago and attempted to evade not just Japanese vigilance, but also that of the Dutch and English Protestants, who, before the signing of the Convention of Goa (1635), used Japanese ruling class antipathy to benefit their businesses and to damage those of the Catholics. English arguments for maintaining their factory in Japan were both the purchase of silk, the import yielding the greatest profit in Japan, as well as trade with other Asian markets, such as Cochinchina, projects which were hampered by the fact that in 1616 Tokugawa Hidetada forced the English to restrict their trading activity to Hirado alone.[32]

The period of English-Dutch maritime rivalry in the East (1618–1619) came to an end, and in 1620 the two countries set up the Defence Fleet, with the aim of combating Iberian interests until 1622,[33] notably in Manila and Macau.[34] During this period, the English took several Portuguese ships, thus obtaining Chinese products indirectly.[35] In 1620, the English vessel *Elizabeth* captured two priests, a Dominican, Luís Flores, and an Augustinian, Pedro de Zuñiga, travelling on the vessel of a Japanese Christian, Joaquim Dias Hirayama, whom they handed over to the Dutch; the latter in turn handed the captives to the authorities in Hirado. The prisoners were burnt alive in Nagasaki in August 1622, and the Jesuits blamed William Adams, "the English pilot", and the other Protestants for the intrigues and misfortunes which befell them in Japan.[36]

In addition to trade with Siam (Thailand) and other ports, setting up the silk trade with China was one of Richard Cocks's major aims, which also met with failure. The president of the English factory in Japan tried, by means of substantial payments, to obtain the cooperation of Chinese traders with a view to setting up direct trade relations with China[37] without having to resort to Macau, where the Portuguese would hamper English plans, as Li Tan,[38] the leader of the small Chinese communities in Hirado and Nagasaki and a trade partner of the English factory, stated: "He sayeth there can nothing cros us in our pursute of entrance but only the Portingales of Amacon & Spaniardes of Manilla, who have greate trade into China, & yf they com to knowledg of our pretence will not want to geave largly to cros our p'ceadings; & therefore hath still desired to pass all in silence".[39] Portuguese Macau, described by Cocks as "a litell point of rock of no importance",[40] held the exclusive right to European trade with China. From Hirado, the English supercargo wished to obtain from the Chinese emperor, through the China captains, the same privileges in Canton which the Portuguese enjoyed. Li Tan, together with two of his brothers, one (named Hua-yü)[41] in Nagasaki and the other in China, cooperated with Cocks in the difficult attempt to obtain Chinese silk. This network of contacts, as well as the supposed influence of the China Captain at the imperial court, were viewed by Cocks as the best way of setting up direct trade with China, although Li Tan did not in fact have any influence over the emperor.

In 1614 Cocks, hoodwinked by the Chinese, informed the Company of the knowledge which the Chinese emperor supposedly had of English trade in Hirado and also of the cooperation of the Chinese trader who would obtain authorisation for English trade in Ningbo.[42] London decided that the Hirado factors should try to set up a factory in China, and in 1615 Cocks was appointed the EIC's official agent in China. However, the English factors tried to emulate the Macau Portuguese, starting from an erroneous view of the relations between the Cantonese authorities and foreigners, allowing themselves to be guided by camouflaged personal interests and by Li Tan's false promises.[43] Initially, Li Tan received an advance from the English, as well as costly gifts, a measure which was criticised by one of the factors, Richard Wickham. The latter travelled from Hirado to Banten in 1617 and presented the Company with a negative image of Cocks's management, despite the damages caused to the factory by the complainant's own private affairs. Before his departure, Wickham wrote to Sir Thomas Smythe (January 1617), praising Li Tan's work and the fact that he was not asking the factory for money before direct trade with China was set up. This was not true, for over the years Tan received large sums of money from Cocks and was the factory's main debtor when it closed down in 1623. Cocks attributed the delay in setting up trade with China to the conflicts with the Manchus[44] and, later, to attacks carried out by the Dutch (pretending to be English) on the Chinese junks which sailed off the coast of the Philippines.[45] In 1621, the factor put forward a new justification, the fact that another English petition had been presented to the new Chinese emperor,[46] an excuse in all likelihood suggested by Li Tan. The fact that the English factory at Hirado never succeeded in becoming involved in the silk trade with China is one of the reasons for its failure, since that same commodity, pillaged by the Dutch from Macau vessels and Chinese junks,[47] would always be profitable in the archipelago. This the English factors knew when they struggled, albeit in vain, to set up trade with China, in which pursuit, according to Wickham, the English "sweat". According to this factor, a further reason for continuing to try to establish direct trade with China from Hirado was that the Chinese would expel the Portuguese from Macau, out of which few Black Ships left for Japan between 1610 and 1616. This absence was interpreted by Wickham as proof of the lack of security and weakening of the Portuguese position in the Far East.[48]

Trade with China was thus one of the major projects of the EIC factory in Hirado, a dream which was never fulfilled, although two years before it closed down Martin Pring affirmed that "if the trade of the Chinese could be drawne to Japan it would prove the best factorie in the world".[49] In 1617 Wickham had informed London that, should the Chinese emperor grant him similar privileges to those extended to the Portuguese, transactions with China would prove to be "the richest trade that ever England enjoyed".[50] This desire, and perhaps increasing knowledge of local reality, led to the English factors in Japan associating, over and over, the verb "to hope", the noun "hope"[51] and the adjective "hopeful"[52] to the project of trade with China. As we will see, the Company, even though not obtaining such privileges in their entirety, would begin its China Trade in 1700, by trading directly with Canton and using Macau as the place of residence for the supercargoes between trading seasons.

The EIC's correspondence contains frequent mentions of the Black Ship voyages between Macau and Nagasaki, of the influence of the Portuguese on the China-Japan axis,[53] as well as of the English desire to invade Macau, whose military defence capabilities were virtually non-existent. Richard Cocks also described Macau's fear of the EIC vessels:

Yt is very certen that w'th littel danger our Fleet of Defence may take & sack Amacon in China, w'ch is inhabeted by Portingales, for the town is not fortefied w'th walls, nether will the king of China suffer them to doe it [...] we are credably enformed that these last 2 yeares when they [the Portuguese] see but 2 or 3 of our shipps w'thin sight of the place, they weare all ready to run out of the towne. [...] And the towne being taken, all the Portingalles' trade in these p'tes of the world is quite spoiled [...] & the King of China would gladly be ridd of their neighbours, as our frendes w'ch procure our entry for trade into China tell me.[54]

The Chinese with whom the factor engaged in Japan managed to dupe the EIC, and Macau proved to be not as vulnerable as had been thought when in June 1622, and with Chinese military help,[55] it defeated a Dutch fleet of fourteen vessels and approximately eight hundred men under the command of Cornelis Reijersz—joined by two English vessels (the *Palsgrave* and the *Bull*) from the English-Dutch Defence Fleet—which attacked the city in an attempt to conquer a trading centre in China.[56] Richard Cocks described the incursion, after which the Dutch strategically tricked the Chinese by saying they were English:

The Hollanders this yeare sent a new fleete of shipps of 14 or 15 seale, greate and small, to have taken Amacan; but they had the repulse with the losse, as som say, of 300, and others say 500 men, and 4 of their ships burned; the king of China now permitting the Portingales to fortefie Amacon, which he would never condecend unto till now, and hath geven order to the vizroy of Canton to assist them with 100,000 men.[57]

Like English sources, Portuguese documents, notably the *Itinerário das Missões da India Oriental* (*Itinerary of the Missions in the East Indies*, 1649), by the Augustinian missionary Sebastião Manrique, refer to the fact that this Anglo-Dutch attack led the Chinese authorities to allow the Portuguese to build walls and to fortify the city.[58] Vessels of the European "enemies" sailed close to Macau's shores several times,[59] and from Hirado Joseph Cockram described the famous 1622 attack and how the Portuguese vessels did not leave Macau because of the Dutch threat in the South China Sea.[60]

A decade after the English factory in Japan was founded, the EIC closed down its trading centre in the Far East, without Hirado ever having attained any role as a centre for English trade with Ming China, as Macau had proven for the

Portuguese. In 1622 Cocks and the other supercargoes did not abide by orders received from Java to close down the factory and declared they needed time to organise the accounts. In the summer of 1623, the *Bull* put in at Hirado, bringing a letter from Fursland which was critical of Cocks's disobedience and stated that the recently arrived Joseph Cockram would henceforth hold full authority. Using his powers, Cockram closed down the factory and tried in vain to recover the sums owed by Li Tan (Andrea Dittis) and the money which had already been handed to him. In December of that year, after ten years of badly run commercial operation and failed objectives, in conjunction with poor staff and financial management of a business always on the verge of bankruptcy, the EIC brought its activities on the archipelago to a close. As we will see, years later the Company attempted to revive its activity in Japan with the voyage of the *Return* (1673), which, unable to trade in Japan, did so in Macau.[61]

Only two European powers remained in Japan: the Dutch, for about two more centuries, and the Portuguese for only about a further sixteen years. In 1636 the Portuguese established in the artificial island of Deshima in the bay of Nagasaki, which became the site of Lusitanian residence in Japan. This meant that they were isolated from the local population and were thus easier to control by the Japanese authorities, as was also the case in the Macau peninsula, easily controlled by the Mandarinate.

In 1637–1638, the Shimabara uprising was organised in the main by Christians. The Portuguese were accused of instigating the rebels, which the Dutch helped the Japanese to put down. The Dutch moved their factory from Hirado to Deshima in 1641, two years after the final expulsion of the Portuguese from the Japanese empire. Macau tried in vain to re-establish trade with the archipelago in 1640 and 1647 by sending two embassies. Essentially depending on the profits of the Black Ship, Macau was intensely affected by the end of this trade, and the city suffered greatly and was forced to look for new market partners, with the EIC profiting from the situation in the medium and long term.

As João Paulo Oliveira e Costa concludes, the arrival and activity of the northern European rivals in Japan contributed to the final decision by the Shogunate to break off relations with the Roman Catholic church and with Christianity,[62] which led to the increasing impoverishment and to the socio-economic crisis apparent in Macau from then on and which English visitors recorded. For example, in 1769 William Hickey visited the enclave and, before travelling to Whampoa and Canton, described it as an unpleasant place where extreme poverty reigned, epitomised in the local soldiers:

> this miserable place, where there is a wretched ill constructed fort belonging to the Portuguese, in which I saw a few sallow faced, half naked, and apparently half starved creatures in old tattered coats that had once been blue, carrying muskets upon their shoulders, which, like the other accoutrements, were of a piece with their dress. These wretches were honoured with the title of "soldiers". Not only the men, but everything around bespoke the acme of poverty and misery.[63]

English visitors and residents described the economic difficulties of the territory from which they benefited, as we will see in subsequent chapters. The English presence was a source of income for the Portuguese and Chinese inhabitants derived from letting properties,[64] trade cooperation and rendering services to the EIC supercargoes. However, the harsh blow suffered in Japan served as a warning to the Macau authorities as regards the possible consequences of their English rivals setting up in trade in China. Mistrust and defence of economic interests thus marked Anglo-Portuguese relations in the Far East from the outset. In the meantime, King João IV directed his efforts and expense towards the war of Portugal's independence against Spain until the 1668 Luso-Spanish treaty of peace and attempted to legitimise the new dynasty in the European courts, especially the English,[65] whose mediation—since 1666—had facilitated talks between Spain and Portugal. The latter country and Britain were, therefore, the oldest allies in Europe, but in the Far East English and Portuguese traders competed.

The Convention of Goa (1635) and the opening up of Eastern ports to the English

Following the "firm peace and concord"[66] signed in August 1604 by Philip II of Portugal and James I of England, in November 1630 Philip III and Charles I renewed the peace accords, which were to be observed in the overseas dominions of both nations.[67] In 1632 Count Linhares, the viceroy of India, wrote to Philip II, informing him of the proposal[68] by the "president of the English by which they would come to an understanding and practise in that State the peace which [the king of Portugal] had agreed with his Britannic Majesty".[69] In his reply, the king counselled peace with the English because "that State [Portuguese Asian Empire] was in such a tight situation".[70] According to the viceroy, this alliance would further result in benefit to the Crown's Customs, through receipt of royal taxes,[71] while the English William Methwold, who had arrived in Surat in November 1633, viewed this arrangement as an excellent strategy to revitalise English trade in Asia, which had fallen into decline.[72]

To face the Dutch forces, whose alliance with the English had ended in enmity after the massacre of Amboina (1623), the Convention of Goa[73] was signed in January 1635. This was a local peace and cooperation accord[74] between Methwold and the viceroy of India,[75] which, together with the 1642 Anglo-Portuguese treaty signed by João IV and Charles I of England,[76] opened up the gate of the East to English vessels. The Portuguese began to trade through EIC's ships, avoiding Dutch attacks, which continued despite the treaty signed between João IV and the United Provinces in November 1641, and which the VOC, operating from Batavia, did not respect until 1645. Peace in the East came after a treaty was signed by the latter establishment and Goa in November of the preceding year.

The viceroy's letter to the king of Portugal described the signing of the "agreement to a truce" with the English, which would make it possible to join forces against the Dutch and the Persians by forming two Anglo-Portuguese fleets to recover Hormuz, Paleacat, Jacatra, Banda, Amboina and the island of Formosa from the Dutch.[77] In 1635, the Convention of Goa put an end to almost half a century of maritime conflicts between the two oldest European allies but did not lead to the immediate weakening of their common (Dutch) enemy.[78] According to Maria Manuela Sobral Blanco:

> Count Linhares lacked a clear vision of the great damage which English interference in the markets under the Crown's control would represent for Portuguese trade. In setting up friendly relation with the former foes, he foolishly opened up the gateway to trade centres such as Kanara and China, until then rigidly reserved for the Portuguese [...] The result of the Truce proved harmful to Portugal's interests, since the English now became rivals in the Portuguese markets for pepper, they infiltrated the Malindi

coast to trade in gold and ivory, and most of all, they carried out a sortie to the Canton fair, seriously endangering the Portuguese monopoly in China. [...] The gateway to the markets over which the Portuguese Crown had zealously held a monopoly for more than a century was suddenly opened up to the avidity of the East India Company.[79]

Maria Blanco further lists the different reactions in the Iberian Peninsula with regard to this alliance, notably that of the Council of Portugal in Madrid, which disagreed with the idea of extending peace with the English to Asia, contrary to the view of Count São João, who agreed with the truce.

A new cycle of trade in the *Estado da Índia* began, as proved by the arrival of the *London*, an English vessel chartered by the Goa viceroy, which, equipped with weapons for defence against the Dutch,[80] set sail for Macau. Its owners' condition was that English supercargoes could trade in Macau, which did not happen, as there were two Portuguese agents on board whose aim was to boycott English trade. The news of the signing of the Convention of Goa might not be favourably received by the local oligarchy, which proved in fact to be the case, since Macau's livelihood came from trade, and trade was its *raison d'etre* from the very beginning, back in the sixteenth century. This basic principle shapes my analysis of the city's administrative framework, its defence structures, its social fabric and its foreign affairs,[81] notably with regard to the English. Indeed, in 1695 the Italian traveller Giovanni Francesco Careri had observed this reality in his description of the enclave's poverty, its dependence on China for food staples and the subjection of its inhabitants to the vagaries of the sea and to the Mandarinate.[82]

As we have already seen, the EIC's activity, together with that of the VOC and of independent European traders, contributed towards the weakening of the Portuguese empire in the East. The English presence gradually took root in Asia, extending as far as Japan, where trade with Macau was banned in 1640 by the Japanese authorities, a measure that abruptly ended the city's golden age, forcing the Portuguese to strengthen their ancient trade relations in ports such as Manila, Makassar, Cambodia and Timor.

3

The arrival of the English in Macau

The Convention of Goa signed between Goa and Surat aimed to face the growing Dutch power in the Far East, gradually opening the gateway to Macau for EIC vessels and those of private English traders. This alliance mirrored the problems with which the *Estado da Índia* had to concern itself in the face of its northern European rivals and the strategies Portugal adopted to deal with the situation. The English visited Macau when the *Estado da Índia* was beginning to contract, but, as we will see, the EIC only established itself in China in the early eighteenth century. From early on, the arrival of these rivals displeased the municipality of Macau, which tried to defend its privileged status with the Middle Kingdom and keep its trade competitors away; four years after the Convention was signed, these would facilitate the expulsion of the Portuguese from Japan, jeopardising the survival of the City of the Holy Name of God of Macau. On the other hand, imperial vigilance over Macau hampered the city's trade activity and its power, since the Chinese authorities viewed the enclave as part of China, under the authority of the emperor; and a perfect place where foreigners could be enclosed and controlled, as we shall see in chapter 6.

The first 'English' vessel in Macau

The Portugall, a watchfull eie and jealousie over us.

—"Henry Bornford at Surat to the Company, April 29, 1636", in
Sir William Foster, *The English Factories in India 1634–1636*,
1911, p. 227

After the signing of the Convention of Goa, a group of Englishmen, accompanied by the Portuguese factor Gaspar Gomes, and as proposed by the viceroy of Goa, Count Linhares,[1] set sail from Goa on board the *London* in April 1635 and arrived in China on 23 July. The group was received in Macau with reluctance by the local oligarchy. Gomes had to ensure that the English sailors did not disturb the city's peace, offend the residents during their religious ceremonies or drink to excess. At first, it was not the residents of Macau who made it difficult for the English to disembark; rather it was the Portuguese factors who had travelled on the vessel, with the two sides becoming locked in a struggle of interests which ended two weeks later when the EIC officials were authorised to settle on dry land. The viceroy of Goa had secretly forbidden the crew to land, as a result of which the English supercargo Henry Bornford advised his directors that, should they want him to carry out a second journey to China, he would sail not to Macau but to one of the other ports or islands in the Pearl River delta.[2]

In February of that year, and writing to Philip II about the benefits of the Convention of Goa, Count Linhares had informed the king that there was a cargo of copper and iron in Macau "which could not be shipped because of the Dutch presence in the Straights [*sic*] of Singapore". The viceroy had therefore chartered, from the president of the English factory in Surat, a vessel (the *London*) on which to carry these goods "because as they [English] are in no danger from the Dutch, they can bring them with great ease, and it does not cross my mind that the said English may divert this cargo, since, besides being men of their word, all their vessels will stand as security".[3] According to the viceroy, the English already knew the environs of Macau, given the countless voyages they had undertaken, including from Japan, together with their former allies, the Dutch. It was agreed that the English would not contact or trade with the Chinese,[4] with Count Linhares defending his position thus:

> my having agreed with this President that no English would land on Macau soil, and we would put in their vessel [...] a captain with fifty soldiers [...]; according to my thought that the Chinamen are treacherous, and that they might want to raid their vessel [...], and, as for the cargo he much complimented me, and in fact it was agreed that I would name the price the vessel would pay to come here.[5]

In turn, and contrary to what the viceroy had written to Philip II, the instructions issued by the English factory in Surat advised the crew of the *London* that some of them would be allowed to settle on dry land:

> to which purpose [they] shall take a house, and cohabite lovingly together. [...] And that no scandall may be given or taken in point of religion (wherein the nation is very tender) lett your exercises and devotion be constant but private, without singing of psalmes, which is nowhere permitted unto our nation in the King of Sapines dominions, except in embassadors houses. Lett our religion appear in our good conversation amongst men, which will best expresse us to be Reform'd Christians. Howsoever, let not your opinions disturb their practise, nor your curiosity to pye into their ceremonies distast them [...]. In briefe, doe not yourselves, nor permitt not any others to give, any offence in matters of religion; but, observing of daies and all other indifferent ordinances.[6]

The viceroy of Goa promised to pay the EIC 10% of the profits yielded by the voyage, the main aim of the former being to bring from Macau 5,000 *quintais* of copper, some iron and artillery pieces from Manuel Tavares Bocarro's foundry.[7] Surat warned the English officials travelling to Macau that the Portuguese might trick them, for which reason the former, when loading the vessel, should give priority to the goods likely to yield a profit; advice was further given on what goods to carry in the event of there being extra space on board, with a total ban on officials' private trade.[8]

In parallel with trade disputes, from the outset religious differences between "Papists" and Protestants also marked Anglo-Portuguese relations in Macau, with the above advice anticipating the difficulties to which the different religious practices and beliefs would give rise between the two peoples in the enclave. These conflicts made themselves felt into the nineteenth century, since it was only in 1821 that the English were allowed to build a Protestant cemetery,[9] and several bishops in Macau railed at the pernicious presence of the foreigners who corrupted the morals of the citizenry.[10]

Methwold's instructions to Captain Willes further advised him that both conflicts between the English and the Portuguese, to which the signing of the Convention had put an end, and the personal interests of the Portuguese community, could bring to the boil adverse reactions on the part of the enclave's inhabitants towards the English during the "first visit of an English vessel". Thus, mistrust and the clash of trading interests marked the first contacts between Macau traders and the EIC. Methwold thus informed the *London*'s captain:

> At his arrival at Macau, the Captain is enjoined to conform to directions
> from the Portuguese governor, particularly in regard to persons sent ashore
> from the ship; and to avoid all occasions of giving offence: for it is to be
> apprehended, that as this is the first visit of an English ship there, under a
> friendly compact, soe fears and jealousies; grounded as the former Enmity
> between the two nations, may be entertained by the Portuguese.[11]

In May 1635, the viceroy Miguel de Noronha wrote to the captain-general of Macau, Manuel da Câmara de Noronha, and announced the truce with the old allies (Convention of Goa), sending a copy of the document describing "what is to be found in the truce, [that] this new friendship can bring great hope to the *Estado*, with it [...] the President has chartered this vessel, which carries 42 pieces of artillery, and has 200 men, he [William Methwold] says, fierce and brave".[12] The viceroy cordially recommended the English captain, also saying that it was important that "no Englishman has conversation with any Chinaman".[13] Six or eight Portuguese men should always remain on board the English ship to assist and guard the cargo. The ship's captain should be cordially invited to dinner and welcomed by the captain-general, who should also supply him with provisions and show him the city. The instructions from Goa were minute, listed the measures to be taken by the Portuguese when interacting with the English crew, and several times re-iterated the need for the English to maintain a distance from the Chinese, for the former carried valuable goods with which to trade with Gaspar Gomes's assistance.[14] The EIC factors were to pay for the vessel's measuring, and the petition to the Mandarin should be made in the name of the experienced Portuguese who accompanied the English officer.[15] Communication between the native population and the newcomers should be avoided at all costs, and the *London* should return to Goa as soon as possible, "before the Chinamen can suspect anything, or any Macau Portuguese warn them [the Chinese]".[16] For his part, the captain-general of Macau informed the viceroy of Goa of the arrival of the *London*, of Gaspar Gomes's performance,[17] of the implementation of the various instructions of the Count Linhares regarding the peace treaty (Convention of Goa), and the "disguised" sojourn of the vessel without raising Chinese suspicion, for the latter had been told that this "galleon of the Armada" had come to guard the remaining galleons awaiting it in Southern China, "because of the [...] European enemies".[18] The captain-general further described the "friendship", the supply of provisions with which he received the English captain before taking him back to the vessel, which was guarded by trusty Portuguese men, as if replying point by point to his superior's letter. Details as to the loading of the copper and artillery[19] were also part of the long missive which proved to Goa that the enclave had carried out its duty.

The *London*, the first English vessel to anchor in Southern China,[20] under the command of Matthew Willis, despite having been secretly chartered by the Portuguese, triggered clashes between the Mandarin authorities and the administration of Macau, which was forced to pay a fine to the former because of the unwanted presence of the "foreign" vessel,[21] after its departure on 20 October for Goa, where it arrived in early February 1636.[22] The English complained that they had been duped by the factor Gaspar Gomes "making things difficult for them".[23] In the meantime, the behaviour of the English supercargoes in Macau was less than professional, and in August 1636 Methwold mentioned the dubious accounting of the voyage by Abraham Aldington, who was found guilty of fraud given the inflated expenses of the crew's stay in the enclave.[24]

On reaching Goa, the crew of the *London* refused to pay customs duties, just as they had done in Malacca, since they had bought their goods from Chinese residents of Macau and had not off-loaded them in India, as they intended to ship them on to England. The new viceroy of India, Pedro da Silva, informed the king of Portugal that he could do nothing, since the contract signed the previous year between Count Linhares and the English did not cover this eventuality, and the former had not informed the Council of his decision.[25] However, the letter sent by Count Linhares to Philip III of Portugal before the *London* had even set sail pointed out the advantages of the "new truce" and of the customs duties "because the English were told that they had to pay duties on all the goods which they bring and take".[26] Manuel Ramos, the administrator of voyages to Japan and Crown agent in Macau, informed the viceroy that, when the English left Goa "they were already determined not to abide by the orders [of Count Linhares] to disembark [in Macau] only when the Captain-general would come for them". The Portuguese factor confessed to have suffered greatly in their company, for "they esteemed [him] very little".[27] In his letter of 30 October 1635, Manuel Ramos described the English as enemies, referring to their open attempts to communicate with the Chinese, as well as to the petition handed to the Mandarin when the vessel was measured, requesting a "port" in Chinese waters. The Portuguese were forced to avoid the rendition of the vessel, an infraction for which, later, they had to pay, as already mentioned, a substantial sum in the Canton fair. The Mandarinate ordered the Chinese inhabitants to leave the city and cut off the supply of food staples with a view to forcing the Portuguese authorities to pay the fine. This strategy to pressure the Portuguese was applied throughout the centuries, and is also mentioned by Courteen's agents in 1637 when they describe the possibilities of future English trade with China. As described by Peter Mundy, Macau was a location to be avoided by those English traders wishing to set up in business in China, given the level of control exerted by the Chinese and by the Portuguese.[28] In 1849 Henry Charles Sirr also mentioned the Chinese permission for the Portuguese to establish themselves in the peninsula of Macau as a strategy to control the foreigners: "The great enemy to be dreaded by the Portuguese would be famine, in the event of a war with the Chinese; for [...] the principal supplies come from the mainland".[29]

After the *London*'s voyage, Manuel Ramos, the administrator of voyages to Japan, advised the viceroy of Goa to guard against monetary losses in Macau and to force the English to leave a deposit in Goa for the vessel's rendition.[30] Fully aware of the threat posed by the English vessels, the enclave at once joined forces with the Canton Mandarinate in order to repel the unwanted foreign presence. As Anders Ljungstedt concluded, right from the very beginning the Portuguese had perceived French and English interests in China as harmful to their trade.[31]

Henry Bornford, "the firste [Englishman] that negotiated [...] business in those parts",[32] affirms in his travel log that while his apparent objective was to assist the viceroy of India deal with the Dutch blockade, the underlying purpose of the EIC's mission was to launch direct trade with China. He further states that this aim was only defeated by the fact that Chinese "superstitions" kept foreigners at bay, as was also the case of the Portuguese in the "iland of Machau",[33] who for their part were not allowed free entry into China. The supercargo concluded: "so far as the English could see, the averseness of the Chinese to intercourse with foreigners is exaggerated by the Portuguese, who also abuse other nations to the Chinese in order to keep the trade to themselves".[34] The comments of the man in charge of the *London*'s voyage to Macau regarding Portuguese attitudes, including the comment I quote in the epigraph to this sub-chapter, constitute the first English image about the city's dwellers, based on actual visual contact and interaction. From the beginning of the English presence in China, the Portuguese carried out a two-pronged strategy of interests which operated on two fronts and consisted of keeping other European nations away from China and denigrating their image among the higher echelons of Canton's provincial administration. However, Bornford listed the goods which could be most easily sold in Macau and reached the conclusion that, should peace between the Portuguese and the English come to pass, the latter would gain a part of this lucrative trade.[35] For his part, Gaspar Gomes, back in Goa, described the voyage to the new viceroy Pedro da Silva and stated that he had warned the English that, under the instructions they had received, they could not trade in Macau. Pedro da Silva was highly suspicious of this expedition and, in a report to Philip III of Portugal, he paraphrased the factor's account,[36] stating that the English

did not wish to abide by this, but would rather have their own factory where they would sell and buy whatever was to be had, and became great friends with the local Chinamen, continuously giving them food and drink [...], taking them many goods and silver, and that they wanted no more than to be allowed to build two thatched houses outside the city and not sturdy houses like those of the Portuguese, and that they would offer them their goods cheaper by 30% and 40% than our prices, and as the Chinamen did not allow them the goods which they requested, which will not be very difficult because those people always seek out their goods in larger quantities, and as those which we buy from them are in little quantity because of the lack of navigation and trade [due to the Dutch embargo in the Malacca Straights] they will easily make friends with the English, in this way harming this *Estado* [da Índia], especially when they [the English] come with such greed to return to China, as Gaspar Gomes tells me, and also here after they arrived I have heard that, even against our will, they will send out two of their brigs during the monsoon, and will do this every year.[37]

These accounts by Gaspar Gomes and by the new viceroy reflected the interest felt by the supercargoes in Surat to approach the Chinese to request authorisation to build a "thatched" and not permanent factory, as were the Portuguese buildings, outside the walls of Macau where they would compete with the city's dwellers. Even before Gomes had arrived in Goa, Manuel Ramos had already warned the viceroy of the dangers of the return of the English and of trade with China and Japan passing into their hands, conveying similar facts to those which the factor would narrate *in loco*, as follows:

(1) the English "intent on continuing this trade", requested Chinese authorisation to send two small vessels to Canton the following year and to build four "very small totally unfortified" houses "with no artillery", unlike those of the Portuguese in Macau, undertaking to sell to the Chinese merchandise at half the price practised by the Portuguese,

(2) the English promised "other things that would benefit them, much to our detriment", and tried to offer a Chinese man large annual payments to the Mandarins and to the emperor, making many other promises on this. Eventually, the Portuguese found out about the plan and convinced the man to take a Portuguese bribe to make him pretend to the English that he would go to Canton to intercede on their behalf,

(3) if the English did not reach Macau from Goa, they would do so from Surat, thus jeopardising Portuguese trade in the Far East.[38]

Pedro da Silva informed Philip III of the threat the English posed to the enclave's trade and of Surat's subversive intentions,[39] although voyages to China were not yet part of the trading policies of the Company in London. However, many of the measures taken and much of the success of English trading in the East derived from decisions made and strategies mapped out by the local factories without the prior approval of the directors in London.

Gaspar Gomes's account and Manuel Ramos's missive prove that the *Estado da Índia* had feared English competition from the moment the first EIC vessel had been sent to Macau, even though this had been the Portuguese wish. Pedro da Silva informed the king that he had admitted to his Council, even before the vessel returned, "how much he felt and regretted, already foreseeing the damage that would befall this *Estado* from sending this vessel to China",[40] describing how, after taking up his post, he had distanced himself from his predecessor's actions and forced the *London* to stay outside the port of Goa to check its cargo and exact the customs duties owed to the Portuguese Crown. The viceroy also wrote to the captain-general of Macau about the major drawbacks of the *London*'s voyage and enjoined him both to make every effort to ensure that no other European nation was received in any other Chinese port, as also letting him know that this voyage had incurred his displeasure; no other English vessel, he further wrote, should be sent to China, nor should any favours be extended to third parties.[41] Four years later, and fighting the Dutch blockade, the same viceroy, in the same type of move adopted by his predecessor with regard to the English, chartered a vessel from the first Danish East India Company, thus weakening the exclusive position of the English.[42]

After the *London*'s return, relations between Pedro da Silva, who for three years did not pay the English for the chartering of the vessel, and Methwold became tense to the extent that the truce enshrined in the Convention of Goa came close to being suspended.[43] For these same reasons, and having banned further English voyages to Macau,[44] the viceroy was considered by Surat as being "irreconcilably adverse unto the English".[45] In the same year, Madras, which would become known as Fort St. George, was acquired by the English, and, because of the Dutch blockade, the viceroy of Goa again proposed to the English that they send two or three vessels to Macau. This support was turned down by Surat, which informed London of the upset expressed by Goa with regard to what it felt was Portugal's abandoning of it, with the Portuguese even being prepared to become the subjects of a foreign king who would protect them from the Dutch. Surat also wrote of the need for English vessels to be sent to the East so as to profit from the advantageous wish expressed by the local Portuguese to cooperate in matters of trade: "wee believe they would readily subscribe to furnish you with pepper, cinamon, and as much freedome & security in some of their forts (if not the fort itself)".[46] In 1636 Surat informed London that they wished to set up direct trade with China, for which London would have to obtain authorisation from Portugal, while the factory would pay the required taxes in Malacca.

The voyage of the *London* and the other Portuguese proposals to use English vessels occurred as a result of the interests and in the name of the Portuguese in Goa. Therefore, this voyage cannot be considered the first English-driven mission to the Luso-Chinese enclave, especially as the EIC directors were unaware that Surat used its capital to send vessels to China, a practice which they later disapproved. London alerted Methwold to the danger of initiatives such as the chartering of the *London*, for the Dutch, should they find out that English vessels were carrying Portuguese munitions or goods, could easily take them in the Malacca Straights and confiscate the cargo,[47] as they did in 1643 when they captured the *Bona Speranza*. This English vessel was chartered by the viceroy of Goa, João da Silva Telo e Meneses, Count Aveiras, from Sir William Courteen's Commercial Association[48] to transport Portuguese soldiers to Macau. The vessel was escorted by two other English ships (the *Lesser* and the *Greater William*),[49] as a result of the difficulties posed by the Dutch blockade. As recorded by the viceroy in late 1643: "The English vessel [...] which had set sail for China is also presumed to have been detained in the same fortress of Malacca, having fought with the Dutch, in which fight the English captain having died [...], this leads us to believe that China must be suffering great hardship".[50]

Enmity and the initial fear of Anglo-Portuguese competition gradually gave way to cooperation as a strategy for the defence of both nations' interests in the face of the Dutch threat in the East,[51] and, thanks to the Convention of Goa, the Portuguese of Macau even started to travel to and from Lisbon via London on board EIC vessels,[52] although peace between the two allies did not make them "the masters of everything".[53] After the massacre of Amboina and the Dutch expulsion of the English from the spice trade, the EIC joined forces with the Portuguese to confront Dutch might, and it was in this context that, as we have seen, the Convention of Goa was signed in 1635.

The beginning of sporadic voyages to Macau and the role of the East India Company factories in the East

Two years after the *London*'s voyage, a small English fleet sent by William Courteen's Association arrived in Macau. This was indeed the first English expedition to arrive in China, the result of private initiative. Conflicts between the crew and the Portuguese and Chinese authorities showed, from the very start, that the English would spare no effort to share with the Portuguese the profits of trade in Canton. During the fleet's stay, one of the traders, Peter Mundy, came to write the first long description in English of the enclave, to which he added pictorial representations. Immediately following the arrival of the first English fleet, Macau defended its trade and economic interests and developed strategies on five fronts for the purpose, notably with the Mandarinate, with Lisbon, the viceroy of Goa, the English crew members, and also with the English king.

John Weddell's expedition and Peter Mundy's diary (1637): The beginning of Anglo-Portuguese relations in Macau

Following the Luso-English truce, the EIC was not alone in sending vessels to China, and in June 1637 four vessels of the fleet of Courteen's Association, under the command of John Weddell, who had participated in the taking of Ormuz, anchored in the waters off Macau after passing through Goa, bringing on board a number of Malacca missionaries, as well as Peter Mundy, who during his stay in Macau wrote the illustrated diary to which I have already referred.[54] In 1637 Courteen, together with Endymion Porter, succeeded in obtaining authorisation from Charles I to trade in the East Indies, momentarily upsetting the balance of the EIC monopoly until his Association was taken over by the EIC around 1649.[55] For a number of years Courteen's vessels had already been fighting against Portuguese supremacy in the Indian Ocean, which made Surat inform London that Courteen's fleet was one of the hurdles standing in the way of success for the EIC's business ventures, notably in Macau: "for Courteen's ships came out expressly to take advantage of the Foundations which the Company, at a great cost, had laid for Intercourse with China, through the Portuguese settlements of Goa and Macau".[56] According to the same source, these circumstances were aggravated by the "jealousy" of the Portuguese in Goa, who tried to boycott the *London*'s enterprise—to which they themselves had invited the English—even evading payment of the charter involved. On the other hand, the powerful Dutch who confiscated Portuguese goods carried by English vessels hampered Anglo-Portuguese cooperation, which was only resumed when the *Hind* was chartered in 1644.[57] This was the year in which the Banten factor proposed to London to set up direct trade with China, in the wake of the Portuguese and the Dutch, an activity which would, no doubt, be successful.[58] For his part, the Surat factor, Edward Knippe, hoped that, even if peace came about between the Portuguese and the Dutch, the former would charter vessels from him to sail to Macau, given the destruction of Portuguese vessels by Malabar pirates.[59]

If we exclude the voyage of the *London*, (disguisedly) flying the Portuguese flag, Weddell's voyage was the first entirely English trading expedition to the territory. For this reason, I will dwell especially on the sojourn of the independent traders, for Portuguese and English sources[60] reveal not only the prejudices and the expectations but also the defensive and trading strategies both of the Macau Portuguese and of the English newcomers, who tried to achieve their aims at all costs. Patricia Drumond Borges Ferreira has studied this episode and states that Weddell's crew members were the first Englishmen to reach Macau.[61] However, and although we cannot be absolutely certain that William Carmichael actually visited the enclave—despite this being highly likely—and if we exclude the sojourn of Frobisher's wife and servant (1620), the *London* was, in 1635, the first vessel to arrive in the city with an English crew on board.

In his report to the viceroy, the Macau captain-general Domingos da Câmara de Noronha described the arrival and sojourn of Weddell's crew as "notably full of greed, and they already came from those parts with this intent, all hatched on the vessel *London* [...], and they had brought with them the intention of also wanting to send some of their vessels to Japan",[62] further remarking on the difficulty of enforcing royal justice in the city and the Chinese ban on any visits to the English vessels.[63] That is to say, each side's initial mistrust marked relations between Weddell's fleet and the Macau authorities, as had already been the case when the *London* put in at Macau.

While still on his way to China, Peter Mundy mentions two female pioneers, Richard Frobisher's wife, Joan Frobisher, and their servant, and the first recorded visit by English women to Macau, around 1620,[64] when the *Unicorn* was shipwrecked in what were viewed as enemy waters, since the English and the Portuguese were rivals in the East until 1635. On 7 September 1637, in response to Macau's protest against the Luso-Chinese confrontations caused by the presence of the *London* in Macau, Weddell and Mundy both mention the conflicts to which the signing of the Convention of Goa had put an end, accusing the Portuguese with regard to the situation prior to 1635:

as it was not enough that you should close and forbid us your ports, but you also exerted every means to prevent us from holding commerce with other kingdoms. At last peace was sought for by you for two or three years, [...] and concluded in the city of Goa in December 1634 [10–01–1635] [...] the articles being confirmed by both parties, by which was conceded to us the free entry and trade of your ports.[65]

Upon his arrival in the enclave, Mundy was invited to lunch at the Jesuit seminary, and throughout his stay, he wrote a detailed description of the city's human and natural landscapes.[66] The English and Portuguese documents gathered both by Sir Richard Carnac Temple and L. Anstey, and by Maria Manuela Sobral Blanco,[67] as well as the *Livros das Monções* (*Books of the Monsoons*), present the trading interests which mark the beginning of Anglo-Portuguese relations in Macau and which would in essence hold true until the founding of Hong Kong. The English settlement in the Pearl River delta was from the outset viewed by the Portuguese authorities as a threat to the city's trade and, as a result, to its very survival.

In the first letter sent by the city of Macau to the English king in July 1637, and in reply to the king's letter brought by Weddell,[68] Domingos de Noronha stated that he had received no notification from the viceroy regarding the Goa "contract",[69] and, further to the letter he had received from the English fleet,[70] he also advised Weddell that he had not been notified of the Anglo-Portuguese peace. However, as proved by Portuguese documents prior to this voyage, the conclusion must be drawn that this alleged lack of knowledge of the signing of the Convention of Goa is a fabrication, for, as already stated, and as early as 1635,[71] Count Linhares had informed the captain-general, the latter having expressed thanks for the news.[72] Once again, Domingos de Noronha strategically resorted to supposed ignorance of the peace so as not to lend support to the entry of trade competitors in China. While Macau refused to honour the Anglo-Portuguese "truce" agreement, with a view to defending local interests,[73] the *London* became a recurring symbol of the problems which the English caused the Portuguese, with the captain-general offering to assist Weddell's fleet only in circumstances of "urgent need", as he was "limited [and without] orders from his superiors", the king of Portugal and the viceroy of India:

> Because when the vessel *London* came to this port, it brought particular
> orders from His Excellency Count Linhares, with a Portuguese Factor
> on board to take from here artillery and other cargo belonging to private
> traders, [...] it caused such losses to the city, and to its conservation with
> respect to the Chinamen, who are so worried that any other nation visits
> these parts that have thus made us suffer great losses,[74] in the estates of the
> inhabitants of this land, because they depend greatly on them, this city
> which is in their land.[75]

If the captain-general stated he was unaware of the signing of the Convention
of Goa, he wrote about the fine that the city had paid to the Mandarins because
of the visit of the *London*, which damaged the enclave's economic interests. In
a three-pronged strategy involving Weddell's fleet, the Chinese authorities and
the viceroy of Goa, Domingos Noronha wrote to the latter in December 1637,
informing him that four English vessels had arrived in the enclave, and why
he had banned any person from contacting the fleet and placed the city under
guard and had sent provisions for the crew. This type of defensive measure continued down the centuries, as can be seen from the protest sent by Macau to
the Mandarinate against the presence of a British warship off the coast of the
peninsula in 1800.[76]

Faced with the Chinese desire to contact the "red-haired barbarians",[77] Macau
strategically informed the former of the unfriendly designs of the "newcomers".
The English eventually decided to visit Canton,[78] which the Portuguese could
only enter to take part in the city's fair and trade directly with the Chinese. The
enclave further feared that the fleet's destination was Japan, that it would attack
the Black Ship (*nau do trato*) and would manage to set up a factory in China
next to Macau. Weddell forced his way to Canton,[79] and the Portuguese conveyed their astonishment to the English Captain, stating that such an act would
bring the crew "many misfortunes with the locals".[80] In the end, the Mandarins
demanded that Macau pay for any damage caused by the English, since they had
arrived in China as friends of the enclave, although the Portuguese had denied
them any type of trade. The Chinese demanded that the English pay the customary taxes, and Weddell's endeavour ended in failure, for which the captain
blamed the Portuguese machinations.[81] Irrespective of the truth of this statement, which up to a point corresponds to the facts, given that the Macau traders
tried to defend their interests by every means, this argument would be used

repeatedly by British historians to justify why the EIC established direct trade with Canton so late.[82]

Since Weddell's was the first entirely English fleet to arrive in Macau, it is interesting to note that, like the captain of the *London*, he discussed with the Chinese the possibility of paying them an annual fee, as the Portuguese did, and dividing Macau with the latter.[83] The English desire to acquire a position and an establishment in China similar to that of their old European allies became immediately clear, this plan only coming to fruition after the Opium War, with the founding of Hong Kong.

On 6 September, Weddell wrote to the city and referred to the "most tedious" and threatening letters he had received from Macau and which led him to think that it regarded the English as none other than "despicable and worthy of no esteem", re-iterating that, one way or another, he would be successful in gaining entry to the China trade. He went on to say that, according to the Portuguese themselves, Macau "is [...] but a possession of His Majesty the King of China" and that in any event all he required for success was the authorisation of the king of Portugal.[84] In effect, the following day the city again stated in a letter to Weddell: "we are not in the land of our King nor did we gain a place in this city by a fair war, rather we have it through the benevolence of the King of China and [...] we depend on him not only in serious circumstances but also in the smallest matters of our government [...] the sustaining of each day".[85] The letter also describes the level of control and pressure exerted by the Mandarins on the territory when the English fleet arrived, repeating "the very great troubles and losses" the Portuguese had previously undergone because of the visit of the *London*, irrespective of the fact that the vessel carried a Portuguese factor.[86] This situation had arisen anew, though in a more serious way, for Weddell's fleet had arrived without the authorisation of the king of Portugal or of the viceroy of India. The city's governing body further feared that the repercussions of all the offences committed by the English would be felt by the enclave, upsetting the trade in which it had been engaged for over ninety years with the Chinese.[87] This would run counter to the principles of the peace treaties signed between England and Portugal, which aimed to preserve both countries' colonial possessions and interests.

The Senate met in October to respond to Weddell's request[88] to trade in order to make up for the costs of his voyage and decided to allow the Englishman to do so, as his requests were "of little consequence" and the goods to be traded would not harm the interests of the local traders. This would stop the fleet from attacking the Macau fleet returning from Japan, which was vital for the local economy.[89] In December 1637 the city informed Charles I of the reasons and interests which had led the Portuguese to assist Weddell's fleet in initiating trade relations with China. It also criticised the behaviour of the remaining English crew who, unlike Weddell, were discredited and accused of shamelessly squandering the monarch's money. Macau affirmed it had helped the crew members like "true friends", although, the latter being traders, it could not provide accommodation for them, nor allow them to set up a factory. This was not for want of friendship or the desire to do so, but because of five reasons, which were explained at length and which had already been put to Weddell:

(1) to avoid Chinese "investigations" and problems such as those which had arisen in 1635 with the voyage of the *London*. The Portuguese had had to pay the Mandarinate many thousands of *patacas* and had been threatened with expulsion from Macau as traitors, since the native population believed the English, with their blue eyes, cast the "evil eye" and would invade the country. If the small *London* had caused such difficulties, four "so large" vessels would cause many more;[90]

(2) trade between England and China would destroy Macau completely, and this could not be done in the name of Anglo-Portuguese friendship, since the city made its living from trading with China, Japan, Manila and India. If the Chinese transferred this trade to English hands, it would mean the end of the territory. The Anglo-Portuguese peace and friendship accord had not been signed by either party with the aim of destroying, rather of preserving Portuguese dominions. Thus, Weddell's fleet could sell wine and textiles to the Portuguese alone, for these goods were not sought by the Chinese;[91]

(3) the Portuguese were not in their own country or in land conquered by them, as was the case of India, where they were sovereign and the English were welcomed. Macau, although governed in the name of the

Portuguese king, was located in the emperor's land. He had authorised the Portuguese to settle there as a favour, and the latter had to rely solely on the provisions sold to them by the Chinese; if such provisions were denied, it would mean the ruin of the city. Likewise, the Portuguese were banned from trading with foreigners (a practice which did not please Macau either), so the English should not blame them but rather the restrictions placed on them by the Mandarins, to whom all were subject;

(4) the four-vessel fleet frightened the Chinese, leading them to fear an increase in the number of foreign vessels. It was also impossible for the Portuguese to secretly supply Weddell with the cargo he desired, without the Mandarinate's knowledge;[92]

(5) the Chinese did not allow other nations to trade in Macau, including the Spanish from Manila. This being so, neither the king of Portugal nor Charles I were in a position to decide which other nations could "endanger this trading post" and destroy Portuguese trade.[93]

The document (fls. 222–227) summarises, from the Portuguese point of view, the advice given to the English and the events which made up this episode. Macau described the damage caused by the crew among the Mandarins when they visited Canton and accused the factor Nathaniel Mountney of deviating from Weddell's diplomatic approach. The enclave even had to send five Portuguese to save the English traders under arrest in Canton.[94] The captain-general of Macau appealed to the English king to preserve the enclave's well-being. The latter would do everything in its power to assist his subjects, provided such assistance did not jeopardise its own situation; all these statements could be corroborated by the crew of the *London*. According to the Portuguese, authorisation for the English to trade in China did not depend on them but on the Chinese, who, even when stating that the English were welcome, would do everything to subject them to extortion and later remove them, since the inhabitants of Macau themselves were subjected to trickery. The city decided to help the English, provided they left and never again threatened its stability and trade with China and Japan, as well as its relations with the Mandarin authorities.[95] The letter further summarised all the assistance rendered by Macau to the fleet and the traps laid by the Chinese. The Portuguese felt offended above all by Nathaniel Mountney and they defined themselves as mediators between the English and the Mandarins, but could not grant the English freedom of movement in Macau, accusing them of behaving ungratefully and in ill-faith. The episode of the *London* was referred to countless times, and Charles I was reminded that the city's decisions were based on prior experience and were in no way designed to break the peace pact between the two European nations. This argument was also used to keep away any type of competition from the city.

Weddell's fleet left Macau in late 1637 after a prolonged stand-off with the Portuguese and Canton authorities[96] which made the London traders' intentions very clear. Thus began the long establishment of English interests on the Macau-Canton circuit, a process which would pick up speed from the early eighteenth century onward. Contravening the edict issued by the captain-general, the departing English fleet carried several priests and Macau residents regarded as "deceitful and traitors", a decision which, according to the Portuguese, would have highly negative results for the *Estado da Índia*, since these vessels also carried concealed goods which did not pay customs duties.[97] Macau's defensive strategy continued, and, three days after the departure of Weddell's fleet, several married men (*casados*), among whom the alderman Domingos Dias Espichel, sent a letter to the viceroy which they titled "Reasons presently to be given about the harms that will result if the English come to Macau". In this document they put forward the reasons why the English must not be allowed to enter China, for they might easily engender among the Chinese "mistrust and suspicion which will mean the complete ruin and perdition of this City"[98] and of trade with Japan:

> if under peace and friendship, the English continued to send [ships] to Macau, and if this city, by interest, engages in trade with them, even if limited, this city and the whole of the *Estado da Índia* will be exposed to great harms, as will happen if they bring silver. They will alter the goods in such a way that what now can be bought for two, we will not be able to find for four, and even the residents and therefore Your Majesty's vassals who come here to trade will not be able to take them [...]. If the English are allowed security of trade among us, India will be lost, and they will become masters of it, and the reason is clear, because if they take the goods that we used to take, which we cannot now because of the impediment in the

straights [Dutch blockade], with them the English will have entry into all the Kingdoms of India and will be well received [...] paying little heed to our friendship.[99]

After Weddell's departure, the Mandarins once again demanded that the Portuguese pay a fine of 80,000 taels.[100] The arrival of the English thus brought about a change in the relations between Macau and the Chinese authorities. In 1638 the viceroy wrote to the king of Portugal and informed him of the presence of the fleet in Macau, of the Chinese attempt to set fire to it, and of the threat that the beginning of English trade posed to the city which was able to "rid itself" of the newcomers.[101] In another letter of the same date, he again referred to the damage which the English vessels would add to that already caused by the Dutch, and the danger of the rivalry pushing up the price of Asian goods.[102]

Since its founding, Macau had become a new type of problem for China. Given the city's strategic geographical location, in the sixteenth century it had become a Portuguese walled city/peninsula that could easily be controlled by the Cantonese Mandarinate. The emperor had therefore chosen the territory as a trading centre and "pre-port" for Canton[103] for all the foreigners who traded in his empire, as this made it easier to control the latter and keep them outside "[Chinese] law",[104] that is to say, foreigners had to be kept as far away as possible from Chinese civilisation. Hence, the importance of Macau for the Mandarinate. Even though Weddell's fleet had entered China without imperial authorisation and had damaged the image of the English, some of the difficulties faced by the crew are included by Earl H. Pritchard in the list of factors which from the outset hampered Anglo-Chinese relations in Canton: cultural differences or clashes which engendered conflicts of opinion and attitudes between the two peoples: political organisation, religion, administrative framework, justice, and Chinese trade organisation, as well as intolerance on both sides.[105] These conflicts and sensitive areas were to remain in latent form especially until the Opium War, during which time the Portuguese authorities were compelled by circumstances and strategic requirements to adopt neutral policies which in essence sought to please the masters of the land, on whom their well-being and their continued presence in the delta of the Pearl River depended.

The beginning of sporadic voyages to Macau and the EIC's diplomatic strategies in the second half of the seventeenth century

> The commodities of Macau come from the sea, and the entire city makes a living from it, there are no other stable goods than what the wind and the tides bring, if these fail, everything fails.
>
> —Fr. Luís da Gama (15–12–1664), BA, cod. 49-IV-56, fl. 204

The taking of Hormuz (1622) was the first great blow dealt by the northern European rivals against the *Estado da Índia*. There followed, from 1640 onwards, a series of events which weakened the Portuguese presence in the Far East: the expulsion from Japan and the negative outcome of the embassy sent there in that year by Macau, the official divorce between Macau and Manila in 1644, after the end of the Iberian Union, and the taking of Malacca by the Dutch (1641), which distanced the enclave from the Indian traders and from the decision centres in Goa and Lisbon. The VOC continued to harm Portuguese interests in Canara (1652–1654), in Ceylon (1656) and in Malabar (1658–1663). In addition to the ruinous end of the Nagasaki trade, Macau faced the crisis brought about by the establishing of the Qing dynasty in China (1644), and the food shortages in the 1650s and 1660s. The Portuguese were aware of the impact of European competition on trade, essential as it was for the survival of the enclave, as shown by the epigraph to this sub-chapter. Faced with this situation, the city's traders therefore strengthened old markets in Makassar, Cambodia, Tonking, Cochinchina and Batavia, among other ports. On the other hand, as we will see, Macau's trade and economy suffered as a result of foreign competition in Canton throughout the eighteenth century. The growth in demand for Chinese products pushed up the prices of these, while the greater availability of goods imported from other Asian ports depressed the prices of the same, thereby reducing Portuguese profit margins.

At first sporadically and as a result of local decisions made by its factors in the East, the EIC attempted to establish itself in China especially through Portuguese Macau, often referred to as "the first land of China".[106] According to A. J. Sargent, during the fifty years after Weddell's visit, the Company made several attempts to set up trade in Canton, although without any results due to the competition and obstacles created by the Portuguese.[107] This argument is also put forward by W. E. Soothill, Earl H. Pritchard and Sir William Foster,[108] who summarise the presence of English vessels in Southern China and English resistance to those obstacles. D. K. Bassett asserts that, given the lack of documentary evidence, little is known of the policies followed by London before 1653 and that, therefore, Pritchard (*Anglo-Chinese Relations*, pp. 54–55) cannot have reached conclusive findings, for even during the seventeen years after 1653, EIC officials were only to be found in Cambodia and Siam.[109] Bassett re-interprets the conclusions reached by Eames, Sargent and Pritchard with respect to the lack of attempts by the EIC to set up systematic trade contacts with China after the Massacre of Amboina. To previously presented factors, he adds Luso-Dutch competition, the absence of an English factory to the east of India, and the Company's overall inactivity and lack of interest in trading with Canton while it developed increasingly intense activity in Java, Sumatra and Borneo. The first English voyages to Macau and to Manila, between 1635 and 1644, stemmed from the opportunities which Company officials grasped locally in the East, given the difficulties faced by Iberian traders because of the Dutch blockade. These were isolated attempts which do not mirror the EIC's *modus operandi* as set out in London.[110] In fact, Surat considered it to be of the greatest convenience to have a further two vessels built, given the trade benefits to be had in the Portuguese ports as a result of the Convention of Goa.[111] In early 1639 the director of Goa's Finance (*Vedor da Fazenda de Goa*) signed a contract with Andrew Cogan and John Wylde for another voyage to Macau, the latter being allowed to invest some capital in the city's trade; the supercargoes alone would be authorised to disembark.[112] Two years later, the president of the Banten factory informed Surat that Dutch fleets surrounded the Portuguese in Goa and Macau, hampering their movements and their trade, ending on this note: "the pore Portugall is like to rue it on every side this yeare".[113]

In 1657–1658 the EIC directors planned to set up a factory in Canton, albeit for a short period. This project was not followed through, perhaps because of the war with the Netherlands, the setting up of contacts and trade centres in Asia also being a matter of regional preference and not simply due to a lack of capital to invest. Even though the first undertakings did not represent a robust effort on the part of the Company to set up trade relations with China, they marked the beginning of Anglo-Portuguese relations in Macau.[114] They displayed trends, interests and patterns of rival interaction between each country's traders, which, as stated by the king of Portugal in a letter to the viceroy *a propos* of Weddell's visit, had to be reconciled by means of "agilities" and dissimulation, "for the terms to which things in general have been reduced oblige us to make peace with England".[115]

The start of the truce between the Portuguese and the Dutch in the East (1645–1652) freed the former from the need for English vessels, but Macau, "abandoned" by Lisbon, endured the consequences of the wars caused by the Manchu invasion. In early 1645 King João IV ordered Goa to hamper the English vessels' room for manoeuvre,[116] given the ease with which they already operated in the ports of the Portuguese *Estado da Índia*, a strategy which was developed especially during the administration of the viceroy Filipe de Mascarenhas and up to the Treaty of Westminster (10–06-1654), after which English trade in the Portuguese Asian ports was once again facilitated. Macau's interests were thus defended subtly so as not to interfere in the kingdom's European diplomatic strategies and in its interests, recently separated as it was from the Spanish Crown, and for which England was a strategic ally. These Portuguese priorities were far removed from the interests of the Portuguese and Macanese who lived and traded in Southern China.

In January 1643, in a letter from Surat to the EIC,[117] Edward Knipe described the absence of trade between Macau and India in the preceding three years because of the Dutch blockade. He stated that these two Portuguese territories were in need of goods and advised London to grasp the opportunity by sending more vessels, since the Portuguese and the Dutch were at war, and the English could thus easily sail the Eastern seas. As regards the second (Luso-) English voyage to Macau, in August 1644 the *Hind*[118] was sent to the enclave by Surat, together with the *Seahorse*, again without the knowledge of the directors in London. Contrary to what some authors have stated,[119] this was not the first English vessel entirely at the service of the EIC to put in at the enclave; its purpose, after due authorisation from the viceroy of India,[120] was (also) to conduct another English trading venture in China. Approximately five months before peace was signed between the Portuguese and the Dutch in India, Count Aveiras issued the *Hind* with a charter in March 1644, following the decision of the Revenue Council (*Conselho de Fazenda*) for this vessel to carry from Macau all the surplus copper,[121] giving Blackman, the captain of the *William*, instructions regarding the voyage, in accordance with the terms agreed under the old contract with the *London*.[122] The arrival of three EIC vessels—the *William*, owned by Courteen's Association, the *Seahorse*, and the *Hind*—in Macau in 1644, incurred Dutch displeasure, seeing as they did the English gain ever greater power and freedom of movement in the East. Basing herself on documents in the Goa Historical Archive,[123] Maria Manuela Sobral Blanco asserts that the *Hind* and the *William* went to Macau at the behest of the Portuguese Crown to take on munitions and gunpowder in exchange for cinnamon.

Initially welcomed by the Macau Portuguese, the crew of the *Hind* quickly felt affronted by the Chinese because of the excessive sum they demanded after the vessel had been measured and which reduced the profits of the voyage.[124] The president of the Surat factory, Francis Breton, described the state of the city, comparing it to the territory to which the *London* had sailed approximately ten years before, paying far lower taxes. What most surprised the *Hind*'s supercargoes was the poverty which had had the city in its grip since trade with Japan came to an end:

> But that which rendered the voyage much less profitable then it might have proved is the extreme poverty of the place, not appearing the same it was at the London's being there; rendered so by the loss of their former Trade to Japon and the Manillas [...]. And now lately (which makes them more miserable) China is wholly imbroiled in wars. [...] which disturbances, with the Portuguese's poverty, have left Macchaw destitute of all sorts of commodities, there not being to be bought in the city either silks raw, or wrought, China roots, other then what were old and rotten; nor indeed anything but China-ware, which is the bulk of the Hinds' lading, the rest being brought in gold. Nor could any thing at all during the ships' stay there be procured from Cantam.[125]

Unlike the *Hind*, the *London* and Weddell's fleet had visited Macau when it was thriving, before the Black Ship had stopped sailing, whereas the vessels which came later arrived in a city undergoing a deep socio-economic crisis due to the end of trade with Japan and to the starvation which ravaged the population in 1648. Nor were these circumstances favourable for English trade in Canton. In the 1640s and 60s the Manchus invaded Southern China, making the city fight on several fronts to ensure its survival, since, after the end of the Portuguese-Spanish dual monarchy, it also found itself officially "divorced" from another trading partner, Manila.[126] The state of disruption in the empire and piracy in the South China seas were known to the English, who therefore avoided these waters. The Manchu conquest, that is, the advent of the Qing dynasty, and the final taking of Canton in 1650, were also impediments to the development of English trade in China.[127]

In London, the Company directors' reaction on being apprised of the voyage of the *Hind*, which left Macau in November 1644, was even more adverse than that sparked by the voyage of the *London*. President Breton, on abandoning the project to set up EIC trading in Macau, was forced to justify his actions by declaring that he had pursued such a course in order to take advantage of the regional circumstances, comparing his initiative to Methwold's during the *London*'s voyage:

> We must confesse it was a bould attempt of us to dispose of your ship-ping unto such remote parts as Maccaw and the Manielies without your especiall license, which we would willingly have attended and gladly have enjoyed for our warrant, but that delaies therin would have been danger-ous, especially in that to Maccaw, the Dutch and Portugals being then upon a treaty of peace, which once concluded, we well *knew that the Vice Roy (when the trade should be open to the Portugals themselves) could not dispense with ours or any other strangers voiaging thither; which induced us to lay hold of the present opportunity*, so fairly offered; whereunto we were encouraged by the confidence we had that a voiage thither for your propper accompt could not prove less advantagious then did the Londons fraight-ing voiage, wherwith you were yet well pleased. [...] The ship returned in safety [...] we doubt not but to render a satisfactory accompt therof. In the interim, you may please to take notice that we never expected a continued trade thither, nor were licensed for more then that voiage, which had we not then embraced, could not now be procured.[128]

The *Hind*'s voyage was profitable, but was in the end an isolated attempt, and Surat decided not to undertake further voyages to China.[129] Despite the signing of the Convention of Goa, conflicts between the English and the Portuguese continued, and the EIC complained in early 1647 about the heavy losses and offences[130] caused by the Macau administration. The city was in a "depressed state" and its trade had stagnated because of the Manchu invasion, which explained why no English vessels were sent to China.[131] In October 1650 Surat stated that China was in such a state of poverty and trade so reduced that "the Portuguese at Macau [were] sinking into poverty".[132]

English complaints about clashes with the Macau administration continued throughout the seventeenth century, notably in the 60s.[133] On 28 October 1649 the EIC again complained, in patriotic terms, to the English Council of State about the violent enmity of the Portuguese in the East, summarising the Anglo-Portuguese naval stand-off since 1602 as follows:

> They [EIC] were opposed by the Portuguese, who "pretended the sole title to that navigation, as well by discovery as donation". [...] By the blessing of God, they not only made good their commerce in their several residences, but came off victorious in several signal fights against their determined enemies, the Portuguese, notwithstanding the incredible advantages possessed by the latter both in men and ships. After thirty years of hostility the Portuguese, finding by dear-bought experience that they could not prevail, and wearing of war, proposed peace, which was accepted and agreed upon in the year 1635.[134]

The document criticised English interlopers such as Sir William Courteen, who invaded the EIC trading territory, competing against it to the advantage of the Portuguese enemies. This document went on to imply that, when the problems caused by the Portuguese rivals had ended, independent English traders arrived with charters issued by Charles I, and that these traders in no way contributed to the development of the nation's trade.

In early 1647 the Macau Senate wrote to the king of Portugal, warning him of the danger, *vis-à-vis* the Chinese authorities, of Goa's sending foreign vessels to the city, once again recalling the reprisals suffered as a result of the *London*'s visit.[135] In that year, king João IV wrote to the viceroy and referred to the very great losses caused by the sending of two English vessels (the *Hind* and the *William*) to Macau in 1644 by Count Aveiras, because "of the great repugnance of the king of China that this nation passed through his land", for which reason "similar vessels must not be sent to that city".[136]

In 1648, after the EIC's fruitless first sporadic voyages to Macau, the Company directors asked Banten to advise them as to the possibility of sending a small vessel on a voyage to China. President Peniston advised against such a voyage because of the pirates that infested the South China seas and given the fact that the Portuguese in the impoverished city did not honour the Convention of Goa:

> The experiment which you desire we should make with one of our small vessels for trade into China we are certainly informed, by those that know the present state and condition of that country very well, cannot be undertaken without the inevitable loss both of the ship, men and goods. [...] And how one of our feeble vessels would be able to defend themselves against such forces [pirates] is easie to be supposed. As for the Portugalls in Macau, they are little better than mere rebells against their Vice Roy in Goa, having lately murdered their Captain General [Diogo Docem] sent thither to them [1651]; and Macau itself so distracted among themselves that they are dayly spilling one another's blood. But put the case all these things were otherwise, we must needs say we are in a very poor condition to seek out new discoveries.[137]

The level of poverty in the city also influenced the English trading strategy, as mentioned by the Surat factor in 1637.[138] In mid-1652, when the ten-year peace between the Portuguese and the Dutch had come to an end, conflicts flared up in the Malacca Straights, and the English were again viewed as allies by the Portuguese, an alliance which was reinforced by the start of the Anglo-Dutch war in that year. The Dutch attacked English vessels, paying special attention to those which might be carrying Portuguese goods between Goa and Macau, while the English regarded Cambodia as a territory where a factory might facilitate indirect trade with China.[139]

In 1655, one year after João IV and Oliver Cromwell signed the Treaty of Westminster,[140] which granted English vessels greater freedom in Portuguese ports in the East[141] with the exception of Macau, the viceroy of Goa Rodrigo Lobo da Silveira wrote about the now common English maritime traffic in Goa, the rituals carried out by the foreign vessels, and their disregard with respect to the Portuguese authorities' demands, as well as the news and letters from Portugal carried by the English ships, stating that the captain of one of these vessels had heard in England that "during this monsoon sixteen Dutch vessels will come to this State [Portuguese *Estado da Índia*]".[142] This was a vital piece

of information for the defence of the territories under Portuguese rule and pro-
vides evidence of Luso-English cooperation in the East.

In November 1658 the Batavia factor informed London that two inter-
loper vessels, the *King Ferdinand* and the *Richard and Martha*, had left Canton
with no cargo and without paying custom duties,[143] upon which the Mandarin
authorities forced Macau to pay a heavy fine, as had happened twenty-three years
earlier in the *London* case and later with Weddell's fleet. The discouraging nature
of these voyages led another vessel, the *Welcome*, not to sail for China as originally planned, but rather to a different destination. In the meantime, the factor
appointed by the EIC to oversee trade with China never took up his post,[144]
the China Trade project thus being postponed yet again for several reasons.[145]
However, the Company had petitioned the Portuguese ambassador to London
for a letter of recommendation to be handed to the governor of Macau.[146]
Diplomacy thus became one of the many strategies used by the institution, both
in Europe and in the East, to undertake the first voyages to China. Already in
1661 Surat informed London that trade with China would yield profits, leading
the directors to plan several voyages and investment in the tea trade, while the
English factory in Macassar bought goods from Portuguese ship owners in
Macau, albeit in small quantities.[147]

Although in 1659 Surat advised London that trade with China would
be neither profitable nor "free", so that it would not be sending any vessels to
China,[148] five years later, and as proposed by the Company's directors, it sent
a vessel, the *Surat*, to the Luso-Chinese enclave. However, after the departure
of the vessel, London forbad its recently appointed agent Quarles Browne to
organise any voyages to China, preferring to see its officials apply their capital
in existing factories. The Banten factor, John Hunter, had suggested the voyage
of the *Surat* to Macau-Canton on finding out that a vast quantity of Chinese
goods had accumulated there over a period of eight years because of the Dutch
blockade. These could be bought lucratively, since the Portuguese did not dare
transport them for fear of the Dutch.[149] The *Surat*, captained by Robert Groste,
left Banten in June 1664 and joined the vessel of the captain-general of Macau,
Manuel Coelho da Silva, in July, shortly before he reached the enclave. The
crew was advised that the scant trade in the city, virtually inactive for the preceding two years, was suffering the consequences of the Manchu invasion. The

authorities attempted to make the *Surat* pay—by means of a 6% customs tax—for the losses incurred by the residents five years before when Macau had been visited by two English vessels (the *King Ferdinand* and the *Richard and Martha*). The enclave's commercial situation was not very favourable as a result of two factors, the Dutch blockade and the difficulties brought about by the Manchu invasion of Southern China, and perhaps for these reasons, in the 1660s the EIC concerned itself mainly with re-starting trade with Japan and not so much with the China trade. The crew of the *Surat* was told by the captain-general not to leave the vessel until he had received orders from Canton for "free trade", but the supercargoes concluded that the Portuguese were unable to do anything without the Mandarins' orders and remained in Macau in the hope of being able to trade. The Portuguese promised to assist the English given the "near affinity of our two nations",[150] but the English only visited the city in August, rented a house and a warehouse in October, and negotiated with the Portuguese, albeit with great difficulty, for the house and the warehouse were placed under guard so as to prevent the crew from fleeing without paying the Chinese tonnage taxes, which would make the latter exact from Macau payment of yet another heavy fine. As had been the case before, the English crew proposed setting up a factory in the enclave, a proposal which was turned down by the Portuguese. In the meantime, the Chinese boarded the vessel to inspect the cargo, and the English responded that if they were not allowed to land and sell their goods, they would leave after carrying out some clandestine trade. The Portuguese benefited from trading with the English and had the warehouse under guard until November, when the English paid a deposit in goods and money.

The *Surat* put in at Taipa in such a way that the Chinese authorities did not detect its presence, for trade between foreign vessels and the city was banned, and on 12 December the crew left Macau, sailing to Banten.[151] According to the factor at Surat, the voyage was not as profitable as had been hoped because of the obstacles placed in its way by the Chinese and the Portuguese in Macau,[152] with the English factory seeking new trading opportunities. However, the urgent need arose for a special permit from the king of Portugal "for ye City of Macaw have writ to him, & ye Vice Roy of Goa, not to give any Strangers leave to [go] thither".[153] Once again, local wishes and the enclave's interests departed from the principles of the Convention of Goa, and the English, faced with these hurdles, opted for indirect trade conducted from other parts of China and from Eastern factories such as that at Ayutthaya in Siam (Thailand). All the while, the EIC attempted by diplomatic means to turn Macau into a strategic space for its crews and supercargoes. However, the factors described trade between Macau, Malacca, Makassar and Manila (1661–1664) and mentioned that the Portuguese would not allow an English factory to be set up in Macau.[154] In September 1661 John South, writing from Siam, informed Surat that he was sending goods to Macau and was trading with the vessels of that city;[155] nine years later the Macau ship *Rosário* arrived in Banten, carrying Fr. António Nunes in an ambassadorial capacity, the English presidencies having become cognizant of the difficulties which the Portuguese were facing in their attempts to develop trade, given the oppression exerted by the Manchus, which led them to trade clandestinely.[156]

In the mid-1660s the new Chinese dynasty, in a strategy designed to consolidate its power, adopted heightened policies to control sea traffic and evacuate the coast, driving away possible rebels and weakening the coastal inhabitants, which led to a significant reduction in Macau's sea-going fleet between 1663 and 1667, since the Chinese burnt and confiscated approximately thirteen of the city's vessels.[157] In 1679 an imperial edict decreed the opening up of trade between the enclave and Canton, and in 1681 and 1684 the territory's trading activity and foreign trade in China were again authorised. Although trade had been opened up, the emperor retained maritime defence measures, notably restrictions on the number of vessels allowed to put to sea and the creation of customs houses to increase imperial revenues, especially in Macau; here the hopu was created (1684), with every vessel in Macau now paying taxes based on its tonnage, to the city's "greater misery".[158] The opening up of Chinese trade in 1684 increased competition on the part of the Chinese traders and damaged Macau. Faced with the difficulty of keeping up its own trade, it was only natural that the then five prominent traders in the city, with seats in the Senate, should try to keep European competition away[159] and, finding it impossible to do so, should charge a percentage of the foreign traders' profits. The Portuguese thus became ever more dependent on cooperation with the Chinese and the foreign traders, notably the Armenians.[160]

After Portugal and Spain signed their peace treaty in early 1668 with England's support, in June of that year the EIC directors, in an endeavour to extend their trade to China and re-start trade in Japan, petitioned Sir Robert Southwell, envoy extraordinary to Portugal, to obtain the prince regent Dom Pedro's authorisation for English vessels to put in at Portuguese ports and for his subjects in the East—especially in Macau—to extend friendly treatment to the English: "We look upon this liberty touching Maccaw, as a necessary help to a larged costly design we have in hand, and is likely to conduce more to the benefit of this kingdom than us the adventurers which design is the establishing a trade at China and Japan for the vent of our cloth and other Manufactures".[161] In early 1669 Southwell asked Dom Pedro to write to the viceroy of Goa requesting his subjects in the East, especially the governor of Macau, "libertie and freedome of commerce to the English [...] good usage [...] freedome of commerce and the libertie of residing".[162] This diplomatic measure on the part of the EIC may have been taken in response to requests such as those addressed to London by the president of the Surat factory, William Methwold, after the voyage of the *London*, attempting with Portugal's involvement to obtain authorisation for the English to trade in the enclave.[163] Following these English diplomatic moves in Lisbon, policies for the defence of the local interests in Macau also became the result of orders received from Lisbon. These very often contradicted English plans, since, in early 1669, a letter from the prince regent ordered the viceroy, João Nunes da Cunha, to ensure that all the captains of the Portuguese fortresses maintained "good correspondence and mutual friendship" with English crews in the ports of the *Estado da Índia*, except that of Macau, where the foreigners had to be barred from any trade:

> because its preservation and trade depend on the favourable support from China, and because of the consequences which will follow as the King [emperor] does not wish to consent to such Trade, and because of the English, the Dutch will also want to use the same concession with which they will become absolute masters of trade in the South; however, if any English vessel sink in those seas, and has to put in at that port and needs some supply or help, you will order it so, which is due in the name of Brotherhood. But in no circumstance is it to be allowed to buy or sell any goods, for the damage that this may cause.[164]

The administration, the strategic importance and the status of Macau differed from those of the other Portuguese territories in Asia, and Dom Pedro drew the attention of Count São Vicente and of the governor of Macau to the danger posed by English and Dutch trade in China, although the political situation in Portugal since the Restoration demanded a two-pronged strategy: obtaining the assistance of Spain's enemies in Europe and not antagonising them in the overseas territories, where their interests obviously ran counter to those of Portugal. The struggle in the overseas territories would not be possible, given the lack of resources, and would also weaken King João IV's position in Europe.[165] However, clashes between the VOC and the Portuguese in the East continued, and this was a situation with an inverse and a reverse: truce in Europe and fighting in the overseas territories.[166]

As regards the exchange of information between the *Estado da Índia* and Lisbon, as also the latter's awareness of the fears of Macau's residents, it is worth remembering the statements presented by the Senate to Goa and Lisbon on the problems caused by Weddell's fleet in 1637 and by other English vessels. While Dom Pedro wrote to the viceroy, the Portuguese secretary of state informed the English special ambassador Paul Methuen of the acts of piracy by English buccaneers which attacked vessels from Macau and sold their spoils in Bombay, urging the English government to take appropriate measures to prevent similar situations.[167]

In Europe, English diplomacy and spying activity, as well as the sending of intelligence from Lisbon on the movements of Portuguese vessels[168] became efficacious strategic measures in the EIC's attempts to establish itself in the East. A year after the signing of the marriage contract of Catherine of Braganza and Charles II and of the new Anglo-Portuguese treaty in 1661[169]—through which Portugal defended itself from Spain and the Dutch, and the English attempted to exploit the weakened state of the Portuguese in the East[170]—Bombay, the so-called English gateway to India,[171] was ceded by Afonso VI to Charles II as part of the Portuguese princess's dowry. However, the transfer was only completed in 1665,[172] the English king leasing the territory to the EIC in 1668.

As argued by D. K. Bassett,[173] Bombay was the first true English "colony" in the East, since all the other factories were merely trading centres. The transfer of the port from the Portuguese led to the presence of an English warship for the first time in the East when the Earl of Marlborough was sent to the island of Salsette for the formal hand-over of this dominion. A secret article appended to the 1661 treaty[174] asserted that, from their base in Bombay, the English would lend military support to the Portuguese dominions in India against the Dutch. This never happened, for, although the latter signed a peace treaty with the Portuguese in that year,[175] between then and early 1663 the VOC captured Kollam, Cranganore and Cochin, before the effects of the treaty made themselves felt in any actual way in the East. The EIC had been in possession of Madras since 1639 and in 1686 it founded Calcutta, but its base in Bombay allowed it to develop a strategic position on the coast of north-eastern India which was more secure than the factory at Surat, the city becoming a port of significant importance for English trade in the East, overtaking Goa as an economic centre in the second half of the eighteenth century.

Macau between Surat and Japan: The voyage of the Return

EIC voyages to Macau were few until about 1675. In September 1673 the *Return*, captained by Simon Delboe, docked in the enclave seeking protection from the Dutch, and the crew remained in the city for about eight months. At this time it developed some trade, limited by the Portuguese, after spending time in Formosa and approximately two months in the bay of Nagasaki in a vain attempt to re-start English trade with Japan,[176] from which the Portuguese were also barred, as we have already seen. Faced with the crisis which engulfed the enclave, its merchants tried to find alternatives to the old trading activity with Japan,[177] and, after a meeting at the house of the captain-general of Macau, António Barbosa de Lobo, and having drawn up seven articles, they authorised the off-loading of the *Return*'s cargo for trade with the Portuguese alone and against cash payment.[178] The seven articles, designed by the Portuguese to safeguard the vessel and crew and to carry on trade without Chinese retaliation, allowed the English to:

> bring their vessel to the false harbour [Taipa] where [...] it can have all its goods taken onto land, being first ... registered and inventoried. [...] Enough houses in which to store their goods will be rented and [...] the captain with six persons will live there [...], and five soldiers will be posted

there as sentries [...] for the Chinamen not to disturb them [...], it is prudent that captain and the six persons who assist him should in any way leave the said houses, nor should they walk in the streets, because it is not public to the Chinamen that they are in this city, that they should not sell more than strictly necessary for their outlays and expenses [...], they should pay the percentages of two hundred taels [...] as the Portuguese dwellers do, [...] for anchorage of the vessel to the Mandarin of the White House.[179]

The crew was kept under surveillance because of the "offences [...] costs and intranquility which this city has sometimes repeatedly suffered with this barbarian and tyrannical Tartar government, when other English vessels came to this port",[180] selling some of their goods to pay off their expenses. However, British sources reveal that the Portuguese authorities initially barred Macau residents from visiting the English warehouse and buying goods there, under threat of being considered traitors and enemies of national interests.[181]

The letter written by the *Return*'s supercargoes to Surat described their arrival in the territory, the way it was governed, both locally and from Portugal, the crew's first contacts prior even to the meeting of the Portuguese traders in the governor's house and their initial decision: "The Portuguese at Macau are governed by six commissioners who represent the city and a captain general, who has the comand over the Manillas for the King, and receives his orders through the viceroy of Goa, but at Macau neither the commissioners can act without the captain general, nor he without their concurrence".[182] From early on, this type of information about the policies and measures taken by the Portuguese with respect to the Chinese authorities interested the English, as we can see from the supercargoes' descriptions of the growth of trade in Macau prompted by the Anglo-Dutch war of the early 1780s, the arrival/departure of Portuguese vessels, the prices of the goods carried, and, for example, the Portuguese embassy to Peking in 1752.[183]

The crew of the *Return* stated that the Portuguese had barred them from trading and they could only off-load their goods in order to safeguard them. These measures were designed to avoid difficulties with the Chinese of the type caused by earlier visits of English vessels:

> the supercargoes of the *Return* sent Mr. Robinson ashore on the ship's arrival, and the chief of the six commissioners sent us word, that we might

land our goods for their security if we desired it, and that the ship might lie in the same road as the King of Portugal shipping did, but to admit us to trade and sell our goods ashore, they could not, for they were under the control of the Tartars or Chinese, who had prohibited trade with the English as well as the Dutch at this place. They added that some of our nation had been several times at Macau, for which the Portuguese authorities had been brought into trouble by the tartars: wherefore they could not admit us to trade.[184]

To the argument of the fine paid by the city as a result of the *London*'s visit, Macau's traders now added the examples of Weddell's fleet and that of the *Hind*, recalling earlier, less pleasant episodes and incidents to justify their barring English vessels from entering until the eighteenth century.[185]

Macau's reply displeased the crew, whose expectations with regard to re-starting trade with Japan had already been dashed and who now feared the attacks of their Dutch enemies on the seas. A second supercargo, Delboe, accompanied by Grimaldi, the governor of Macau's messenger, went ashore to renegotiate with the authorities. This second contact, further to which the above cited meeting at the home of the captain-general was organised, allowed the English to dock in the "false harbour" of Taipa and off-load the goods registered and stored in a godown (warehouse, cellar), guarded by five soldiers paid by the crew. The account is a translation of the seven articles (presented above) from the Portuguese source and describes the demands which the city presented to the supercargoes because of the fines paid to the Chinese when English vessels had visited the city in earlier times. The crew members admitted that they only acquiesced to the Portuguese because of their fear of being attacked by the Dutch should they put out to sea, adding that, with Lisbon's authorisation, it would be easy for the English to remain in Macau alongside the Portuguese.[186] In November the English requested the freedom to trade, to which the Portuguese replied that they should "in every matter adhere to what had been agreed".[187] In May of the following year the crew requested permission to move the vessel closer to the city to a position from which it might be protected by the city's forts from possible Dutch attacks, a request which was denied. Finally, in early September 1674 the vessel left for India, not without first having attempted to trade with the Chinese in Lampacau.[188] The Macau Portuguese were able to extract some benefit from the expedition in that they forced the crew to negotiate in accordance with the city's trading interests. Cross-referencing Portuguese and British sources regarding this episode, it is possible to arrive at conclusions differing from those of Patricia Drumond Borges Ferreira when she affirmed that Portuguese documents "do not refer to the case [of the *Return*] and English documents do not go into detail on the matter".[189]

According to John Bruce,[190] the incident which led the vessel to the territory gave rise to great speculation by the supercargoes concerned, for the latter counselled Bombay to negotiate with Goa on freedom of trade and the founding of a factory in Macau, where a considerable amount of EIC goods could be supplied to the Chinese in exchange for local products, easily saleable in India and in Europe. The author's conclusion is that this incident is probably the origin of the EIC China Trade; however, the episode merely represents yet another of the initial attempts to trade with China, and one of the countless occasions when the English supercargoes gathered first-hand information on the business activities, the *modus vivendi*, *modus operandi* and the local interests of Macau, contributing, as had other previous voyages, to the permanent establishment of the EIC in the Pearl River Delta approximately twenty-seven years later. According to Bassett,[191] it is following upon the failed attempts to re-establish direct trade with Japan and, later, in the conflicts in Tonkin that we must situate the turning-point of the Company's interest towards maritime dealings with China. In the case of the *Return*, the ensuing trade was the result, not of a plan carefully laid out by the English, rather it came out of the desire to conduct some trade and of the crew members' defending themselves from the Dutch peril in the seas of Asia. Macau thus operated as a familiar haven in the Far Eastern seas and an alternative location for trade with the Portuguese, when the latter permitted it.

The last English voyages to Macau in the seventeenth century

The EIC's first voyages yielded reduced profits, but after its charters were renewed by Oliver Cromwell in 1657 and King Charles II in 1661, the activity of the English interlopers in the East was weakened, Dutch competition was controlled by the Navigation Acts,[192] and Portuguese hostility was controlled through trade and diplomatic accords such as that which marked the marriage of Catherine of Bragança to Charles II. Under these accords, Bombay and Tangier were ceded to the English, while the role of the English factories in India was strengthened, a context which allowed the EIC to take a different view of trade with China and contributed towards making Britain the greatest maritime and colonial power from the middle of the following century onward.

In 1681, the directors considered the establishment of trade with China as "desirable" and "profitable", for Canton silk was better than that of Amoy, and English products were more easily sold in Canton. However, two doubts persisted: obtaining a Chinese permit for the Banten factory to trade in Canton which would guarantee the security of the vessels, and the possibility that sending vessels to the Pearl River delta might offend the Chinese in Amoy. The EIC already traded with the latter, and trading in Canton might jeopardise established commercial interests.[193] According to a EIC letter to Banten (1680) considering the treatment meted out by the Chinese to the Dutch in other parts of China, the Company regarded with some suspicion and reservations the invitation extended by the viceroy of Canton for the English to set up a factory there.[194] Precisely the following year, the Company decided to send a vessel to Canton and advised Banten that if the Manchus invaded Amoy, the factors should find alternative ports, notably Macau and Lampacau.

From that year onward, vessels from Banten carried a supercargo—who together with the captain, formed a "joint council"—who was not allowed to reside in Canton and returned with the vessel.[195] Although it had attempted to set up a factory in Canton in 1673, 1682–1683[196] and 1689, it was only after 1699 that the EIC tried to develop the China Trade in a systematic manner.[197] Up to that time, its vessels had sailed sporadically from Banten to Amoy and Formosa,[198] ports where continental Chinese products were to be found and where the supercargoes bought silk, china and pearls, among other goods. While Macau attempted to overcome its economic crisis, in 1670 the EIC factor in Banten, Henry Dacres, managed to obtain authorisation to trade in Formosa and later in Amoy, both under the control of Cheng King until 1683[199] and 1680 (respectively), when the Manchu troops took these ports. In 1685 the Chinese emperor opened his ports to foreign vessels. The appearance of a new EIC in 1698 increased rival activity between the two companies,[200] with the older-established one concentrating its trade in Amoy and the recently formed in Canton, where in 1699 its vessel, the *Macclesfield*, arrived. In 1709, the two rival Companies, the "old" one created in 1600, and the "new" founded in 1687, merged into a single entity, the New East India Company.

The trading activity of the EIC factories in the different macro-regions of China[201] did not achieve the desired results, and, after several voyages planned by local factors such as Henry Dacres, in 1683 the Company decided to attempt to establish itself near Canton, sending the *Tywan* and the *China Merchant*. The crews of the two ships were prevented from trading by the Chinese and the Portuguese and were driven away from the city.[202] Agents of the Eastern factories, such as Dacres in Banten, were pivotal in the turning-point in Company policy with regard to China, as they made decisions based on local reality and experience. Expansion of trade to China in the years 1675–1682 thus derived from initiatives taken by these traders, the London directors only learning such decisions sometimes a year after the event. Isolated attempts to set up trade in China did not achieve any immediate results, since self-sufficient China closed itself to the outside, and the Portuguese continued to defend their interests at all cost. This was the case of the voyages of the *Carolina* in 1683 and the *Loyal Adventure* in 1684,[203] which were attempts to begin trade relations with China both through Macau and Lampacau. In the meantime, the crews on the initial voyages gathered information of use for future expeditions, notably on how long English vessels could remain off the coast of Macau with a view to obtaining goods from Canton, the supercargoes on board the *Loyal Merchant* reaching the conclusion that private trade had to be controlled to prevent the prices of Chinese products from rising.[204] On the other hand, and according to the EIC supercargoes, the establishment of the English in China was hampered by the Portuguese, who advised the Mandarins that Macau was in danger and requested that they expel foreign vessels from the city; this they did by ordering the English to dock at outlying islands, where Chinese traders would go to negotiate.[205]

The crew of the *Carolina* left London in 1682 charged with founding a factory in Canton, aiming to avoid Macau should the Portuguese hinder their dealings with the Chinese; they would try their luck in other ports on the Chinese coast such as Taipa Quebrada[206]—where the Chinese would meet them—or even the alternative ports of Amoy and Formosa. In the second decade of the eighteenth century, the supercargoes held their preference for docking at "Typa

Quebrada harbour (which was a safe place for a ship to ride in near Macau, and yet out of the power of the Portuguese or Chinese)",[207] where the *Carolina* arrived in June 1683. The English were received by the governor, who stated he had been informed that the crew was Dutch, hence foes, and added that he could not authorise any type of trade unless he was so instructed by the viceroy of Goa, under pain of arrest and execution, Macau not having enough goods to allow for transactions, given the tight control of the Mandarinate, under whose orders almost every aspect of the city lay.[208] According to the Chinese officials who visited the vessel, the Portuguese governor had warned Canton of a Dutch presence in Taipa, requesting that warships be sent to expel them. The Chinese authorities accepted the evidence that the crew members were English but told them of the emperor's displeasure with regard to Dutch and English trade with the king of Formosa, as this activity allowed the latter to acquire the munitions with which he fought against China. The Mandarinate ordered the *Carolina* to leave, and the vessel left Macau in July 1683. It carried the message that no European nation should attempt to establish itself in China,[209] for the Portuguese had bought exclusive rights to foreign trade and had informed the emperor that the English and Dutch were helping the king of Formosa against him.[210] For its part, the *Delight*, sent by London in January 1683 to join the *Carolina*, was given the same message by the Chinese when it reached the vicinity of Macau in mid-1684, the crew concluding after six days that any trade in the enclave would be impossible. They therefore sailed to Amoy,[211] once again viewed as an alternative for direct trade with China. Whereas the previous trade endeavours had come as a result of the Banten agents, the EIC's attention shifted definitively from Japan to China between 1674 and 1684, given the impossibility of re-starting trade with the archipelago, and not as the outcome of a pre-existing plan on the part of the Company.[212] In 1684 Fort St. George concluded that English trade in Lampacau had become ever more difficult, for the "Portugueez of Macoa had prevailed with the Tartars to prohibit all Trade aboute the Pampacoa islands".[213] Indeed, in 1682 and 1685 the Macau Senate, as an institution comprising traders with commercial interests, informed King Pedro II of the harms of foreign competition,[214] and in early 1686 the king banned foreign vessels from the city,[215] while the English factors in Madras had been attempting since 1684 to invite Chinese traders to set up residence there.[216]

In September 1689, a year after the fruitless voyage of the *Rebecca* and the *James*[217] from Madras to Macau, the master of the *Defence*, William Heath, contributed, as had Weddell, towards maintaining the negative image of the English in China, until more direct contacts and the Chinese traders' commercial interests made it fade. This is the first major incident in the history of the English presence in Macau. In 1689 the Chinese demanded that the crew of the *Defence*, sent to Canton by the Madras presidency, hand over the vessel's mast, an order which Heath refused, sending a group of sailors to the island of Taipa to recover it by force. The English, some of whom had taken up quarters in the Forte da Guia in Macau, were stoned by the native population, responded by opening fire and ended by killing one Chinese man. A Chinese vessel and some of the island's inhabitants opened fire on the English and arrested some of the men who had remained behind. Heath decided to leave the enclave in May 1690 and left a sum of money with a Chinese man to ransom the captive crew members.[218]

Since the end of the 1680s to the 1750s, the Portuguese traders of Macau had had close dealings with the English country traders, especially in Madras, to where they sailed annually,[219] and in 1712, the year which saw EIC supercargoes' private trade again banned,[220] the Macau Senate wrote to Edward Harrison, the newly arrived governor of Madras, welcoming him and advising him that

> vessels of the inhabitants of this city who go to that port have always been very well accepted there, both on account of the mystical friendship which exists between the crown of Portugal and that of England and the good correspondence which has existed up to now between this city and that [...], we hope [...] to receive greater demonstrations of accord for in the same way [...] Your Excellency will have them guaranteed for anything you please.[221]

The city foregrounded the principles of the old alliance governing Anglo-Portuguese relations, including in the East, thus also defending the interests of Portuguese traders in the British Asian ports, while the English defended their priorities in attempting trade with China via the enclave. In 1739 English traders from Madras mentioned the Portuguese trade competition and justified such trade on the basis of its longevity and of its profits; this activity was therefore also to the advantage of the EIC itself, with the Company directors employing Portuguese traders to supply tea to Madras, as they already did to the VOC in Batavia.[222]

An anonymous description of Macau in the 1600s (c.1693) mentions the increase in the Protestant presence in the second half of the seventeenth century, as well as the Portuguese attempts to keep the foreigners away from the city, where only the Portuguese were allowed to buy property:

> how the Macanese proceed with the Batavians and the English, and their trade with China: The City of the Holy Name of God [of Macau] does not permit any of the vessels of the English and Batavian Heretics to enter the port of Macau, although some of the Chinese Magistrates requested it, and such permission might bring not inconsiderable temporal gain. For this reason, the vessels of the Heretics stay at anchor for some months in the Islands closest to Macau, there facing the great danger of the region's terrible storms. In that time, the Macau Senate, despite allowing some of them to visit the City occasionally, nevertheless, rarely allows them to stay overnight. [...] And there were very few English vessels which sheltered there, from the year 1626 to 1692.[223]

The revenues derived from the English presence in impoverished Macau became essential to its economy. As we will now see, this presence increased from the beginning of the eighteenth century, for the Chinese authorities only allowed foreign traders to remain in Canton during the "trading seasons" (September–March),[224] and so the EIC officials, and later European trading agents and interlopers settled in Macau for the rest of the year. The enclave became a strategic territory for the Chinese authorities in terms of regulating the presence of the "barbarians" and benefiting from their trade, their control over the city growing ever more stringent. Macau's own survival depended on respecting the will of the Mandarinate, and the city's submission to Chinese wishes was a constant feature in its history, which the English referred to in their attempts to turn the weight of Chinese power to their own advantage with a view to legitimising their presence and trade in a place administered by the Portuguese. The English also knew that if they took Macau by force the Mandarins would order the closing of the Barrier Gate (Porta do Cerco) and starve them to death, forcing them to leave the city.

4

The beginning of regular East India Company trade with China

Throughout the second half of the seventeenth century, the EIC's initial attempts to set up direct contact with China stemmed above all from the strategy of Eastern factories, whereas the Portuguese tried to defend their privileged position in the Pearl River delta, to the detriment of English interests. Between 1690 and 1696 eight EIC vessels made their way to Chinese ports, this number rising to twenty between 1697 and 1703 and to forty-three between 1698 and 1715.[1] At the end of the seventeenth century, the success of the voyage of the *Macclesfield* marked the beginning of the permanent settling of the supercargoes along the Macau-Canton axis, forcing the Portuguese to adapt to new trading circumstances arising in Southern China. The initial turning away of northern-European competition was part of the strategy for survival adopted by Macau, which was compelled to adjust to the new situation brought about both by the arrival of the EIC and increased European trade with China from the beginning of the eighteenth century onwards, and by the development of the port of Canton,[2] all of which factors affected Portuguese trade in the Far East[3] and turned Macau into an increasingly multicultural city. Although the different communities in Macau did not interact as much as we would think, due to linguistic, religious and social obstacles, the city was, at the time, as cosmopolitan as it could be, a platform where Asians, Africans, European and American traders and travellers met and mingled to a certain degree.

According to Brother José de Jesus Maria, in 1745 there were in Macau "twelve thousand men who at the same time dwelt there, [...] between Portuguese, half-castes, *Nhons* [Macanese], Malays, Canarins, Timorese, Mozambicans, Malabars, Moors, Kaffirs, and other nations of which all is composed, as well as some foreigners who reside here, and here get married, French, English",[4] testifying to the cosmopolitan character of the enclave and to the presence in the city of married English men. Indeed, the Dutch Andreas Houckgeest, head of the VOC factory between 1790 and 1795, stated that it would be impossible to find such an amalgam of nations anywhere else and such bizarre figures or such a variety of races as in Macau.[5] In 1744 the captain-general of Macau put before the Portuguese king the case of an Englishman who wanted to marry a Portuguese woman, which constituted a "bad example", since this might lead to "so many getting married, that in a few years' time they will outnumber the Portuguese".[6] One year later, King João V banned the marriage of foreigners in Macau, since within a few years the latter would outnumber the Portuguese. Ten years later, the Macau Senate advised the king of Portugal that Portuguese trade in the city was virtually non-existent, given the number of foreign vessels sailing to Asian ports, which made the Portuguese feel unprotected.[7]

The success of the *Macclesfield* (1699–1700) as a turning-point

Ou-Mun [...] is, in truth, a territory important for coastal defence and an excellent strategic position for foreign vessels.

—Tcheong-Ü-Lam and Ian-Kuong-Iam, *Ou-Mun Kei-Lok. Monografia de Macau* [*Monograph of Macau*], 1979 [*c.*1751], p. 116

After a series of failed attempts to set up trade with China and because of the growing difficulty of trading in Amoy and Formosa in 1699, the EIC directors, displaying some urgency,[8] decided to send another vessel to Canton, a voyage which would alter the status and position of the English in the Pearl River delta.

On 26 August 1699 the *Macclesfield* reached Macau, where the Portuguese, who had lost four vessels to English pirates, searched the vessel minutely and offered to defend it with their forts, "a thing never before granted to any European ship".[9] Not wishing to appear mistrustful of the Portuguese overture, the supercargo thanked the Portuguese for their generosity and replied that they did not yet know whether the hopu and the Chinese traders would provide him with a reason to stay and that it was for the moment advisable for the ship to remain outside the harbour. The supercargo John Briggs went ashore to greet the

Portuguese governor and visit the hopu,[10] requesting them to advise the Chinese authorities of the arrival of the *Macclesfield*. On being visited aboard his vessel by the hopu's secretary and some traders, the head supercargo Robert Douglas requested samples and prices of silk and stated that he would only respond to matters after ascertaining the position of the hopu. The Portuguese approached the vessel, displaying curiosity and their suspicions that it might belong to pirates. After the exchange of gifts with the hopu and the measuring of the *Macclesfield*, a number of Cantonese traders with whom Briggs had negotiated on an earlier voyage visited the vessel. Among these was the Mandarin of the White House, who communicated in Portuguese with no need for interpreters from Macau. On 5 September Douglas and the captain visited the enclave and were received by the governor, several aldermen, the hopu's secretary and the Mandarin, saying that the latter "showed us more respect than is usual for one of his quality to do, for he received us at the door of the Hall, and at parting went down with us to the first landing almost 10 or 12 steps".[11] Before setting off for Canton, Douglas became aware of the change in behaviour of the Chinese and of their interest in the possibility of setting up contacts with their new trading partners, a conclusion which the English supercargo spun in his favour, not hesitating to make demands of the Chinese and the Portuguese, the latter ever more powerless in the face of the wishes of the Mandarins.

The Canton hopu sent a chop to the English guaranteeing them security and freedom to trade and asking the supercargoes not to leave before he arrived in Macau, which he did on 7 September. The vessel was again measured, and the sum of taxes was reduced from 1,200 to 480 taels. Meanwhile some supercargoes went ashore in Macau with three of the latter absconding. These were captured and returned by the Portuguese, who made provisions available to the English. On 3 October the *Macclesfield* sailed up to Whampoa, and six days later the crew members moved from a trader's house to their own hong (warehouse) in Canton, recruiting local workers. All these attitudes on the part of the Chinese showed to what extent the Mandarinate wished to please their English partners. As already shown, trade in Macau proved to be difficult, and the crew decided to set off for Canton, signalling the beginning of regular English trade in this city, henceforth a destination to be preferred over the two previous ones, Amoy and Formosa.[12] The supercargoes enjoyed some freedom of movement in Canton, and, assisted by a French agent and French Jesuits, and, already more aware of how to act towards the Chinese, they contacted a local trader and did business until the viceroy ordered their definitive departure from the city in July 1700, on the grounds that they had to be confined to Macau.

This was the first truly profitable EIC voyage to China, giving rise as it did to the permanent setting up of the English along the Canton-Macau axis. The *Macclesfield*'s success marked the beginning of a new phase, for, from 1700 onward, the English no longer needed Portuguese trading and political media-tion in China, but approached the Chinese traders and authorities directly. From then on, trading interests were shared by the English, the Chinese and the Portuguese, to the great dismay of the latter, who submitted to Chinese designs and attempted to extract maximum profit from the sojourn of the English vessels in the Pearl River delta. For their part, and given their direct contact with the Chinese, EIC officials concluded that Macau could do nothing in the face of Chinese interest in trading with recently arrived partners. The trade monopoly enjoyed by the Portuguese was now under threat, and they were totally depend-ent on the Mandarin authorities, as Robert Douglas concluded in September 1699: "This city is at present miserable poor; and although the Portuguese have thee name of the government, yet the Chinese have thee Chief Power, and all thee Customes of the Port, excepting some small privileges that the Portuguese Ships enjoy".[13]

Determined to strengthen EIC privileges, Douglas had for the first time secured the hopu's authorisation for English supercargoes to go to Canton[14] and negotiate with traders designated by the Mandarin authorities. If large-scale trade was carried out in Canton, English interests were also defended in Macau by means of economic relations set up with independent traders, the Jesuits and the city's authorities. However, the supercargoes attempted to limit the time they spent in the enclave to the minimum, since it was in Canton that they developed their business, the English presence in China during the period under analysis concerning itself above all with trade. There then began the English cycle of trade in Canton, which in turn gave rise to Anglo-Portuguese relations in Southern China on a permanent footing, the enclave becoming from then on the place of residence for English officials during part of the year.

The first fruits of the China Trade system: The growing influence of the British in Macau and the conflict of interest between the Senate and the governor

In November 1699 the new Company appointed Allen Catchpole president of its Council in China, a post he held together with that of English consul-general.[15] Faced with the impossibility of founding a factory, the Council was charged with finding other ways of setting up trade relations with China[16] and gaining a market for English textiles and lead, notably in northern China. Catchpole set out on the *Eaton*, the vessel being loaded with pepper in the recently founded English trade centre of Borneo and meeting up with the *Macclesfield* on the island of Sanchuan in October 1700. Here both vessels were detained by the hopu, until in December the diplomat set out for Macau in order to engage in the business pertaining to vessels sent from Borneo. He travelled to Canton, where he remained temporarily. However, personal trade and interests sparked conflicts between the supercargoes and the Mandarinate, cancelling out any positive results the voyage might have had. In February 1702 Catchpole and the members of the Chusan Council were relieved of their duties.[17]

As already stated, from 1700 onwards the Company, which in 1709 changed its name to the United Company of Merchants of England Trading to the East Indies as a result of the merger between the "old" and the new East India Company, began to send several ships to Canton on an annual basis.[18] According to Hosea Ballou Morse, in November 1700 the Company sent five vessels to Canton, among which the *Seaford* and the *Rising Sun*. As early as 1700, the Company was faced with the obstacles which prevailed throughout the eighteenth and nineteenth centuries: the difficulty of selling English products and of obtaining the silver demanded as payment by the Chinese.[19] Because of the monsoons and the Mandarin authorities' demands, English ships had to reach the Pearl River delta between the end of July and the middle of September and leave before the beginning of February, the period of the so-called trading season. For reasons of internal security, foreigners were not allowed to learn Chinese or remain in the Canton factories beyond the trading period, and the Chinese were not allowed to leave China in foreign ships, although they did so illegally. Macau, besides being the gateway for Westerners to enter China, was from early on a platform for the meeting of the English crews of several vessels, the destination of EIC correspondence,[20] including through use of Portuguese ships,[21] as well as being the staging-post where:

- British vessels could be re-provisioned,[22] repaired [23] and seek protection in the event of storms,[24]
- officials and crews could wait and gather intelligence on the situation in Canton[25] while the comprador prepared for the arrival of the supercargoes in the city,[26]
- initial meetings could take place with the hopu and trading contracts could be signed with the Chinese, and Chinese documents could be translated,[27]
- goods could be warehoused,[28]
- refuge could be sought and officials and crews could wait while problems or crises were worked out in Canton,[29]
- intelligence from Canton could be received for the benefit of recently arrived British vessels and where accounts of the arrival of European vessels originated,[30]
- communication with the British presidencies in India could be carried out.[31] It also offered opportunities for residence, convalescence and rest,[32] learning Chinese, buying slaves from the Portuguese,[33] jailing British offenders in China,[34] and also gathering and sending Chinese flora to India and Great Britain.[35]

The enclave became a strategic space used by the Mandarin authorities to confine and control foreigners, as attested by the different opium crises (1815, 1820, 1839) and the incident of the *Lady Hughes* (1704) in the city, as will be shown. From 1710 onwards Company vessels and "country ships" sailed to Canton via Macau.

Although initially Macau was the first Western port in China and above all a location for brief sojourns while crews hired a Macau pilot and received information and the hopu's permission to sail up the Pearl River, there was a gradual increase in requests by supercargoes to remain there, as shown by the letters exchanged between the Senate and successive governors. The aldermen (senators), the major traders in the city, tried to prevent the competition from setting itself up in the enclave, and we see successive governors being forced to justify authorisations for foreign traders to enter the city and remain there. This tension between the Macau governor and the Senate dragged on throughout the eighteenth century, and in 1773 the viceroy of India and the Senate ordered the governor to expel from the city all the foreigners living in rented houses, for which they paid high sums of money.[36] In a letter to the Senate, the governor listed European residents and stated that only the European Companies had been renting expensive houses in the city since 1758 for periods of three to ten years.[37] He added that if the Europeans lived there illegally, the Senate too was to blame, as it had never taken any measures on the issue.[38] In fact, accepting or expelling foreigners from the city was the joint responsibility of the governor and the Senate; however, and as stated by António Vale,[39] the demarcation line between each body's powers in this matter was not defined, which gave rise to mutual accusations of interference.

Two months after the signing of the Anglo-Portuguese "offensive and defensive alliance in Asia",[40] in October 1721 a ship arrived in Macau carrying British pirates whose objective it was to attack Spanish vessels, and it presented to the governor a letter-patent from the British king requesting every port which was friendly to Britain to assist the vessel, which the captain intended to have repaired or sell in order to return to Europe on an EIC ship. The governor informed the Senate that it would be advisable to grant such permission to the crew so as to prevent them from attacking local vessels sailing from Manila[41] and justified his policy[42] on the basis of the Senate's earlier request for the arrest of the British who often took vessels in the vicinity of Macau.

As already shown, since the English arrived in the seventeenth century there had been conflicts between the Portuguese and the Chinese over vessels which sought to dock in the port. The Senate, not without underlying trading interests, took precautionary measures for this not to happen, that is to say, if the governor deployed arguments of a diplomatic nature or invoked the external security of the territory, the Senate traders resorted to maintaining a balanced relation with China to try and keep European rivals away.[43] Thus, in March 1758 the governor wrote to the Senate to explain that he had authorised the presence of a British interpreter in the city to prevent him from running risks in Canton and also "because [the latter] had sought the flag of His Majesty the King of

Portugal, who in the terrible Earthquake, received, so many benefits and offerings from the [British] monarch, that [...] will tell our own king that his vassals are ill-treated in the dominions of which he is such a friend".[44]

The Senate replied and referred to the commercial losses the city and the Canton traders could incur should the interpreter concerned later travel to Ningbo.[45] Authorisation for foreigners to enter and live in Macau is thus one of the reasons for the constantly tense relation[46] between the governor and the Senate in the eighteenth century, although the aldermen also successively flouted the king's ban on long-term residence of foreigners in the enclave, given the high profits derived from letting houses,[47] since, as stated by the Dutch supercargo Andreas Everardus van Braam Houckgeest (1739–1801), the main source of income for Macau residents was house rents and the supply of concubines for foreigners.[48]

However, in the early 1730s, the British consulate in Lisbon complained to the Portuguese secretary of state for foreign affairs that the Macau authorities had banned foreigners, including British, from living in the city,[49] a measure which was obviously temporary. The city's complex interests defined the relation between the local oligarchy and European residents, and successive governors developed different policies. For example, in 1759 Diogo Pereira admitted to the Senate that he would not allow entry of a foreign vessel expelled by the Chinese in Canton, for the British presence in the city "had always been abhorrent to him".[50] However, a number of EIC ships—such as the *Prince Augustus* in 1727—docked in Taipa Quebrada while its supercargoes went to Canton. According to Earl H. Pritchard and Paul A. Van Dyke,[51] the first half of the eighteenth century saw important developments in Anglo-Chinese relations, notably: all trade was concentrated in Canton, the tea trade grew immensely, local institutions developed and were regulated as were trade practices and the residence of British traders in China, and there was an increase in the hostility towards foreign traders and in their financial exploitation by the Chinese traders. To these factors I would add the fact that the British presence became constant in Macau and significant for the enclave's economic and cultural life, especially until Hong Kong was founded.

5

The gradual growth of the British presence in Macau in the early eighteenth century

After the trading seasons in Canton, the supercargoes made their way to Macau, where they lived during the summer in relative quietude, thus being able to prepare contracts for the following year and attend to EIC interests without having to return to Europe. These prolonged sojourns of traders in the city gave rise to the production of increasingly well-informed descriptions of it, allowing the Company to become better acquainted both with the policies of the Portuguese and Chinese authorities and with the trade and interests of the remainder of the European nations in China, and to shape its trading strategy in a more informed and efficacious manner.

In 1703 Alexander Hamilton captained a country ship on its way to Amoy, when the vessel was hit by a typhoon off the coast of Macau, forcing him to put in at Taipa. The Canton hopu visited the vessel together with traders, who bought goods. The Portuguese refused permission for the crew to return to Macau unless they were handed the 10,000 silver taels which the vessel had carried on its earlier voyage from Canton. Hamilton decided to arm the crew who were in Canton with a view to storming his way into Macau where he would be able to finalise the deal with the Chinese. Two British men made their way to the enclave in order to complete the formalities of the trade contract and found out that among other products, eighty baskets of Japanese copper were missing from the goods purchased from the Chinese in Canton; as a result, the crew later took a junk laden with goods as compensation. As would become customary in Western travel accounts, Hamilton described the geographical position of Macau, its ports, the human landscape, the many illegitimate children, the religious orders and the weakened physical and military defences, as a result of which the enclave no longer was the fortress it had been in its golden age, of which there merely remained the majestic churches and other prestigious buildings.[1] The episode involving Hamilton exemplifies the conflicts which marked business dealings and Anglo-Chinese relations on the Canton-Macau circuit, while the information gathered *in loco* was pivotal for the EIC. In 1704 Charles Lockyer arrived in Macau on board the *Streatham*, visited Canton and, seven years later, published a set of suggestions for future traders engaging in trade with China, *An Account of the Trade in India*.[2] In his "Dedication" to John, Earl Powlet, Lockyer states that he had written down his observations on several parts of the East Indies for the entertainment of the curious and information of those wishing to develop trade in Canton, teaching them how to react to Chinese customs and impositions,[3] and how to flatter and strategically evade the Portuguese administration in Macau:

> hoppos have always officers at Macau, who will conduct you by Water to the city, in about 24 hours' time. But it would not be amiss on your going ashore, to visit the *Portuguese* Governor, and other Gentlemen of that Nation, who will receive you kindly, give you the News, and persuade you to go no further up. Hear every one's story and let them think you intend to lie there, unless you are forced to *Amoy* by the *Hoppos* unreasonable Demands for measurage, which by means of their Spies will soon come to their knowledge, and make well for that affair.[4]

Five years after the voyage of the *Macclesfield*, Lockyer's arrival in the city represented another trading success in China, with the *Streatham* carrying one of the first shipments of opium from India that was sold in Canton.[5] Within the sphere of the China Trade, Macau was a strategic location when it came to waiting before sailing up the Pearl River, as was, for example, the case in 1703 when the supercargoes of the United East India Company vessels, the *Kent*, *Eaton* and *Loyal Cook*, acting jointly, remained in Taipa and in the enclave, engaged an interpreter, visited the Macau hopu and assessed the new trading policy of the recently appointed "emperor's Merchant", who had bought the monopoly of trade with foreigners.[6] The supercargoes concluded that they had to set out for Canton as speedily as possible instead of staying in Macau[7] where the Portuguese, contrary to what they stated, were unable to offer them security, for they themselves were "hardly masters of the place".[8]

In 1715, having gained increasing independence and power to trade and pose demands in respect of the Portuguese administration in Macau, the EIC super-cargoes were allowed to build a factory in the suburbs of Canton, by the river,[9] met twice weekly for "consultation" and eventually demanded greater freedom to trade,[10] with the threat of removing their business to Amoy. The founding of the factory was an important step of the so-called "Canton system" of the China Trade, which the British tried to change, fighting against the demands of the Mandarinate and of the Cantonese merchants and resisting the power and control of the Portuguese authorities in Macau. In 1716 the supercargoes of the *Marlborough*, *Susanna* and *Stringer* waited in the enclave for news as to whether they would be well received in Canton,[11] acquainting themselves with the situa-tion and recent developments in that city, that is to say, as already stated, Macau operated as a centre for gathering information both with regard to trade with the Chinese[12] in mainland China and in other ports such as Amoy, Ningbo and Tin-Hai. Availing themselves of the monsoons, the British arrived in Macau at the end of the summer, engaged a guide or pilot[13] and remained there until their vessels were measured[14] and they had received the usual privileges, after which they set out for Whampoa and Canton. As early as the middle of the eighteenth century, British vessels were also measured in Whampoa.[15] The captain of the *Marlborough*, after docking at Taipa, exchanged letters with the Portuguese authorities and with the Chinese traders, who asked him to sail up to Bocca Tigris so that they could meet; the captain was threatened by the Portuguese that, if he followed this course, there would be repercussions for British trade. In Canton, Fenwick contacted some Chinese traders and the hopu, who gave per-mission for his vessel to dock, as he did not come from Madras and was not going to trade in Amoy. The recently arrived *Susanna* accompanied the *Marlborough*, sailing to Whampoa in July 1716, as was the case of the *Stringer* in August. The supercargoes of these vessels were instructed by London to rent a shared resi-dence and approach the Portuguese and the Chinese as a group, mistrusting Macau's intentions, "to whom they did not give entire credit", and considering the time they had spent off the coast of the enclave as wasted.[16] The importance of the British presence in the Pearl River delta thus gradually increased, to the detriment of Portuguese trading interests, since the traders and authorities in Canton became aware of the high profits they accumulated as a result of the ever more numerous visits of European vessels to their port. The British concluded that they could progressively do without the linguistic services and know-how/why of the Portuguese, long-established in China, for French missionaries also served as interpreters and lent their assistance to EIC trading. For example, in 1793 Brother Jean Baptiste Grammont (1736–1812?) counselled the ambassador Lord Macartney on the emperor's protocol and expectations as regards gifts to be given. At the time of the embassy, Grammont, who had lived in Canton between 1785 and 1791 (during which time he had assisted British traders and diplomats), wrote to the ambassador, warning him that the Portuguese priest and embassy interpreter, José Bernardes de Almeida (1728–1805), would do everything to harm British interests in China and offering to join the embassy and control the Portuguese missionary's activity; this offer was ignored.[17]

In 1716 the first formal "convention" took place between the British and the hopu, the latter guaranteeing freedom for the British to approach him whenever necessary, to develop trade in a freer manner and to choose Chinese workers.[18] In 1718 seven ships were chartered in Macau to carry tea from China to Batavia, and 1730 saw a further six such arrangements. In 1780 the British bought small boats in which to carry opium and supercargoes to Canton,[19] and such transactions pleased the Portuguese ship-owners and traders who thus saw a new source of revenue appear in the city, deriving from the needs and expenses of virtually every British crew who stopped off in Macau on the way to Canton.

6

Macau as a centre for Chinese control of the European "barbarians"

In 1719, the Kangxi Emperor (1662–1722) proposed to the Portuguese that foreign trade be centralised in Macau, where Western merchants would thenceforth reside. The city, relatively impoverished since the suppression of trade with Japan, viewed the imperial edict as permission for European rivals to enter an area in which the Portuguese still held a privileged position, and the Macau Senate, despite the profits it would gain from the sojourn of foreigners, refused the proposal, as it would again in 1733. In 1720 the viceroy of India rebuked the Senate for having refused the imperial proposal for the anchorage in Taipa, as the proposal would have allowed Macau to absorb a part of the enormous sums of money which the British annually spent in Canton; it would also have allowed for closer control of British trade. The Senate replied that it had merely attempted to avoid greater control of Chinese monitoring of the territory.[1] Profits would derive from the totality of import duties offered by the emperor to the city, as well as from letting houses and the names of Portuguese trading businesses, a strategy which allowed the British to conduct their business in the enclave, for Portuguese law banned any foreigner from owning landed property or from opening businesses in Macau, which led to the Portuguese letting or selling the names of their businesses to British traders. In the meantime, the Portuguese administration concluded that the Qing dynasty's efforts to control and keep foreigners away from mainland China were affecting business and everyday life in Macau, for in 1723 the emperor expelled all missionaries in China to the enclave and in 1725[2] he limited Macau's sea-going fleet to a maximum of twenty-five vessels.[3]

In 1720, after the EIC formed its rotating and seasonal Council in China, a Chinese "guild" was formed in Canton. The security (hong) merchants system turned into a cartel in 1760 called the co-hong[4] (to which the supercargoes raised immediate opposition), which was constituted by the hong traders[5] with a view to controlling foreign trade, its thirteen regulations defining the rights and duties of Chinese and Western traders.[6] Created as a regulatory instrument, the co-hong was responsible for collecting taxes, keeping a distance between foreigners and the native population and regulating trade prices and transactions. From the 1740s onwards, this system also became a controlling mechanism used to enforce the Mandarinate's orders, altering its *modus operandi* so as to respond to foreigners' movements and demands, and upholding the *status quo* demanded by Chinese tradition. Faced with all these changes, in 1722 the EIC appointed a permanent Council in Canton, headed by James Naish.[7] The Council's objective was to demand from the Mandarinate and from local traders ever more favourable conditions for its regular trade. From this moment, the management mechanism of the EIC in China began to develop, and it would remain relatively unchanged up to the end of its trade monopoly in 1833.

Since the British presence had been building up since 1700, Macau and Canton were subjected to greater control by the Mandarin authorities, for the Luso-Chinese enclave, besides being a port, was inhabited by foreigners who could shelter missionaries and rebels. Thus, in May 1723, on the arrival of the *Walpole* in Macau, the crew members were advised by the Chinese traders that they were not allowed to sail up to Canton because they were carrying firearms on board.[8] The Portuguese governor offered the vessel his protection against the Chinese, but the British once again concluded that "so far from being able to afford protection against the Chinese, they themselves are hardly masters of the place, and the ships would be as safe in Canton River as here".[9] The supercargoes made their way to Canton where they rented accommodation and mentioned episodes of Macau's political life which obviously influenced the British presence in China: "Received [July, 4, 1723] advice from a Macau of the arrival of a Portuguese ship of 250 Tons from Goa, with orders to reinstate the old Governor turned out last year".[10] In 1732 the governor, António do Amaral e Meneses, knowing of the coming visit of the viceroy of Canton to decide on the plan to centralise foreign trade in the enclave, wrote to the bishops of Beijing,

Nanking and Macau and questioned them on whether to receive foreign ships in the enclave and Taipa. The three prelates replied in the negative, justifying their response by citing the city's inability to defend itself militarily from such a presence, the need to avoid greater control by the Chinese, and the bad morals of the Protestant Europeans.[11] According to the bishop of Macau, João Casal, the foreigners, finding themselves in the city, would be in a better position to take it. Later, in 1776, another bishop, Alexandre da Silva Pedroso Guimarães, stated that foreigners, especially the Armenians and the British, were ruining the territory's trade, a reality to which the Senate testified, having sought advice from the prelate on the possibility of petitioning Goa to expel the foreigners from the enclave in order to save its trade and its morals, to which the latter replied that the emperor had given his authorisation for the "barbarians" to remain in the establishment ten years previously. The appendix to the bishop's letter informed that in 1776 eight British supercargoes and two private traders rented houses in Macau which were scattered around the parishes of Sé, São Lourenço and Santo António.[12]

In 1733 the emperor, with the aim of continuing to gather in the profits of trade with the barbarians, all the while attempting to keep them as far away as possible from mainland China, again put to Macau his predecessor's suggestion whereby foreign trade should thenceforth be channelled through the city, a proposal the bishop also turned down, hoping as he was to see the Protestants, many of them single, as far away as possible, since they corrupted morals in the enclave.[13] This position received the support of the viceroy of India, Pedro Mascarenhas, Count Sandomil. According to British sources, the territory's trade that year remained weak, there being only nine Portuguese ships there, conducting reduced trading activity with India and the Malay archipelago.[14] In a letter to the Senate, the viceroy of India listed some of the "harms" which could come about if all foreign trade in China was concentrated in Macau:

> the foreigners being more prosperous than we are, they will naturally call unto themselves all the trade of China, and the Chinamen placing a customs house in Macau to receive the duties on that trade, it would seem, that our customs house will see a considerable decrease to the great detriment of the city [...], and if the Chinamen realise that all goods come from foreign parts, for the profit that results in their favour of receiving from

them the 16 per cent, the city will easily lose the privilege it has attained of paying only 6 per cent.[15]

The Portuguese refused to "host" the British on any permanent basis because of the loss of power to manoeuvre and to invest which the arrival of the foreign vessels caused in the Macau trading community. The latter thus tried to prevent its privileged position from being weakened should the China Trade begin to be conducted in the city and the British take up permanent residence there.[16]

7

The visit of the Centurion

In November 1742, with merely four EIC vessels in Canton, the HM *Centurion*,[1] under the command of Commodore George Anson, was the first Royal Navy warship to arrive in Macau for the purpose of re-provisioning. It had sailed from Southampton in 1740, within the context of the War of Jenkin's Ear against Spain, with the aim of upsetting Spanish interests in South America. Anson participated in what is viewed as the first war waged by Great Britain for colonial reasons, at a time when Britain was fighting to assert its naval and colonial power, an aim achieved, above all, after the defeat of France in 1815.[2] One of the crew of the *Centurion* described the arrival of the vessel in Taipa, as well as the (increasingly nominal) power of the Portuguese in Macau:

> Macau is a large handsome town situated at the entrance of the great River Canton on a narrow point of land, and has several large forts which command the town and all the adjacent country. It belongs to the Portuguese, and is the only settlement any Europeans have on the whole coast of China, but the Chinese have lately so crept into the town and introduced their own laws and government that the power of the Portuguese is now become little more than a name. Mr. Anson on his arrival here sent one of his officers to wait on the Portuguese Governor, who soon returned the compliment, and after the little points of ceremony were settled they mutually saluted each other.[3]

The city operated as a familiar and safe post during the long voyages of European ships, and Boyle Somerville states, with regard to Anson's voyage: "at last, after more than two years of an incessant sea-journey, or of camping on uninhabited islands, [...] we find the small but still indomitable remnant of Anson's

83

Expedition in friendly waters once more, and amid the amenities of civilised life. And here at last were letters from home."[4] The author further affirms that, to understand the episodes which took place during the *Centurion*'s sojourn in China, it is necessary to describe beforehand the geographical position and the joint administration of Macau, laying emphasis on the importance of the enclave and of Portuguese assistance to European vessels which needed to re-provision or undergo repairs, as was the case of the *Centurion*. The ship's visit is cited in Chinese sources in the context of British naval might, as are the cunning of Anson, the battles with Spain (1743), and British thieving and their cannons, which had struck fear in the Far East since the arrival of Weddell's fleet.[5]

The captain of the EIC ship *Augusta* informed Anson of the customary procedures undertaken by foreigners on arriving in Macau, notably the request for the Chinese authorities to authorise entry into the Canton river and the customs taxes to be paid, and advised the commodore to seek the governor of Macau's counsel.[6] Fearing Chinese reprisals such as those suffered in the past by the city when receiving British vessels, the governor persuaded Anson to put in discreetly at Taipa and not to enter the river, for if he did, he would have to pay customs taxes to the Mandarinate.[7] Once again, foreigners profited from the Portuguese know-how/why. On the second day of his stay, Anson landed in Macau to enquire of the governor as to the possibility of acquiring supplies and repairing the vessel.[8] The governor replied that Anson would have to request authorisation from the Mandarin authorities, and the commodore, realising that only the viceroy of Canton could authorise the re-provisioning of and repairs to the *Centurion*,[9] chartered a small junk and sailed to Canton, where, after consulting the supercargoes, he tried in vain to speak to the Mandarin through the co-hong before returning to Taipa. In Macau, Anson handed to the hopu a letter addressed to the viceroy of Canton, and threatened the Macau customs house official that he would sail up the river should the letter not be delivered to the *destinee*, showing how determined he was to obtain the assistance he had requested of the Chinese authorities. Shortly afterwards, a fleet of eighteen junks sailed down to the Taipa Canal carrying envoys from the viceroy of Canton to meet Anson, who intimidated the Chinese authorities and, indirectly, Macau with his warship.

The crew were living in tents on the islands off Macau[10] when the viceroy's permission arrived at the beginning of January 1743. In mid-April Anson left the Macau Roads and affirmed strategically that he was sailing to Batavia, returning in July with the Spanish galleon *Nuestra Señora de Cobadonga* laden with goods which he had taken a month earlier in the Philippines[11] while this vessel was travelling between Acapulco and Manila. The commodore again resisted Chinese demands and, not wishing to remain in "so remote a place as Macau",[12] he sailed to Bocca Tigris where he requested supplies and remained for a number of months; he visited Whampoa and Canton and then returned to Macau before leaving—after a stay of six months in the China seas—for Britain, where he arrived in June 1744. According to Austin Coates, Anson's account of the voyage, supposedly written by Richard Walter,[13] HM *Centurion*'s chaplain, and published in 1748, reveals at a glance British attitudes of superiority vis-à-vis China, considered a backward and intolerant country,[14] while the Mandarinate reinforced vigilance over Macau to prevent the entry of more "barbarian" ships into China. Anson's circumnavigation is one of the best known, on a par with those undertaken by Sir Francis Drake and Captain Cook. This stems from the publication of the account attributed to Richard Walker, and from the spoils captured, which led to greater Chinese control over Macau, as had been the case when the Dutch attacked the city in 1622 and would again occur during British attempts to occupy the territory in 1802 and 1808. The author of the account describes the crew's sojourn and, as the authors of the several accounts of Lord Macartney's embassy would later do, refers to the riches which the city had enjoyed during the first years and the state of decay in which it now was, the Portuguese remaining in the enclave subject to Mandarin authorisation, who, when they so wished, blocked the supply of food and forced the Portuguese to obey them.[15] The crises in the legitimacy of the dual administration and author-ity in the city between the Chinese and Portuguese characterise the history of Macau; it was a phenomenon of a structural nature,[16] easily explained by the fact that the enclave was situated in Chinese territory and was co-administered by the Portuguese. This situation influenced relations between the old European allies, for the Senate was forced to pay the "ground rent" (*foro do chão*), or tribute,[17] and ultimately obey the Mandarinate chops where the British presence in China was concerned. The tenacity, the capacity for dialogue and the adjustments of the Portuguese in the Luso-Chinese enclave have led several authors to compare metaphorically the historical identity of the territory to a plant which is closely linked to it, the bamboo, for like it, Macau "was able to bow to the ravages of bad weather, waiting for the typhoon to pass and allow itself to raise its elegant stem to the heavens again".[18]

As regards the consequences of the *Centurion*'s visit, works like *Navigantium atque Itinerantium Bibliotecha: or, a Compleat Collection of Voyages and Travels* (1744–1748), by John Campbell, applauded the expedition's results, glorified British maritime exploits and described the growing interest felt by European nations in trade with China:

> as appears by the great number of European ships that Rear-Admiral Anson met with in the ports of Macau and Canton; which is a circumstance that deserves to be attentively considered. This therefore is a time, if ever there was a tie, that we ought to exhort ourselves, and endeavour to strike out some new branch of commerce, into which our neighbours cannot so readily fall. History affords us no instance of a maritime power that remained long at a stay. If we do not go forward, we must necessarily go backwards; and, as we rivalled in almost every known branch of commerce, except that to our own plantations, it is not our interest only, but absolutely necessary to our safety, to support and extend these; and if it be possible, open some new channel, both for the benefit of this country, and of our plantations; which can never be done, if we do not encourage long voyages, and the perfecting ourselves in every kind of navigation.[19]

Campbell further uses the many hurdles faced by Anson in Macau, the difficulties of this circumnavigation and the relations with the Chinese authorities to prove British naval capability, advising other adventurers to follow the commodore's example on the seas, to the honour of Britain. In the 1750s several works appeared exalting Britain's maritime and trading valour, as well as the advantages of trade in bringing peoples together.[20] Such exhortations for the British nation to consolidate its trading and naval presence in the four corners of the earth on an equal footing with other European powers echo in the countless documents of the sixteenth and seventeenth centuries published by Richard Hakluyt and Samuel Purchas which I mentioned at the beginning of this study.

8

British relations and conflicts with the Portuguese and Chinese authorities in the second half of the eighteenth century

From the second half of the eighteenth century on, Lisbon tightened its control over Macau, and, in the context of the EIC's project for expansion in the East, conflicts heightened between the supercargoes—whose economic power became ever more visible in the enclave—and the Portuguese and Chinese authorities. In 1749, in the face of the development of British interests in China, Goa banned foreign trade in Macau, an order which was never enforced by the Senate, notably with regard to the trafficking of opium; this was acknowledged in 1795 by the governor of India, Francisco António da Veiga Cabral, when he affirmed that this drug was entering Canton freely and that trading in it might revive the enclave's economy.[1] However, between 1764 and 1788 the governor of the Portuguese *Estado da Índia* reiterated the ban on foreigners' living in Macau, the latter being allowed to remain there only to repair their vessels and avoid shipwreck and attacks.[2]

In the spring of 1754, the president of the EIC's Select Committee in China, Frederick Pigou, returned to Britain and proposed to the directors that the Company send an embassy to Beijing, suggesting that the emperor be petitioned for freedom of movement in Canton and especially between this city and Macau, as British trade was growing at such a pace that in 1750 of the eighteen vessels reaching Canton, half were British.[3] In 1757, a year of transition as regards the European presence in Macau, foreign trade in China was completely restricted to Canton,[4] and the Luso-Chinese enclave saw the enacting of several laws against the presence and trading activity of foreigners, which were revoked that very same year as per the request addressed by the Senate to the viceroy of India. With respect to the British presence in Asia, in June of that year General

Robert Clive's victory at Plassey paved the way for British supremacy in India. The fact that up to that time British living arrangements in Macau had not been official for the Portuguese central authorities justifies the relative lack of references to EIC early business in Macau in Portuguese sources. This is especially so if we bear in mind the larger number of documents dating from after this year and which relate mostly to (non-) compliance with Portuguese law on the part of both the foreigners and of the city's residents, notably on the matters of the (banned) purchase of ships from Portuguese nationals, attacks on Portuguese vessels, and the illegal opium smuggling. In January 1757 the governor, Pereira Coutinho, banned the city's residents from letting houses to foreigners so as to annul the "masking" of the latter, who declared they were only going to rest or re-energise themselves in Macau between the Canton trading seasons. With a view to evading EIC control and "enjoy[ing] the privileges of the natives" of the enclave, several British traders[5] and doctors petitioned the Portuguese king for Portuguese nationality, as was the case of Jacob Francisco Vandermond in 1733,[6] with the granting of such requests surely being facilitated by the services rendered by these doctors to the Macau population. Some British became Portuguese subjects in Goa, thus being able to settle in the enclave, as was the case of Captain Robert Jackson in 1772, who married in Macau and rented a house there with the authorisation of the city authorities.[7] In 1773 the viceroy of India once again banned the letting of houses to foreigners in Macau, a measure which, to a certain extent, pleased the Senate, which wished to protect local trade.

An imperial edict decreed eight regulations for Chinese trade with the "barbarians", which became fully effective in the 1760 trading season, with the British still being forced to return to Europe or continue living in Macau after the trading periods.[8] To avoid frictions in the Chinese ports, the emperor determined that only the port of Canton would remain open to Europeans, that all vessels had to remove their weapons before entering the city—where foreigners were not allowed to take up permanent residence—and that trade, always effected through the co-hong, had to be finalised and debts paid before the end of the trading season. In Canton, the supercargoes were restricted to the area of the foreign factories, being allowed to move within restricted areas and not entering the city.[9] Western women, too, were not allowed in the city, which led to some British forming amorous attachments with Chinese women, especially in Macau.[10] As with earlier imperial edicts, some of the terms of these regulations had no practical effect, with infractions continuing, especially with respect to foreigners employing Chinese labour.[11]

The City of the Holy Name of God of Macau became the sole Western residential area in China, where, in addition to European, Indian, Parsee[12] and Armenian[13] traders, among others, branches of the French, Swedish and Dutch East India Companies were opened[14] between 1728 and 1761.[15] In the 1750s the Company's affairs were looked after by a resident Council of Supercargoes. As I have already said, up to this time any dealings deriving from each vessel were entrusted to six supercargoes who accompanied the vessel to and from Britain, and after 1715 these officials began to work as one entity (the Council of China). The practice of leaving one of them in China had been adopted since 1753, albeit sporadically, and in a more general way from 1757; this was the year which saw the appointment of the Council comprising three permanent agents who from then on stayed in the territory during the trading seasons on a permanent basis, renting houses from the Portuguese, with whom they negotiated[16] and took out loans,[17] also attending to the Company's interests in their relations with the co-hong. The latter owed ever-increasing sums of money to the Company,[18] despite the fact that the 1760 imperial edict banned the British from being creditors of the Chinese.[19]

In 1773 the EIC rented another building to serve as its branch in Macau[20] and later also the Casa Garden[21] to house the Select Committee president. Despite the fact that, under Portuguese law, no foreigner could acquire landed property in the territory, some British traders bought houses in the name of Portuguese individuals whom they trusted.[22] In 1775 two supercargoes became involved in a legal dispute with the governor due to the renting of a house, a practice which had become widespread among EIC members. The supercargoes Lane and Henry Browne rented a house where they planned to live during the following rest seasons, and the governor addressed the president in friendly terms to advise him that the British could not take up residence "independent of those who were supposed to have some control on their behaviour",[23] that is to say, outside the Company's branch. Henry Browne had tasked his comprador with employing Chinese workers to get the house ready and had no intention of giving it up, even if he was threatened by the president of the Council with being banned from taking his seat at the Company's table. From then on, Browne's meals would be sent to his "apartment", a measure which aimed to punish and coerce the prevaricator, who, should he insist on taking up residence in the house, would be suspended from his post until such time as the London directors made their decision known. The young supercargo demanded to see the statutes which forced him to live exclusively in his room at the Company's house,[24] and once again the Council was forced to discipline one of its members in the face of non-compliance with the Company's rules and of a complaint lodged by the Portuguese governor because of this infringement of Macau law. Again in March of the following year, the governor informed the "English House" that the supercargo George Cuming had become involved in a fight and had been brought before him by guards, for which he requested adequate transport to take the young man back to his house.[25] EIC documents describe some of the clashes between the supercargoes and the Chinese and Portuguese authorities in Macau, as well as the British experience of living in the city, especially during the periods between the trading seasons.

In December 1787 the Senate described the geographical distribution of the supercargoes in Macau houses, mentioning that they did not live in the Company's house as determined by law and that they rented approximately fourteen houses in their individual names.[26] In another letter addressed to Queen Maria I in the same month, the Senate referred to the luxurious lifestyle introduced into the city by the British, where the Company took up twelve of the largest dwellings.[27] With regard to the luxury surrounding the supercargoes, in 1800 the Senate's representations to Dom João, Portugal's prince regent, informed him that if the supercargoes settled permanently in Macau they would "bring with them"[28] their different religions, adding that their riches "have unfortunately led many poor Damsels to prostitution: their luxury, customs, their vices too [...] lead to much expense".[29] The document echoed the words of Bishop Marcelino José da Silva in 1793 when he stated that some residents sold the sexual services of their daughters, wives, sisters and nieces to the foreigners, railing against the latter when they did not accept such services.[30] As early as 1777, a report drawn up by Bishop Alexandre Pedroso Guimarães for the Senate on the admission of foreigners asserted that the city would only be able to expel private traders and never the supercargoes of European Companies, for the latter had authorisation to live in the city from the Chinese authorities, the veritable masters of the land who profited from European trade. He added that their expulsion would lead to retaliatory measures by the Companies, such as removing the supercargoes from the control and vigilance of the Portuguese authorities of Macau. On the other hand, expulsion would damage the Portuguese who also invested enormous sums in the opium trade and who would be deprived of the taxes paid by the British, who could easily find persons to represent them directly in Canton.[31] This shows that many of the measures decreed by Lisbon were not efficaciously applied in Macau, for local interests spoke louder than the laws and orders received from Portugal.

The luxurious lifestyle, the cultural and religious differences of the British and their growing power displeased certain interest groups in the city (the traders in the Senate and Catholic priests), whose economy already depended substantially on the supercargoes' investments and expenses and those of other Western traders. In 1778 the recently formed Select Committee replaced the former permanent Council of Supercargoes in China and from then on represented the EIC in Canton and Macau. Until the end of the eighteenth century, the British were forced to stand up to and constantly fight for their interests with the Cantonese Mandarinate, especially with regard to trading restrictions and the lack of freedom to act, an undertaking which, as we shall see, included Lord Macartney's embassy to China. The power of the Portuguese authorities was also a source of displeasure for the supercargoes, who complained in 1787 both to Bombay and to the viceroy of Goa about the abuses of the governor of Macau. In turn the viceroy informed Bombay that he had reined in the governor and had ordered him to respect the EIC officials.[32] The Company appealed countless times—and by means of diplomacy—directly to Goa, the decision-making centre of the *Estado da Índia*, with a view to improving and solidifying its presence in Macau, while the Senate and the other local authorities informed Goa and Lisbon of the decline of trade and of the losses caused by the establishment of foreigners in the city.[33]

According to the Chinese chops and official letters exchanged between the Canton Mandarinate and the Senate Procurators between 1749 and 1847, the two foremost authorities in Macau discussed several times how to manage foreigners in the territory and in Macau, as well as the imperial "codes" on which Luso-Chinese consensual relations were based. The documents exchanged between Macau and the Chinese authorities with respect to the British trading presence engaged above all with Chinese restrictions, the entry and sojourn of vessels and traders in the enclave, including during Lord Macartney's embassy to China, the payment of customs duties,[34] and the enforcing of Chinese law on the conduct of foreigners. When the time came to apportion responsibility for illegal trade, the prolonged sojourn of British vessels in Macau, and the sale of opium against the "Law of the Emperor",[35] the Senate and the Mandarin of the White House exchanged charges of negligence and defended their personal interests with regard to Chinese charges that the Senate was involved in the "concealed" trade. The Senate defended itself frequently,[36] and in 1798 the hopu accused the "Christian Lorcha[37] drivers" of drawing up illicit contracts with the British, whose business deals they ended up abetting, a charge returned by the Senate to the hopu and to the Chinese traders.[38] The personal economic interests of the city's residents thus ultimately facilitated British permanence in the city and their legal and illegal trade. In 1784, when the Commutation Act[39] was passed with the aim of defending the importing of tea by the EIC, the Select Committee again decided to retain a permanent representative in Macau after the positive experience enjoyed by one of its agents in the city during the two previous years, a measure which the London directors viewed as unnecessary two years later.[40]

Captain John MacClary's abuses (1781–1782) and the *Lady Hughes* incident (1784)

Ultimately, the problems caused by some of the independent British traders in the second half of the eighteenth century affected the EIC,[41] since the Portuguese authorities and the Mandarinate held it responsible[42] for the disorderly conduct of the country traders, as was the case, for instance, of Captain John MacClary who, on board the *Dadaloy* (*Calhariz*), captured a Portuguese vessel[43] and prevented a further two from travelling to Manila in 1781. He was later arrested in Macau,[44] for the good of the "public interests of the Traders and Inhabitants of this City"[45] and forced to pay the latter an onerous sum.[46] The enclave's governor asked the supercargoes to convince the British to pay for the damage he had caused, or the Select Committee would have to do so,[47] with this body responding that it had no authority over the country traders.[48] This resulted in the governor calling the British "a lying and troublesome people", and he informed them that they were responsible for any action carried out by their compatriots in Macau. At the end of 1781, on being freed, the British captain again took two of the city's ships, the owner of which complained to the Committee.[49] In 1782 MacClary again took Portuguese vessels,[50] thereby affecting relations between the EIC and the local authorities.

The case of the Bombay country ship *Lady Hughes*[51] is one of the most famous British incidents off the coast of China in the eighteenth century.[52] On 24 November 1784, the year which saw the arrival in Macau of the first North American vessel,[53] the *Lady Hughes* was in Whampoa when, in the course of the usual gunfire salute on the arrival of a ship, this accidentally hit a small boat and injured three Chinese nationals, two of whom died as a result. The Mandarin of Guangdong and the hopu's secretary presented several requests to the president of the Select Committee, asking that the crew member who had fired the shot be handed over for execution; to this the president replied that he had no jurisdiction over country traders and that the British had gone missing in Macau. The imperial authorities demanded that a British man, regardless of his guilt, be handed over, and Pigou advised the Chinese governor to contact George Smith, who was in charge of the *Lady Hughes*; eventually trade in Canton was suspended, the foreign factories were surrounded, exit by sea was blocked, and foreign houses were deprived of food. The foreign community was united in its support for the British and informed the Mandarinate that the deaths had been accidental. Finally, faced with Chinese inflexibility in the matter, Pigou asked the vessel's captain to hand over a man. Since the "guilty" party had absconded, the oldest crew member was taken to the Chinese authorities, and the reprisals ended at the beginning of December, with the *Lady Hughes* setting out for Bombay on 7 December, the British officials realising once again how vulnerable their situation was in China, where, for instance, they and their families had to remain in isolation in Macau, the only place where foreign women were allowed to enter and reside from the end of the eighteenth century onward.[54] The supercargoes feared for their lives and safety should there be another accidental death, which proved the precarious nature of the status of the British in China and which, as we shall see, made them ever more eager to find an enclave of their own, as Macau was under Portuguese administration.

The supercargoes were themselves a source of discontent for the Portuguese authorities when European vessels sailed along the city's coastline, removed plants and stones from the coast, as also reported in the British press,[55] carried weapons, fished and (off-)loaded goods without paying any tax. In 1778, confronted with such illegal activity, the British replied to the Senate that, as foreigners, they were not bound by Queen Maria I's laws. The viceroy of Goa deplored this reaction, advising the city to punish the foreigners' "insolence" by expelling them, as they were "transgressors of the Laws of the Country to which they must adhere".[56] A group of supercargoes attempted to defend itself before the Senate, with the institution responding that the foreigners "live in Macau under the Flags of His Majesty the King of Portugal".[57]

If from the time when they set up their interests in China in the early 1700s, the British were forced to depend, to a certain extent, on the cultural and linguistic know-how/why of the Portuguese who had settled there approximately one and a half centuries before, British trade quickly attained a volume of growth which was the envy both of the Macau Portuguese and the other foreigners. Since trade relations between foreigners and the Chinese took place mostly in Canton, and given the growing contact between the native population and the "red-haired barbarians"—each side being barred from learning the other's language—there soon arose in the Pearl River delta a pidgin aimed at meeting trading needs. Chinese Pidgin English (CPE), also known as "broken English", "Canton jargon" or "Canton English", eventually replaced the Portuguese language (or the Portuguese lexically based pidgin) in trade relations, although CPE did adopt some Portuguese words, as we shall see. In 1715 the Chinese already spoke CPE, whose vocabulary was in the main English and which quickly became the *lingua franca* of the China Trade.[58] However, just as the Portuguese had concluded in the sixteenth century, the EIC realised that it was essential to have a good command of Cantonese, and in 1746 the Company employed the young James Flint as an interpreter. Flint had lived in China since 1736 in order to learn Cantonese,[59] just as Thomas Bevan and Barton did in 1753; their Chinese teacher was pressured by the local authorities into desisting from teaching them. In 1793, faced with this linguistic blockade, three young men, Benjamin Travers, Thomas Charles Pattle and John William Roberts secretly learnt Cantonese in Macau with a Chinese teacher, far from the EIC's headquarters.[60]

As the Company's translator, Flint eventually became a threat to the position of the Cantonese traders and of some of the authorities; foreign supercargoes would no longer need the services of Chinese interpreters and would be able to communicate with the hopu and even with the Chinese viceroy, as well as nego-tiate more freely, as was the case when Flint travelled to Ningbo and Tientsin in 1759 to present the Committee's complaints against the hong traders to the emperor. On his way back, Flint was escorted overland to Macau where he was arrested by the Chinese and expelled in 1762.[61] Acting on Flint's com-plaints, the emperor ordered an inquiry into events in Canton, and the hopu was sent to Beijing in disgrace. Flint's linguistic proficiency helped the British in their attempts at opening up trade routes with ports such as Ningbo, while the Canton traders had been successful in 1757 in obtaining an imperial decree restricting foreign trade to their city. The British did not want to trade only in Canton and used Macau as a strategic port from which to (try to) sail to other already mentioned Chinese ports where they avoided onerous customs duties. However, the Canton authorities controlled British attempts to expand their presence, confining the supercargoes to the Pearl River delta, hence the need for and the importance of using the Sino-Portuguese enclave until Hong Kong was founded. The EIC tried to by-pass the obstacles of the Chinese Canton system by means of stratagems such as that of James Flint and initiatives such as Lord Macartney's embassy, a process which culminated in the Opium War, the founding of Hong Kong and the Treaty of Nanjing (1842) which opened up five Chinese ports to Western trade.

Learning Cantonese was necessary, for if CPE met basic trading require-ments, the Company needed employees who were fluent in this language in order to lodge complaints or to petition the authorities in the event of conflicts or when dialogue had to be engaged. Macau therefore functioned as a centre for learning Cantonese and for translating Chinese language documents into English,[62] a strategy which consolidated the trading independence with regard to Chinese and Portuguese translators developed by the EIC, who over the course of the years sent countless Chinese works to London both in the original and in translation.[63] However, it was only the first British embassy to China in 1793 which allowed for the education of the young George Thomas Staunton, regarded as the first British sinologist and who, acting on his father's wishes and with the assistance of Chinese teachers, began to learn Mandarin in London in 1792. If learning Cantonese became an ever more pressing need, CPE was the fruit of the commercial and cultural interchange prompted by the British trade and economic interests in China. It is proof of British and Chinese adjustment with a view to making communication easier both commercially and between employer and employee, especially with the comprador.[64] British and American traders used CPE even when they spoke with other English speakers, and North American female diarists like Harriet Low (1809–1877), who resided in Macau between 1829 and 1833, used it in the letters she sent back home to her family. Terms and expressions from this pidgin spoken in the Macau-Canton circuit— like "savvy" (to know, from the Portuguese verb "saber"), "Same old, same old", "long time no see", and "no can do"[65]—were imported to Great Britain and the USA by the Old China trade merchants and their relatives. These influential businessmen, many of them from the Forbes and the Delano families, used those expressions after they returned home, and were imitated by social climbers and other people around them. I believe, this was how words such as "savvy" and expressions such as "long time no see" and "no can do" were introduced into the English language all the way from Macau and Canton in the nineteenth century and are still used by English speakers all over the world.

9

The "scramble for the use of Macau"[1]

Throughout the eighteenth century, the EIC became dependent on private trade conducted between India and Southern China whereby Indian opium reached Canton, the purchase of tea requiring silver earned through the sale of that drug. Since the previous century the Portuguese had been importing opium into China, and Macau ultimately became a strategic space for British smuggling until it moved to the island of Lintin. This move affected the revenues of the enclave's traders, who defended themselves from the competition on finding themselves deprived of one of their major sources of income and fearing that the Lintin island might be occupied by the British.[2] The Chinese traders also profited from this trafficking, which therefore rendered ineffectual the imperial edicts banning the importing of the drug into China. In its first phase, this situation dragged on until the Opium War, after which Britain finally succeeded in founding an establishment in China.

In the 1760s, Britain already held the largest European percentage of the China Trade. British vessels arriving in Canton belonged either to the EIC and to interlopers using passports bearing the names of Portuguese businesses and residents,[3] or to independent traders[4] who engaged in the country trade between India and Southern China,[5] with the Company wishing to control the activity of the latter.[6] British trade was thus conducted by three discrete entities: the Company, which regulated every trading activity; private agents or traders who sailed between Britain and China via India under licence from the EIC; and the country traders, residing in India and operating in the main between India and the south of China, authorised to do so by the Company and the Indian traders,

97

and trading also with the Chinese who operated outside the hong system and who were not legally authorised to do business with foreigners.

Asian products, notably cotton imported from Bombay, pepper and opium supplied the EIC with approximately 30% of the capital needed to buy tea in China up to the second half of the eighteenth century, when opium trafficking became predominant. At first the Company imported opium from Bengal,[7] the drug becoming a threat to public health in China; thus a 1729 imperial edict decreed that trading opium was illegal.

The EIC banned the importing of opium from Calcutta, although this had no practical effect since the supercargoes trafficked the drug through their private trade and country traders smuggled the drug to China. In addition, the Chinese traders were not willing to give up such profitable transactions, which continued in a clandestine manner via Macau and later, Lintin.[8] On arrival in the Pearl River delta, the British vessels docked at Taipa, and their tonnage was ascertained in the enclave or in Whampoa before the supercargoes reached Canton. Here the purchase of tea would have been impossible without the drug trade which also supplied significant profits to the British administration in India. One of the Company's first major challenges was finding—besides textiles for which there was little demand—British products which were saleable in China, a self-sufficient nation, with a view to financing the purchase of tea. Until the Commutation Act, Swedish and Danish traders[9] smuggled tea into Great Britain, avoiding the high taxes which British traders had to pay.

The British opium was exchanged for silver in Canton by the country traders, and the EIC received the precious metal from them in exchange for letters of credit payable in London, by means of which the institution was able to pay for the tea it purchased.[10] This system made for interdependence between the Company and the traders, and the amount of opium transported to Canton and the institution's and the traders' profits grew gradually until the first clashes of the Opium War (1839), when the Chinese authorities decided to try and put an end to the illegal trade of the drug.

Controlling the country traders became difficult, given the Company's economic dependence on them and on trade agents, some of whom also began to take up residence in Macau between trading seasons. The traders and some of Macau's governors gained part of the profit yielded by smuggling opium[11] and trading tea, collaborating successively with the British.[12] In so doing, they benefited their interests and avoided problems between the British and the Chinese,[13] although, from the second half of the eighteenth century onwards, the Portuguese tried to defend themselves from the ever-increasing interference of the British in the illegal drug trade,[14] until then conducted by the city[15] from whence, at the beginning of the nineteenth century, it was moved to Lintin. Ângela Guimarães has analysed the regional importance of Macau in this activity and asserts:

> the enclave offered conditions which were favourable to this trade, given the trading privileges it enjoyed and its location. The opium was brought in the main from Bengal, was easier to move into Macau than into Canton, it was subject to less onerous duties since it belonged to Portuguese traders, and it was easier to move from Macau into the Empire whether by land or by boat. The regional situation and every other difficulty endured by the residents increasingly led these to act as "fronts" for the foreign traders, to such an extent that in the mid-1790s, foreign opium accounted for two thirds of the opium in circulation in Macau.[16]

Macau thus served as a strategic location for the EIC's profitable trafficking in opium, with some residents availing themselves of the opportunity to profit from the sojourn of British vessels, which led the Senate in 1764 to ban the purchase or off-loading of opium carried by foreign ships. This collaboration led the hopu to advise the Senate, in late 1782, not to receive "foreign vessels by fraudulent means".[17]

Some Portuguese traders by-passed the Chinese and Portuguese ban by purchasing the drug carried by the British off the coast of Macau, as if they had obtained it themselves, and although between 1764 and 1796 successive governors of the *Estado da Índia* ordered the Senate to confiscate the opium, residents continued to defend their personal interests, despite the fact that the Macau aldermen demanded that Goa ban foreigners and non-resident Portuguese from this practice.[18] In June 1787, when Captain Cheminant was jailed by the governor for having docked at Taipa and disembarked without permission, the supercargoes described how important this island and the peninsula under Portuguese administration were for the EIC, and also the competition of the Portuguese:

the Typa being the only place where a ship can lie with safety for any length of time without entering the harbour, the Portuguese are apprehensive of foreign ships lying there for the purpose of carrying on a contraband trade to their disadvantage for which it is very convenient and are more particularly jealous of ships from Bengal which they suspect to have opium on board. They pretend an exclusive right to it as part of the Portuguese Dominion but this is very doubtful as it is entirely without the reach of any of their guns and it is not so much as within sight from any of their forts, has within it no marks of possession and it is pretty certain the Chinese would not suffer any to be exhibited there. This is the only place a ship in Macau Roads can retire to in stress of weather and every commander of a ship [...] is liable to the treatment Capt. Cheminant has received, should he ever go on shore at Macau—the claim of the Portuguese appears of sufficient importance to merit a thorough investigation.[19]

In 1795 the Senate denounced the situation whereby Portuguese nationals were acting as "agents" for the British,[20] and the governor of Goa advised this body to ensure that the drug trade was conducted in such a way as to benefit the interests of the residents and not those of foreigners; difficulties with the Chinese were to be avoided at all costs. The latter, for their part, were tightening their vigilance over British vessels and foreign residents in Macau. If, on the one hand, British competition was detrimental to the territory's trade, the profits derived from EIC trading and from private traders became essential to its economy. Portuguese/British collaboration, notably in smuggling, heightened from the 1780s onwards, during the time of greatest control exerted by Lisbon over the Macau finances. The monarchy's "officials", that is, the governor and the judge,[21] represented the interests of the Crown, while the Senate defended local interests, and throughout the eighteenth century there was a certain amount of tension and a struggle for power between successive governors and the Senate. Controversies over the remit of the governor continually reignited, and in 1735 the Overseas Council (*Conselho Ultramarino*) even attempted to reinforce the powers of the captain-general (which had until then been merely military); these attempts were always hampered by the aldermen.

The intensifying of European trade in Canton and the continued, reformist policies of the Marquis of Pombal led to a renewal of Lisbon's interest in Macau in the 1760s. In 1783 the Instruction issued by the Portuguese minister

for the Navy and Overseas Territories, Martinho Melo e Castro, openly criticised Lisbon's and Goa's negligence and the opportunism of the aldermen of
Macau and their excessive submission to the Mandarins' demands, advocating
that the *ouvidoria* (judge) be reinstated, the creation of a customs-house—set
up the following year so as to prevent the channelling of Crown taxes into the
hands of private parties—and the reinforcement of the governor's authority,
who from then on was consulted on the management of the city's public funds.
The Senate, which protested against these measures, was criticised for giving
loans without proper recording of the procedures, and the coffers of this institution were renamed *Cofre da Fazenda Real* (Coffer of the Royal Treasury). In
actual fact, the governor's powers remained unchanged, for he lacked the means
to stop the Senate's deliberations from being put into practice,[22] and the measures adopted caused residents—now more keenly "watched", and prevented
from having their goods released from the customs-house and from requesting
new credits while they still had outstanding debts to the Senate or to the Holy
House of Mercy—to invest more and more in smuggling, notably with foreigners, thus increasing the latter's power and the sharing of interests between the
Portuguese and British residents of the city. Competition among the Portuguese
traders contributed towards their greater dependence on the foreigners, whose
economic power became ever greater than that of the Portuguese. There was
also an increase in the transport and off-loading of foreign goods as if they were
Portuguese, in the use of the Portuguese flag by British vessels, and in smuggling,
notably of opium. If Martinho de Melo e Castro's Instructions were designed to
strengthen central authority in Macau, ultimately they resulted in intensifying
the dependence of local traders on foreign trade, hampering implementation of
the measures put forward by the document itself:

> not to be admitted that Vessels of Foreign Nations do Trade there, and that
> such Vessels should only be allowed entry for provisioning According to
> the laws of hospitality: That such Foreigners not even be allowed to set up
> domicile in that City [...] and that any other trading Vessel of any other
> Kingdom, should cast anchor in the Port of Canton, and pay their dues, in
> their totality, to the Emperor.[23]

At the beginning of 1799 the bishop of Macau advised the Secretary of State that
the measures of 1783–1784 and the subsequent reinstatement of the *ouvidor*

(judge) and the greater decision-making powers granted to the governor made it easier for European agents to arrive in Macau and go about their business, negotiating under the names of Portuguese residents, trading companies[24] and ships flying the Portuguese flag (*navios embandeirados*)[25] in exchange for small sums. In early 1783 the governor of the British presidency at Fort William wrote to the Select Committee and referred to the intense competition by Macau residents in the sale of opium, as well as the strategic measures taken in India to stop them from hindering the Company's trafficking:

> We are concerned that the opium which we consigned to you by the Nonsuch did not turn out to better account. The Competition of the Private Macau Merchants for the sale of their opium would no doubt impede that of the Company's, and were aware of this circumstance before we dispatched it but we knew that the Traffick of the Macau ships was not extensive, nor could it be in this Article when the greatest part was engrossed for the Company.[26]

Three years later, the rector of the Seminary of São José in Macau, Manuel Correia Valente, denounced the opium smuggling carried out through Macau with the governor's assistance,[27] showing the value and the great quantities of the smuggling, a situation which was also described by the Select Committee: "The imposition of opium being strongly prohibited by the Chinese Government and a business altogether new to us it was necessary to take our measures with the utmost caution; [...] this article is frequently disposed of at Macau where it can be landed without interruption".[28] In 1788 the Portuguese António Botelho wrote to the Select Committee, in Canton at the time, informing it that Henry Lane had filed a complaint against him in the Macau court. Botelho, in terms pointing to a strategic threat, accused the British man of smuggling opium against the regulations of the EIC,[29] a fact which, were it to become public, could cause problems for the supercargoes. The enclave thus made it possible to develop parallel and alternative trade both for the supercargoes and for the EIC itself.

The network of interests around the opium smuggling united the supercargoes, the trading agents, and the country traders who carried the drug and other goods to Southern China[30] and whose residence in Macau the Committee was unable to prevent, given its officials' private interests, its dependence on private trade, and the strategies of the agents who entered other nations' diplomatic services, evading the Company's legal control.[31] Independent agents and traders such as Daniel and Thomas Beale, John Henry Cox,[32] Charles Schneider, David Reid,[33] William Jardine and James Matheson[34] arrived in the enclave in the late eighteenth century, using the names of Portuguese traders and the diplomatic posts of other European nations with a view to trading and by-passing the law and the EIC's orders of expulsion. In the meantime, in Britain traders and manufacturers began to demand that the government allow direct access to trade in China in vessels other than those of the EIC, so that they could thus practise more competitive prices than the Company's. The minister Sir Henry Dundas (1742–1811) affirmed that the EIC's China Trade was in a precarious and fragile state and that the presence of new, independent traders might upset the situation by giving rise to cultural and economic conflicts; the Company's monopoly should therefore be upheld until such time as new privileges could be obtained from the emperor.[35]

In the last two decades of the eighteenth century, problems intensified in the opium trade to China conducted by the British.[36] At the beginning of the nineteenth century, the Company faced difficulties arising from diminishing remittances of silver from London and from India to China. This metal was essential to keeping the balance of British investments in Canton, and the Company's business became even more dependent on trade in Indian products and in opium carried out by the country traders. In March 1792, a Canton Mandarin visited Macau to remind the Senate of the regulations governing foreign trade in China and stated that "the European Ships, which dock in China to trade must follow the old customs and the rules already laid down",[37] and must pay the taxes due to the emperor.

The growing trafficking was met by a new imperial decree in 1799 banning imports of opium, which was just as ineffectual since the drug smuggling continued through Macau and other locations on the Chinese coast, far from imperial control. In that year, the governor of Goa, Francisco Pimentel, in a letter to the Minister for the Navy and Overseas Territories, Rodrigo Coutinho, made reference to the increase in opium smuggling via Macau and that "the English are at this time masters of that vast province, named Benares. [...] The English lack a place of their own such as Macau, to take into China that merchandise [opium], they depend on the Portuguese who at this very moment get the

best revenues of the customs-house, to pay the costs of that colony".[38] Despite
growing British competition in the opium trade, the trafficking explains Macau's
economic prosperity at the beginning of the nineteenth century,[39] and in 1804
the judge Miguel Arriaga, faced with the importance of this economic activity, proposed to the Ministry that certain foreign goods, among which opium,
be traded by Portuguese nationals on board the enclave's boats, thus channelling part of the profits of Canton's foreign trade, and that the tax per crate of
opium be increased to over twice the sum then being practised.[40] Drug trafficking united Portuguese and British interests and, until the Opium War, operated
as yet another strategy for the city's survival; the latter was adjusting gradually
to the changes in maritime trade and in the regional economy of the Pearl River
delta, to a large extent dictated by the EIC. Faced with the impossibility of pre-
venting the British smuggling and of competing with the EIC, the Senate, whose
members took an active part in the trade, attempted to concentrate this activity
in Macau from the late eighteenth century onward.[41] The pressure put on the
British by the Mandarinate because of the opium smuggling intensified in the
first half of the nineteenth century and, as is known, gave rise to the Opium War.
During the War the British planned to occupy Macau (1840) as a strategic military location,[42] although the Portuguese opted for a policy of neutrality so as
to please both their old European allies and, most of all, the emperor of China,
"the proprietor of the land"[43] where they had first settled nearly three centuries
before.

10

"Guests and old allies"[1]

The permanent and growing influence of the British supercargoes and independent traders in Macau gave rise to conflict between these and the Portuguese administration in incidents which, together with the restrictions imposed by the Mandarinate and the co-hong, led the EIC to seek a territory in Southern China, for if Portugal was an old ally of Britain in Europe, in the Far East Macau's trading interests and those of the Select Committee clashed.

At the end of each trading season, the supercargoes came down from Canton, set themselves up in Macau and continued to manage the institution's interests, regulate the country trade, control those British traders who had diplomatic posts,[2] certify that the British abided by the eight imperial regulations, attempting to prevent a repetition of the events of 1764, 1779 and 1789,[3] when the independent trader George Smith refused to leave Canton, whereupon he was expelled to Macau. In 1780 the Portuguese governor, incurring the Committee's displeasure, refused to banish or arrest Smith,[4] and the supercargoes advised London as to the losses sustained by the Company as a result of the bad behaviour of the private traders in China.[5] Thus, as had been the case in 1771[6] and 1773,[7] in September 1783 the EIC, which two years previously had complained of its lack of authority to take action against private traders,[8] banned any British from residing in China, with the exception of the supercargoes.[9] However, and as already stated, the British traders resorted to diplomatic positions in the service of other nations and to the names of Portuguese businesses to carry out their trading activity outside EIC jurisdiction. For instance, in 1779 the Company informed Captain John Alexander that British ships had to abide by Chinese law, "or the Hon'ble Company's affairs will be thrown into the greatest confusion, and nobody can determine where the affairs may end".[10]

There were several clashes between supercargoes and the enclave's Portuguese authorities, the latter reminding the Select Committee as to who was in authority, as was the case, for instance, in 1779 when a young British clerk was arrested for making a noise in the city and was freed after lengthy talks, or when, in December of the following year, the captain-general, Francisco Xavier de Castro, appealed to the Committee against the insolent behaviour of a number of British captains towards the flag of the king of Portugal when they took a Portuguese ship[11] and burst into the home of Francisco Paula Miranda in Canton. The governor demanded an explanation from the supercargoes and informed them that he would punish their countrymen by means of sanctions against British vessels in Macau.[12] For its part, the Committee, then in Canton, accused the governor, in a letter to him, of insolence and of using rough language in his letters, reminding him that the British were in Canton, outside Macau's jurisdiction, and, like the Portuguese, it also dependent on the will of the Chinese. The supercargoes further justified their position with regard to these accusations, threatened the governor and informed him they would lodge a formal complaint with his superior, the viceroy of Goa, through the British presidencies of Fort St. George and Bombay:

> You assume the air of vice-roy of the Province of Canton, instead of governor of the *dependent* city of Macau. What right have you Sir to interfere with the government of this Province—we are not accountable to the Portuguese in this part of the Kingdom [Canton]. [...] The flag of your king has never been insulted. The ship boarded by our boats was the Eliza English country ship—she entered, and paid the port charges as such [...]. The complaint in the house of Mr. Francisco Paula Miranda, we never heard of until this moment. Mr. Miranda lives in the House of a Chinese merchant and not in a factory of his own. [...] Your master [viceroy of Goa] may be a judge of the improper and unhandsome manner in which you have conducted yourself toward us.[13]

The above excerpt shows that the British stated that they did not acknowledge Portuguese authority in Macau, for the territory was under the jurisdiction of the Mandarinate, a strategy which explains in part both successive references by

British travellers to the (merely) nominal authority of the Portuguese in the city and attempts by the British to occupy it militarily in 1802 and 1808.[14]

The governor responded to the Committee in early 1781 and accused it of having misunderstood his letter through ignorance of military obligations, as it was an exclusively "mercantile" body, which prompted the Select Committee to accuse him of behaving as if he were the viceroy of Canton. Francisco Xavier de Castro threatened the supercargoes and stated ironically that he did not fear the latter's complaints to the viceroy of Goa: "you tell me that even in Macau you are only subject to the Chinese laws, I shall show you the contrary whenever you may come here. If you gentlemen wish to send duplicate or triplicate of your complaints please send it hither, as one of our *moradore's* [resident's] ships is nearly sailing to Goa".[15] The Committee responded to the governor's sarcasm and stated that his authority was confined to the enclave and that the British were independent: "we shall have no occasion to trouble you with any Letters to Goa, as we shall send our packets to the Presidency of Fort St. George and Bombay by one of our ships now in this port".[16] Fearing reprisals on their return to Macau, the supercargoes recounted to the presidency of Fort St George the clashes they had had with the governor, as well as the three recent incidents which marked their relations with the Portuguese administration, thus: the transport of ten slaves who had fled the city on the *York*[17] and who were immediately returned to their Portuguese owners; the search carried out by the supercargoes on the *Eliza*; and Captain Fenwick's forced entry at the Canton home of Francisco Miranda. The Select Committee asked the British presidency to inform Goa of the governor's improper conduct and to defend the EIC's interests in China, for the supercargoes, when in Macau, were at the mercy of Portuguese wishes. The document went on to repeat some of the arguments put forward in another letter sent earlier to the British presidencies in India:

> that the vice-roy may think expedient to give him [governor of Macau] orders to conduct himself to the English with decency and manners. Gentlemen we should not have troubled you on this subject but [...] the company's servants here are obliged to the Chinese, to go every year to Macau for three or four months—it is in the power of the governor, let them be ever so careful in their conduct to insult them as many occasions if through petulancy, pride, or folly, he is inclined to do so, and this man

by his late behaviour, sees much disposed to show a disposition, overhear-
ing and insolent—that your representation [to Goa] will have every good
effect, that can be described. We have not the least doubt, as we had an
instance in the year of 1763 of a positive order from the viceroy of Goa
to the governor and senate of Macau, to be very circumspect and courte-
ous in their behaviour to the English which was sent in consequence of a
spirited remonstrance of Mr. Pigot in a complaint they received from the
Government of that place.[18]

Clashes between the British, the Senate, and the governor continued. In late
1781, after the incident involving Captain McClary, the Committee once again
informed the presidency of Fort St. George that it had already complained
to London about the high-handed behaviour of the governor and of Macau's
Senate, calling the aldermen "lawless people". The supercargoes acknowledged
their isolation and their dependence on the Portuguese, given that the Chinese
refused to become involved in conflicts between Europeans:

> such are the mortifications and insults, we are exposed to, at Macau, where
> the Chinese force us, every year, to pass some months, and we beg that
> you'll represent our situation to the government of Goa, to obtain for
> us some privileges which may place us out of the power of the people of
> Macau; as consequence may follow being left in so neglected a situation
> that will prove very embarrassing to the affairs of the Company, for should
> it happen that we were to be imprisoned by the infatuation of these people,
> the Chinese do refuse interference, we know of no alternative but using the
> force of our ships to release us [...]. Our situation, which we cannot but feel
> to be disgraceful to us, as individuals, to the Company as our Employers
> for in no part of the world, we believe are English subjects, who are in any
> trust, left so devoid of protection.[19]

We see here a clash of wills which flared up every time the British felt their
honour and integrity to be under threat. Francisco Xavier de Castro replied to
the supercargoes that he would not be disturbed by them, since "the supercargoes could not pretend to any jurisdiction in Macau".[20] In April 1782, when all
British would return from Canton to Macau, and acknowledging their power-
lessness, the Select Committee members tried to persuade their Chinese peers
to intervene should the Portuguese "molest" them; the trader Poan Khequa
promised to lay the matter before the authorities should the Portuguese "be

foolish enough to molest them",[21] reducing the supercargoes' fear of returning to the city. In the second half of the eighteenth century and up to the Opium War Macau became, as Jacques M. Downs states, "the Ascot, the Monte Carlo, the Riviera, and even the home of tired traders after a busy tea season at the factories".[22]

The Committee defended itself and tried to obtain security and defensive measures from London, from the British presidencies in India, from the Portuguese viceroy,[23] from the EIC resident in Goa,[24] and from the Canton merchants. The relation between the Senate and Goa was also contentious; the actions of neither part were immune to pressure exerted by economic interest groups such as the British, so that in the 1790s the aldermen complained that the viceroys of Goa were protecting the interests of British traders.[25]

In 1783 one British man called Leslie, having been jailed for causing a disturbance in Canton, was freed by the governor of Macau and complained to Calcutta of the oppressive treatment meted out to him by the same governor. At the beginning of the following year, as directed by the Senate, the Macau judge, Manuel Homem de Carvalho, ordered the supercargoes to return the house they had rented, where a Portuguese official was to take up residence. The British regarded this request as offensive, given that they had already paid $200 in rent; they refused to hand over the house voluntarily and reminded the Senate of the alliance between Portugal and Britain, while again informing Madras of the dispute.[26] Two years later, the buccaneers Robert Watson and William Grandy, after arriving in Macau in a Chinese junk and having admitted to capturing the vessel of Roger Darvale, a British resident in Masulipatam, were arrested at the request of the Select Committee, who praised the speed and determination of the governor, Bernardo Faria. The British later petitioned the governor for the prisoners to be handed over to them, and the governor made it clear that authority in the city was Portuguese and that the criminals would be sent to the viceroy of Goa for trial, with the Company having to pay the costs of their detention.[27] The governor informed the Committee that, should they not pay the costs of the detainees, they would suffer the consequences of such an attitude when their members came down from Canton to Macau,[28] and the supercargoes threatened the governor with the military might of the British presidencies in India: "should it be your intention to offer us any personal indignity you ought to know that the English East India Company's governments in India want neither the power nor the spirit to resent it in a manner that may be severely felt by the city under your command".[29] In his reply, Lemos e Faria accused the British of being inconsistent and of affronts to Portuguese law:

> you are not interested with any character in this city and do not repre-
> sent the Noble British Nation, being merely the servants of the Honble
> Mercantile Company appointed to manage their interests in Canton, and
> that you retire to this city to pass the months in which you cannot reside
> at this port certainly you could not have so much arrogance as you have
> shown for even though you should be desirous to appear as representatives
> of your nation I must treat you as individuals, in so much as you have never
> presented me your credentials.[30]

The governor also replied to the supercargoes' threats and concluded that they were:

> mere individuals without any public character whatsoever, I shall treat
> you always as the Portuguese are treated in the English colonies you being
> subject to the Laws of Her Faithful Majesty while you remain in this city
> [...]. I do not fear them [British presidencies in India] because what I do is
> founded on reason and the Law of nations & supported with these I shall
> severely punish those whom I find presumptions.[31]

This incident sparked a lengthy exchange of letters, and the governor informed the supercargoes that he would have taken the same action if the criminals had been Portuguese, for the British man had captured a ship and had offended "society" in general and not just the EIC.[32] The British demanded that Macau hand over the prisoners or send them to Bengal. The governor asserted that the British were insulting both him and the viceroy of Goa, for, in affirming that the captives would abscond during the journey, they were accusing them both of being liars, concluding yet again: "from this may be seen that you are much better informed in the science of trade than in things of this nature [justice, poli-tics]".[33] The Select Committee again informed the British presidencies in India and the viceroy of Goa[34] of the insults and the abuse of power on the part of the "insignificant government" of Macau[35] with regard to the British nation[36] and replied to the governor, deconstructing his "unfounded" arguments, conclud-ing with an already much used argument: "we are altogether independent and unconnected with you, and therefore have a right to expect that if you should address us in civil language, and not in the terms you would use towards inferior officers and persons under your immediate orders and control".[37] The viceroy of Goa, in his response to the Committee's complaint, minimised this dispute and stated that it stemmed from an error in semantic interpretation, "for there are peculiar phrases, which in the idiom of one language are perfectly polite, & admit but of the best interpretations, which in others will only admit of the reverse".[38]

In July 1789, during the Select Committee's summer residence in Macau, this body became involved in another clash with the local authorities when the supercargo Samuel Peach was dragged out of the house he had sub-let from his colleague Roebuck, at the time away in Bengal, and was arrested for not having abided by the orders of the Senate and the judge to depart from the house, as this was needed to house one of the Portuguese king's officials. Peach replied to the judge that he had paid rent on the house and would only leave it by force, which is indeed what happened. The Committee took the view that the British men had been unfairly treated as if he were a criminal of the worst kind.[39] The supercargoes accused the governor of having committed an illegal act and questioned his decision, with the document describing yet further cases of abuse of power by the Portuguese authorities; they had already taken over the Company's branch as a residence for the governor, although the British had paid a high sum in advance rent.[40] The same situation arose in respect of a house rented by the Swedish supercargoes in 1795. Samuel Shaw, an American trader and future first US consul in Canton, described these incidents, as well as the issue of ownership of the island of Taipa, for the Portuguese kept every foreign vessel away from this territory, with some captains ending up in prison for docking there without permission,[41] much as had been the case of Captain Cheminant, as described above. According to Shaw, cases involving house leasing showed the injustice of the Portuguese and the submission of the other Europeans, for the former saved money and refurbished their homes by means of an ingenious stratagem:

> these are generally in a wretched condition when let to the Europeans. As soon as a house is put in good repair, which is done at the expense of the tenant, the proprietor, although the lease may have been given for a number of years, demands his house again, or else an addition to the rent.

> Unless one of these conditions is complied with, the owner takes posses-
> sion the moment the tenant leaves it to go to Canton and the latter is then
> obliged to look out for another house.[42]

The US trader exemplified his statement, using a whim of the Portuguese governor's wife during an incident involving the Swedish supercargoes:

> the Swedes' house was the best in Macau, and for repairs and improvements
> had cost their company upwards of eight thousand dollars. The governor,
> or rather his lady, took a fancy to it, and the Swedes were under the neces-
> sity of consenting to an exchange, which was in every respect unfavourable
> to them, for the governor's house is not worth half the money which the
> mere improvements on the other have cost.[43]

Foreign residents were thus the victims of Portuguese abuses of power, for "in
matters where an individual European is concerned, they do not use even the
ceremony of asking consent".[44]

  To return to the case of the supercargo Samuel Peach, the British wrote to the
governor, petitioned to pay bail and admitted that they were turning to him as
this was the only defence they could adopt while they were residing in Macau,
hence the importance of such an action.[45] The governor promised to help them
in any way he could, referred to the relative independence of the magistrates and
later concluded that Peach should have abided by the orders he had received
instead of verbally insulting the officials;[46] such an attitude would have justified the use of force and the fact that the case would be prosecuted, with several
supercargoes being called as witnesses to the fact that the British man's house
had been forcibly broken into.[47] The Committee accused the governor of not
helping them, and Peach asserted that he had no dealings with Portuguese residents in Macau,[48] a situation which was true of the overwhelming majority of
English-language residents, even in the nineteenth century. As had happened
in previous clashes, the Select Committee complained to the British presidencies in India and to the viceroy of Goa, later thanking them for their help.[49] The
latter wrote to Bombay, alluded to the good friendship between the Portuguese
and British, apologised for the incident, stated that the governor could have
done nothing as he had neither criminal nor civil jurisdiction, and informed the
Committee that he would launch inquiries to ascertain the truth and prevent
such cases from happening again.[50]

In 1791 and 1800, the Select Committee, still feeling insulted and unwelcome, again complained to London that it was forced to travel to Macau at the end of the trading seasons and of being insulted there by the Portuguese, finding itself at the mercy of the Chinese and Portuguese authorities, with no room for manoeuvre and appeal:

> From what is here mentioned & the ill treatment of the Select Committee last year, the Hon'ble Court may judge of the situation of their Servants at Macau. We are driven there by the Chinese & cannot escape from it without Mortification & Insult [...] should it happen, that we were to be imprisoned by the Infatuation of the People of Macau; & the Force of our Ships to release us [...]. Our Situation, which we cannot but feel to be disgraceful to us as Individuals & to the Company as our Employers, for in no part of the World are English subjects who are in trust, left so devoid of protection. [...] Macau is so little known to the Court of Lisbon and has so neglected by the Government of Goa, that it is now the fit resort only of Vagabonds and Outcasts. It has lost the valuable immunities formerly granted by the Chinese, & the Head Mandareen of a neighbouring Village exercises in it almost the Powers of Government [...].[51] A place so little valued might perhaps be easily procured from the Court of Lisbon, and should it ever fall into the hands of an enterprising People, who knew how to extend all its advantages; we think it would rise to a state of splendour, never yet equalled by any Port in the East.[52]

Once again impoverished Macau was the target of British desire; according to the Committee, the British could turn the city into the most important port in the East, criticising the Portuguese administration and the degenerate population. In the second half of the eighteenth century, British influence and power, ever-growing in the enclave, displeased the local religious authorities, and some of the clashes between the governor and the supercargoes can be viewed in the light of the control exerted by the Portuguese over the British, a measure held as essential by bishop Alexandre da Silva Pedroso Guimarães (1772–1789) who, as acting governor, considered that the city's government needed an independent man,

> a friend to the Portuguese, respectful of the natives, a friend of the Chinamen, with little affection for foreigners [...], and very skilful in dealing with the mandarins and hopus, and Foreigners, and who is at the

same time liberal, for otherwise, he cannot reconcile friendship with the Chinamen, contain the Foreigners, favour the residents, advance the trade which has been destroyed, and prevent disturbances of the peace.[53]

According to local interests, the ideal governor would meet with the approval of the Chinese authorities, would defend the traders' interests and curb the power of the foreigners. The bishop's words are a sign of the growing prominence of the British in the enclave and also of the need for measures such as those taken by Bernardo Lemos e Faria in June 1787 when he jailed Captain Cheminant in Guia Fort, after the latter had anchored the *Laurel* at Taipa without permission.[54] The prelate further considered that the continued presence of the Portuguese in Macau depended solely on good relations with the Chinese;[55] his words reflected the policy of defending local interests to the detriment of foreign trade, for at the end of 1763 the Select Committee had already complained to the presidency at Fort St George:

> The Portuguese Governor and Senate of Macau, have for some time past behaved so extremely ill to foreigners (which particularly affects us) that we think it is now become necessary to have such treatment represented to the Vice Roy of Goa, that his orders may prevent in future the embarrassments their rudeness at present subjects us to, and as a Representation of this sort, can come from none so properly as the Company's Presidencies in India where these People are allowed the privileges of a beneficial trade, and treated with Civility and good manners.[56]

The Committee reported concisely on the clashes with the Portuguese authorities and referred to the fact that the Senate, acting on Chinese orders, had expelled James Flint on his return from Ningbo (1758), with the British asking for the governor's protection. Two years later, the Senate banned Portuguese residents from letting houses to foreigners, advising them that the latter would not be able to remain in their residences unless they "humbly" petitioned the Senate and the governor; the British would be forced to live on board their vessels until such requests were made, and, according to the British themselves, would be exposed to theft and the unpleasant climate. In 1761, too, Captain Skottowe, after docking at Taipa without permission, was threatened with jail by the governor.[57] These measures were designed publicly to reinforce Portuguese power and control over foreigners, which the viceroy of Goa justified as proceeding from the orders of the king of Portugal, due to Chinese complaints about the excesses of the Europeans in Macau and Canton.[58] Cooperation with the Mandarinate, with a view to the survival of Macau, was thus a constant priority for the Portuguese authorities. Financial local interests were obviously more important than laws received from Lisbon, and foreigners were never expelled from Macau and were always able to rent houses and offices.

11

The importance of Macau for the British China trade

As shown, throughout the second half of the eighteenth century EIC officials clashed with the enclave's authorities. The former were, however, forced to abide by the decisions issuing both from the Chinese and the Portuguese and acknowledge the fragility of their position in China. Following the clashes between the British and the governor analysed above, Fort William wrote to the Select Committee in 1783 and acknowledged the importance of that port for the EIC trade in China.[1] On the other hand, the fact that the Chinese exerted ever increasing control over Macau was stressed by several British visitors, for instance the captain of the *Charlotte*, which arrived in Southern China in 1788, carrying new orders from London for the Select Committee:

> the city of Macau, which is situated on an island, at the entrance of the river Canton, belongs to the Portuguese. It was formerly richer, and more populous than it is at present, and totally independent of the Chinese; but it has lost much of its ancient consequence; for though inhabited chiefly by the Portuguese, under a governor appointed by the king of Portugal, it is entirely in the power of the Chinese, who can starve or dispossess the inhabitants whenever they please.[2]

The image of the city's dependence with regard to the growing control of the Mandarins, also due to the presence of other foreigners, was an argument repeatedly used by the British when referring to the increasing room for manoeuvre enjoyed by them, an issue which was also engaged by the Senate Procurator, António José de Gamboa, in a chop sent to the Heungshan Mandarin in 1793, informing him that the Chinese hopu could not supersede Portuguese law in the matter of the other foreigners:

we complained that the hopu proceeds to attack our Laws, which are those which govern all Christians here, who are subject to our Government, and our Justice, and we have used all our authority for more than two hundred and fifty years because this city was founded by us, and the privilege of living in it belongs to the Portuguese, and not to other foreigners from Europe, who are only here while we find it useful to allow their entry.[3]

The Senate Procurator developed this idea in another chop addressed to the hopu himself:

it [Macau] having been founded by the Portuguese almost three centuries ago in houses, walls and fortresses we have always been governed by our Laws in every matter and they govern every other foreign Europeans while they are residents here [...]. For the other Europeans reside in Macau with permission and our authorisation we being free to receive them here or make them leave this city, and we have full authority to punish them when they disturb us, and do not live according to our Laws, and so we send away those same foreigners.[4]

In June 1807, the Senate's procurator answered the Mandarin of Heungshan's chop, stating: "You know that if any British, or any foreigner, are admitted in Macau it is because they were allowed to live here between the trading seasons by your own Government, and they are there treated as guests, without any suspicion".[5] The numerous British who flocked to the territory at times became involved in clashes with the Chinese,[6] and these matters were resolved not just by the Portuguese administration but also by the Mandarin of the White House who, when a native Chinese died, and in keeping with the precepts of imperial law, demanded a guilty party for execution. This was the case in 1773, when the Mandarin asked the Portuguese to hand over Francis Scott, who had allegedly murdered a Chinese man. Scott had already been judged under European law[7] and had been found not guilty by the Senate,[8] a body which was accused by Goa and Lisbon of not defending Portugal's honour and of easily bowing to the orders of the Chinese authorities.[9] Faced with Macau's refusal to hand over the accused man, the Mandarin once again issued an order for the Chinese residents to abandon the city and banned provision of victuals through the Barrier Gate until the British man was executed. Confined to Macau and Canton and totally dependent on the Mandarinate, the Europeans were forced to meet these demands, under threat of having to leave the city. As Bishop Alexandre Guimarães concluded in 1777, on addressing the Senate: "submission to the [Macau administrative] regime, is mixed, depending on His Majesty the King [of Portugal], and on the emperor of China, [...] direct Master of Macau, the city paying him a rent [...]. The land was not acquired through conquest, and therefore our residence is not firm, ad nutum sine".[10] The governor and the Senate often curbed the activity of the British in the city, which displeased the supercargoes, who, as already shown, informed the British presidencies in India both of the "abuse of power" by the Portuguese authorities and of the importance of Macau for the Company's trading activity, asking them for protection:

> we must beg leave to remind you that the Company's affairs place us under the absolute necessity of retrieving to this small establishment of the Portuguese during nearly half the year, we trust therefore as this is not a matter of choice in us we have a claim to the protection of the Company's establishments in India from the injuries and insults we are exposed to.[11]

A year later, after the above clash between the Macau judge and the supercargo Peach, the Committee repeated the same arguments in a letter to Bombay, describing the singularity of their situation in the enclave, where they were at the mercy of Portuguese wishes; the letter adds that the latter did not perpetrate more abuses of power due to their fear of the British presidencies in India: "the unavoidable consequence of our peculiar situation, compelled as we are to take our residence under a Foreign government, and among people but too much disposed to insult us, were they not in some degree kept in awe by the protection which they know we can have recourse to".[12]

In 1788 the Committee reaffirmed the unpleasant situation in Macau, the Portuguese "pride of power" and the need to convince the latter that the Committee had the means to defend itself from insults past and to come, concluding that the British are forced to live "under a foreign government in a grating and unpleasant circumstance, but to be exposed to insult without means of redress, and left to the mercy of stupid prejudice, and brutal ignorance."[13] The strategic importance of Macau for EIC trade in China can also be observed from the fact that most of the references to the territory in the Company's records occur in descriptions of juridical matters and clashes involving the supercargoes and the Portuguese authorities, above all in the second half of the eighteenth century.

Events in Europe also influenced relations between Portuguese, French and British traders in the East, and with Britain at war with France between 1793 and 1802,[14] each nation's vessels attacked the other's in the eastern seas, affecting British trade in China. The Portuguese and British formed an alliance in China to fight off attacks by French and Spanish vessels which united against Britain during the US War of Independence[15] and the Napoleonic wars, the Macau vessels resorting on their way to India to the security provided by the British Royal Navy fleet, which marks the rhythm of the enclave's trading journeys, in the main from 1797 onward.[16] The loss of ships, from early on one of the greatest scourges for the city's economy, was thus provoked not just by weather conditions and by piracy in the South China seas, but also by the conflicts between the European powers, in the event France and Britain. Macau's trade and economy found themselves ever more dependent on European Companies' trading activity, and, as already shown, the increase in the opium trade and the involvement of traders and aldermen in it made it impossible for the Portuguese authorities to fight off foreign competition, attempting rather to concentrate this activity in the territory. If Macau was a strategic position for the China Trade, British trade became essential for the territory. According to the governor, Vasco Luis Sousa Faro, at the end of 1792 British capital represented approximately 90% of the trade which moved businesses in the city; the governor feared that the EIC would set itself up on Lantau Island and harm Macau's trade if it began to use the island to sell the goods it brought from India, notably opium.[17] Despite this growing relation of dependence, during the second half of the eighteenth century the enclave's government and the supercargoes were in constant face-off, the former not failing to demonstrate to the British that Portuguese law was the only (European) one prevailing in the city.

Despite the "humiliating" conditions under which the Company was forced by the Chinese to conduct its trade, the supercargoes, acting independently, took gold and iron from Canton to India, and opium from India to China, and did—or were able to do—little or nothing to alter the situation they were in, fearing the Mandarinate's reactions and the effect of these on their private trade or the Company's. Even the British monarch intervened, trying to set up direct diplomatic relations by sending the embassy led by Lord Macartney, who after the mission acknowledged the strategic importance of Macau, the disadvantaged situation of the British with regard to the position of the Portuguese, and described the annual traffic of the supercargoes to and from the enclave at the beginning and end of the Canton trading seasons:

> The English come to Canton not to Macau, where they have no business. Yet as soon as the ships are loaded at canton, all the English are obliged to leave it, to desert their factory there [...] and to be at considerable expense in removing to Macau, paying for a house there besides hiring new servants and other inconveniences. They are obliged every time they must thus go to and from Macau to pay fees or duties on the same furniture and books and clothes for which the duties have been already paid several times. They are also obliged to pay duties for the provisions and liquors which they bring with them though entirely for their own consumption.[18]

The situation of the supercargoes, as well as payment of customs duties dated back to when the British had first set up in this trade, and from early on the latter fought to improve their living and working conditions and for the abolishing of such duties.[19] Thus these issues were not new at the end of the eighteenth century, and in 1795 the supercargoes concluded that the Chinese practice served to prevent smuggling, since Westerners could carry goods from Macau to sell in Canton, declaring them as consumer goods.[20] At this time the supercargoes—in vain—petitioned the Mandarinate to allow them to sail their vessels directly to Bocca Tigris without stopping in Macau; they would no longer engage their pilots there, rather they would engage them in Lintin, sailing to Whampoa without stopping,[21] that is, the EIC attempted at all costs to remove itself from the sphere of Portuguese influence in order to gain more freedom and trading independence in Southern China.

Macau thus presented itself both as a gateway into China, a place to prepare and rehearse trade in Canton, and as a Western frontier-space, where Europeans could reside when they were expelled or were fugitives from Canton or mainland China. However, the British attempted to gain ever greater freedom with regard to Portuguese and Chinese authorities and resented the excesses of both sides. The enclave was also used both by the Chinese and Westerners for the trafficking of opium, with the Portuguese profiting from the sojourn of these traders and their business.

12

Lord Macartney's embassy to China, 1792–1794

The ever growing importance of the China Trade for the British economy and trade, especially after the Commutation Act, incidents such as those of the *Lady Hughes* (1784), the tight control of the Portuguese and Chinese on the Macau-Canton axis, the high prices practised by the Chinese, and the demands of the co-hong and the hopu led the British, "the first people in the world",[1] to attempt to set up diplomatic ties with China and obtain from the emperor a territory of their own on the Chinese coast, like Macau, where they would be governed by their own laws and from whence they could expand their trade. The first two British embassies reflected this desire for expansion.[2]

The first British attempt at diplomatic contact had failed in 1788 due to the death of the ambassador, Charles Cathcart, on the journey to China, in the Bangka Straights, but the instructions and the letter he carried reveal Britain's trade interests in China and Macau, the diplomat having been tasked with gathering information from the supercargoes which might serve him in achieving his aims.[3] Cathcart was to seek permission from the emperor for the British to set up in trade preferably in Macau or, failing that, in Amoy.[4] In Lt-Colonel Cathcart's preliminary proposals dated August 1787, the following was put forward:

> If Macoa [*sic*] was ceded to us by the Portuguese, it does not follow that the Chinese would confirm us in the Portuguese privileges. The possession of the Island is not wholly in the Portuguese hands, and there is only one port which from its Harbour is important. It would be attended with some Inconvenience, in removing the Hong Merchants from Canton, but their capitals which have overcome the local inconvenience of Canton which is remote from the Raw Silk, China Ware and Tea Countries, might render Macau a valuable depôt, and overcome its defects.[5]

These words testify to early British interest in occupying Macau or gaining a similar position to that of the Portuguese and justify the fear and the constant alert of the enclave's authorities.[6]

In a second attempt, and with a view to transmitting to the emperor the requests of George III, Sir Henry Dundas appointed Lord George Macartney (1737–1806) as head of the first British embassy to the court of Qianlong emperor (r. 1736–1795) in 1793.[7] This was also done with the aim of achieving greater trade freedom in Canton and an establishment similar to Macau for the British,[8] thus trying to evade Portuguese and also Chinese control.[9] With this aim, and to study the conditions under which the Portuguese had settled in Macau and their situation there in 1790, the Select Committee drew up and sent to London the "Memorandum & Heads of Information Required, Respecting the Portuguese Settlement at Macau", which had been requested by the directors by means of fourteen points. Throughout the document, the supercargoes gave a concise account of Sino-Portuguese relations, trade with other parts of China, duties and rent paid to the emperor, the means of communication with Beijing, the defence of the enclave with Chinese help, and the benefits gained by the Portuguese from their privileged position, whereas the remaining nations which visited Canton annually were not permitted to set up permanent trade in China. On this latter point, the document advised as follows:

> very considerable—all goods prohibited at Canton are admissible at Macau, they can purchase goods at more reasonable rates—and sell to greater advantage. Every other European nation being in some degree, only allowed to reside for a certain period of the year at Canton, during which they are of course compelled to dispose of their cargos and purchase their returns in some measure at the mercy of the Chinese merchants being freed from the expense of linguists and compradores independent of the Chinese subjects purchasing and exporting goods from Macau into China; pay duties to the Chinese government on all such goods 20 per cent, less than if the same goods were purchased from any other European nation.[10]

The eleventh point advised London as to the annual revenue of the Portuguese administration, notably that derived from customs duties, while the following point indicated the annual outlay on the establishment's upkeep. The last two points covered the city's military defence and the revenues which the Mandarinate demanded from the Portuguese.[11] This information was surely gathered to prepare the embassy led by Lord Macartney, a former governor of Madras, who arrived in the enclave in June 1793[12] accompanied by the embassy's secretary-general, Sir George Staunton (1737–1801).[13] The members of the embassy made their way to Beijing and, after the "culture shock"[14] and the failed attempts to negotiate with the emperor,[15] they returned to Macau in January 1794.[16] Lord Macartney stayed in the Casa Garden[17] until March, at the time the residence of James Drummond,[18] and was aware that he had not been able to achieve the purpose of his mission.[19] Once again, Britain looked at Macau as a territory to be "conquered", and Macartney himself asserts in his travel diary:

> the Portuguese who, as a nation, have been long exanimated and dread in this part of the world, although their ghost still appears in Macau, hold that place upon such term as render it equally useless and disgraceful to them.[20] It is now chiefly supported by the English, and on the present footing of things there the Chinese can starve both it, and those who support it, wherever they please. If the Portuguese made a difficulty of parting with it to us on fair terms, it might easily be taken from them by a small force from Madras [...] or with as little trouble and with more advantage we might make a settlement in Lantao or Cow-hee, and then Macau would of itself crumble to nothing in a short time.[21]

While the ambassador suggested that Macau be taken or annihilated from the vantage point of other British factories to be set up in China, the enclave's authorities and priests and friars, as well as the missionaries in Beijing, once again defended Portuguese interests at all costs. The Portuguese priests who took part in the embassy fiercely criticised British actions and designs. Later, in a representation to the emperor led by the Beijing missionaries in about 1802, Father José Bernando d'Almeida and other priests, having been warned by Macau's Procurator, advised the emperor both of British false designs when they occupied Macau in that same year, purporting to defend the Portuguese against the French, and of the "calamities" and "dire" consequences which might derive from British entry into China:

> among the different nations [...] which come to trade with China, there is a kingdom named England whose people, in the West, have the distinctive feature of being deceitful and hypocritical. For the best part of the past dozens of years, this nation has been proposing and retains the ambitious

design of absorbing into itself everything there is, to which end it often resorts to the apparent and hypocritical title of trade, with which it covers up its hidden and captious instincts. [...] And in the year fifty eight of Emperor Qianlong, they sent a large vessel with gifts for the Emperor, and among the many things, which the English hypocritically asked for, [...] that an adjacent island be ceded; all of this in order to be able to execute their premeditated stratagems. [...] Not only in this place [Bengal], but in many others the English have used the same stratagems[22] [...], and if they succeed in obtaining what they seek in China, peace and tranquillity will not be durable in this empire. The Portuguese, however, have existed in this empire for more than two centuries, without having until now motivated any distrust or disquiet of any kind.[23]

Besides the negative image of British designs, drafted in terms and phrases such as "evils and captiousness", "hypocritically" and "astute enterprises", the document's authors also compared, by dissimilitude, the British presence and activity with those of the Portuguese in the Pearl River delta.

Macau's political power had long feared the growing British presence, and the governor, Vasco Luís Carneiro de Sousa e Faro,[24] pre-empted the arrival of Lord Macartney's embassy by informing the governor of India, Francisco de Cunha e Meneses, at the end of 1792 that:

the English are repeating for a second time an ambassador to China [...]. It is public knowledge that the purpose of said embassy is the wish of the said English [to obtain] the island of Canton, there to establish themselves and, when they achieve this, which I do not doubt they will for we have in that court no-one to hamper this project, this neighbouring power will do Macau no little harm, unless we take measures for the future.[25]

Macau's fear dragged on until after the founding of Hong Kong, and in 1811 judge Miguel de Arriaga recounted to the Portuguese Minister for the Navy and Overseas Territories, Melo e Castro, British attempts to set up in trade in China, to the detriment of Portuguese interests[26] and justified the governor's words transcribed above.

Lord Macartney's embassy gave rise to several descriptions of China and of the city of Macau, such as John Barrow's, which refers to the scheming of the Portuguese missionaries in Beijing[27] and, in its second edition, to British attempts to occupy Macau in 1802, as had been the case in Goa that same year and in 1799;[28] these strategies had been presented by the British as "succour" in the face of the French threat,[29] and in 1806 still remain implicit in British "colonial" discourse:

> towards the close of the last war [1802], when it was found expedient to take possession of some of the Portugueze colonies, and an expedition for this purpose was actually sent out to secure the peninsula of Macau, this missionary [Bernardo Almeida] lost no time in suggesting to the Chinese court, that the designs of the English in getting possession of Macau might be of the same nature as those they had already practiced in India,[30] and if they were once suffered to get footing in the country, China might experience the same fate as Hindostan. [...] The Chinese at Canton (and a great deal depends upon their representations) would have no objection to see the English in possession of Macau; for they cordially hate, I believe it is not too much to say despise, the Portugueze, and they speak with horror of the French. What a moment then is this for England to turn to its advantage![31]

Barrow's concluding remarks on Britain's position towards Macau reveal that British designs had not changed since the arrival of the first EIC officials in the enclave in 1635. As has been shown, Britain did not completely recognise Portuguese sovereignty in the territory, and its (British) occupation was from early on referred to as a relatively easy—and even advisable—undertaking, given the state of neglect and poverty in which it had been left by Lisbon; hence the Jesuits in Beijing had attempted to ensure Lord Macartney's embassy would bear no fruit, which would thus keep religious and trade rivals away both from Macau and from the rest of China.

In 1802 and 1808, a period which is beyond the scope of this analysis, and following Macartney's diplomatic failure, two British attempts were made to occupy the territory militarily, under the pretext of defending it from the French threat. However, in 1808 the Canton governor-general Wu Xiongguang made it quite clear that British occupation of Macau was an affront not just to the Portuguese administration but also to China, a fact which hampered British movement and designs: "Macau which is not Portuguese, is part of our territory of the great Qing Dynasty, how dare they [British] invade our land? If there are alarms on the frontiers, China is able to confront the situation. Do not go to any trouble because our people might be frightened by your manoeuvres".[32] That year, the same imperial official approached the emperor with a view to putting into retrospective context the arrival of the British in Southern China and their interests, as well as those of the Macau Portuguese, accusing the latter of allowing their northern-European rivals to disembark in China:[33]

> the English, seeing that those of Xiyang [Portugal] enjoy this privilege of exemption from customs duties, have for a long time nurtured the ambition of occupying the place of those from Xiyang. At this time, when Xiyang is weaker than ever, the English, on the apparent pretext of providing protection for those of Xiyang, are trying to cause the occupation of Macau to happen, and those of Xiyang, fearful of British might, have begun to tolerate the presence of the English in Macau. They [British] will ultimately try to expel the barbarians from Xiyang, achieving their ambition of occupying the totality of the territory of Macau. English ambition is more than obvious. Besides which, on the one hand, it is imprudent to let the English, being rebellious and indomitable, stay in our interior territory.[34]

The Jiaqing Emperor (1796–1820) also accused the viceroy of Canton of cowardice in not being more forceful in the face of the British soldiers.[35] Located on the periphery of the Portuguese empire and on the maritime fringe of China, Macau also enjoyed imperial protection, which strengthened the Portuguese position in the face of British attempts to occupy it; the latter would have to face not only Lisbon's diplomatic reactions but also Portuguese and Chinese military forces in the East. If the British described the cut-off in the supply of victuals to the city ordered by the Mandarins to make the Portuguese abide by their demands, they realised that, after their occupation of the territory, China might isolate them in the same way, making British military strategy ineffectual—which would equally displease their old allies, the Portuguese. Thus the latter realised that support from Canton and Beijing was indispensable if they wished to remain in China, and they made full use of their centuries-old knowledge of Chinese culture to defend themselves against British interests. The "barbarian" enclave was used strategically by the Chinese authorities to control all foreigners, hence their interest in retaining the Portuguese there.[36] The episodes of British attempts to occupy Macau were mentioned at the end of the nineteenth century and early twentieth century in Portuguese publications by authors whose spirits were "inflamed" by the British Ultimatum (1890)[37] and who wished to review Britain's position as so-called "faithful ally"[38] and "sister nation",[39] accusing Britain of pretending to be an ally when, in reality, it was trying to take over Portuguese territories.[40]

Lord Macartney's embassy to China did not bear diplomatic fruit, but as already shown with regard to the changing of China's image in Britain, it had direct cultural repercussions in Europe and indirectly in Southern China in the long term, for the young George Thomas Staunton (1781–1859), who took part in that expedition, exemplified the British desire to set up in trade in China, later becoming a Sinologist, a supercargo and EIC administrator in the East. In 1793, aged twelve, George Thomas accompanied his father, Sir George Leonard Staunton (1737–1801), deputy secretary and minister pleni-potentiary in Lord Macartney's embassy, as a page to the ambassador. Before and during the sea voyage, the adolescent studied Chinese with Pol Ko and Lee, two Chinese missionaries from the Propaganda Fide [Roman Catholic College for the Propagation of the Faith], quickly becoming at ease with Chinese char-acters, to the extent that during the meeting with the emperor, he was the only one who spoke with him. Later, in April 1798, Staunton was appointed clerk of the British factory in Canton, promoted in 1804 to EIC supercargo, and the following year took part in introducing vaccination in China by translat-ing the Treatise written by the Company's surgeon Alexander Pearson. In 1808 Staunton was appointed factory interpreter, and in 1816 he became president of the Select Committee, living in Macau between the trading seasons. That year, together with William, Earl Amherst (1773–1857) and Sir Henry Ellis (1777–1855), the supercargo was appointed King's commissioner in the second British embassy to Beijing (1816–1817);[41] his mission was to try once again to defend the rights and interests of British traders in Canton and Macau, a diplomatic undertaking which also bore no fruit. The know-how/why he had accumulated ever since his adolescence, as well as the fact that he had a fluent command of Chinese, allowed Staunton to have a successful career, which also symbolises British persistence as regards the valuable China Trade.

After Lord Macartney's embassy, a more negative image of China began to appear in Britain and Europe; it was now represented as a weak and vulnerable nation which should be forced to modernise. In the first decades of the nine-teenth century, the British government concluded that, in order to achieve the aims underlying Lord Macartney's embassy, it would have to resort, not simply to diplomacy but also to the use of force, a strategy which, after the end of the EIC monopoly, took the 1839 opium crisis as a pretext. The clash of interests between the Chinese and the British thus led the prime minister, Lord Palmerston (1784–1865), to declare war on China, a conflict which became known as the first Opium War and during which Macau remained neutral, defending its centuries-old interests and its privileged position in China.[42] On these grounds, writers such as Alexander Michie criticised the Portuguese attitude during this war, which, in the end, allowed the British to seek "a home of their own in the Canton waters".[43]

Historians such as Vincent T. Harlow,[44] thinking back to the war of American independence, Britain's naval battles with Spain and France, the French Revolution and the British Industrial Revolution, have developed the theory known as the "swing to the East", that is, the image of a first British (Atlantic) empire giving way to a second (African and Eastern) empire in about 1763, thirty years before Macartney's embassy, a shift which Michael Duffy[45] situates at the end of the 1790s, already after the diplomatic expedition. According to P. J. Marshall,[46] the "old empire" system co-existed with that of the "second" (Eastern) empire, as the structures of the first empire did not collapse entirely to make way immediately for the "conquest" in the East. British interests in Asia only replaced the country's Western interests in the early nineteenth century, the shift to the East thus running parallel to British imperial policies in the Western hemisphere, notably the development of trading activity in Brazil and in the American Spanish colonies. In this same context, Lord Macartney's embassy to China appears in 1793 with the aim of promoting exports of British products stemming from the Industrial Revolution, developing conditions favourable to EIC trade in China, and in some way to make up for the loss of the North-American colony markets.

Conclusion

At the end of the eighteenth century, Britain took on the role of a mighty power in the East; the British role and status in Macau at that point were very different from those of a hundred years before when the EIC set itself up in China. The foreign population and trade ultimately became essential for Macau's economy, but the local and religious authorities accused the British of constituting—through their higher standard of living than that of the Portuguese—a trade and moral threat, of driving upward the prices of the city's products, of keeping prostitution active and of introducing a taste for excessive luxury in private and public life. If on the one hand, local economic interests depended on British investment in the city, through the letting and purchasing of houses and vessels, as well as loans, the Macau Senate also wished to control foreign activity and competition, aims which were difficult to reconcile. On the other hand, from 1700 onward the Portuguese could do nothing against the designs of the Chinese authorities and Canton traders, who increasingly encouraged the setting up of trade relations with other European partners.

The British and North-Americans, the two largest foreign communities in Macau from the end of the 1700s until the first Opium War, had a representative social impact on life in the enclave, from fashion to cultural customs, and further contributed to the accumulation of wealth and to the intense cultural activity in Macau, a multi-ethnic enclave since the Portuguese had founded it. In addition, as a geographical-cultural referent, Macau served as a backdrop to countless fictional adventures in British literature,[1] a phenomenon closely linked both to the development of the EIC China Trade, whose picturesque and exotic dimension attracted British writers and painters,[2] and to the founding of Hong Kong. If the members of the Anglophone communities influenced the *modus vivendi* and progress in the Portuguese-ruled territory, the latter played a pivotal role in these English-speaking communities' trade and cultural relations with China, a status acknowledged by Alexander Michie in 1900, when he listed some of the pioneering "glories" of Macau within the framework of Sino-Western relations:

> the influence of Macau on the history of foreign relations with China extended much beyond the sphere of mere commercial interests. For three hundred years it was for foreigners the gate of the Chinese empire, and all influences, good and bad, which came from without were infiltrated through that narrow opening, which served as the medium through which China was revealed to the world. It was in Macau that the first lighthouse[3] was erected, a symbol of the illuminating mission of foreigners in China. It was there also that the first printing-press was set up, employing movable type instead of the stereotype wooden blocks used by the Chinese. From that press was issued Morrison's famous Dictionary, and for a long series of years the *Chinese Repository* [...][4] conducted chiefly by English and American missionaries. The first foreign hospital in China was opened at Macau, and there vaccination was first practiced.[5] It was from Macau that the father of China missions, Matteo Ricci, started on his adventurous journey [...] in the sixteenth century [...]. The little Portuguese settlement has therefore played no mean part in the changes which have taken place in the great empire of China. [...] St Francis Xavier [...], [...] Camöens,[6] who in a grotto formed of granite blocks tumbled together by nature, almost washed by the sea, sat and wrote the Portuguese epic "The Lusiad".[7]

If the trading population of the "diminute settlement"[8] initially wished to hamper foreign infiltration in the China Trade, such a design became impossible in the face of the interests of both the Chinese traders and those of the enclave's population who profited from the seasonal presence, in the case of the EIC supercargoes, and annually, in the case of private traders and their families; the English-speaking residents did not, however, often mix with the Portuguese.

Macau was the Western gateway into China for British traders and supercargoes and their only permanent residence there until the early 1840s. In the late 1700s it was also a base where independent traders could set up in trade and compete with the EIC's monopoly until 1833. The City of the Holy Name of God of Macau thus played a basic and unique role in every phase of British trade in Southern China, from the arrival of the *London*, chartered by the viceroy of Goa from the EIC in 1635, through the permanent establishment of the super-cargoes to the arrival of the interlopers and independent merchants who upset the Company's monopoly. This inconvenient situation for the EIC was similar to that of the Portuguese when faced with the arrival of their northern-European rivals in the *Estado da Índia* in the early seventeenth century and which marked the beginning of the period of downsizing and decline of the Portuguese empire in the East.

If British interests in the enclave never fully came to fruition, notably the occupation of the city, this must be attributed to the geographical and political situation of Macau and to the vigilance of the Portuguese and especially the Chinese authorities. In August 1842, to mark the end of the Opium War and nine years after the cessation of the EIC monopoly, the British—"a community in search of a colony"[9] in China during a century and a half—signed the Treaty of Nanking. The British had demanded the cession of Hong Kong, a "Macau of their own" where they could trade without third party restrictions. The founding of the new colony and the opening of the five Chinese ports, following upon the entry and establishment of the British in China through Macau and Canton,[10] transformed the Western foreigner's way of life in China and in the Sino-Portuguese enclave;[11] hence the designation of Old China Trade for the historical period up to 1842. After the founding of the British colony, the presence of the "red-haired devils" in China changed, becoming not exclusively commercial but also administrative. This led to greater British proximity to Chinese culture and to a new image of Macau, no longer seen as a commercial hub, but increasingly as a place for leisure, convalescence and tourism for Hong Kong residents and visitors. The Sino-Portuguese enclave rapidly lost much of its economic and political strategic importance in regional and international terms as Hong Kong rapidly became the leading trading city in the Pearl River delta.

The Anglo-Portuguese alliance, as shown, gradually extended to the Far East, and relations between the two Western allies regarding trade and imperial interests in China were marked by diplomacy between the two European kingdoms, by the clash of interests of local traders, and also by both the "Portuguese and Imperial Laws",[12] with the Macau Senate and governor finding themselves compelled to negotiate and justify their actions to Canton and Lisbon as regards the British presence in China, while Macau fought for its own survival on the maritime fringe of the province of Guangdong. The oldest alliance in the Western world was also influenced by the policies of the Chinese administration, with whom the Portuguese were forced to negotiate, often using Chinese law to defend their own status in the Pearl River delta *vis-à-vis* the British. The Protestant interests and presence contributed to the formation of the historical and socio-cultural identity of Macau, especially in the first half of the nineteenth century. The city operated as a decompression chamber for the Westerners who travelled to China and for the Chinese travelling to the West, giving rise to the multiplicity of contexts in which Portuguese, Chinese and British encounters, interactions and conflicts took place.

Notes

Introduction

1. The Macau English Tavern/Hotel was strategically located in the Praia Grande during the 1830s and was owned by two former East India Company supercargoes—Richard Markwick (1791–1836) and Edward Lane (d. 1831)—who established a firm called Markwick and Lane. It was also called the "Beach Hotel" in Anglophone sources and "English Tavern" in both Anglophone and Portuguese documents [B. L. Ball, *Rambles in Eastern Asia*, 1856, pp. 409–410; Harriett Low, *Lights and Shadows of a Macao Life*, 2002, pp. 104, 568; and Jin Guoping and Wu Zhiliang (eds.), *Correspondência Oficial Trocada Entre as Autoridades de Cantão e os Procuradores do Senado: Fundo das Chapas Sínicas em Português (1749–1847)*, vol. 8, 2000, pp. 30, 37].

2. On the British Museum of Macau, established in 1829 by EIC supercargoes and North American and British traders and missionaries, see *Canton Register* (02-03-1830); Eliza Morrison (ed.), *Memoirs of the Life and Labours of Robert Morrison; Compiled by His Widow*, vol. 2, 1839, p. 424; Harriett Low, *Lights and Shadows*, pp. 92, 157, 228, 241, 286; George Bennet, *Wanderings in New South Wales*, 1834, pp. 35–36, and Rogério Miguel Puga, "The First Museum in China: The British Museum of Macao (1829–1834) and its Contribution to Nineteenth-Century British Natural Science", *Journal of the Royal Asiatic Society*, series 3, vol. 22, nn. 3–4, 2012, pp. 1–12.

3. The EIC Library of Macau and Canton was maintained between 1806 and 1834.

4. British Library, *India Office Records (IOR)*, G/12/32 (1731), fl. 15.

5. Paul Van Dyke's seminal *The Canton Trade*, 2005, pp. 35–48, 77, 119–167, is the only study that devotes more than a few paragraphs to the importance of Macau in the context of the China Trade.

6. The Chinese considered the Portuguese "Macau barbarians", long since established in the enclave and easily controllable due to their "fixed residence" [cf. "Memorial of Qi Ying" (1845), in António Vasconcelos de Saldanha and Jin Guoping (eds.), *Para a Vista do Imperador: Memoriais da Dinastia Qing*, 2000, p. 96], but they were differentiated from all other Europeans who stayed there temporarily. I use the term "foreigner" from the Portuguese, and also English, point of view in Macau, to designate residents who are neither Portuguese nor Chinese as described in Portuguese and English sources in the seventeenth and eighteenth centuries, given that the territory was jointly administered by the Portuguese governor, the Senate, the Chinese Mandarin of the White House and the Tongzhi magistrate. Chinese Macau answered in juridical terms to the *zongdu* (viceroy of Canton), who delegated competences to the Mandarins of Xiangshan and Qianshan (the White House Mandarin) to resolve the problems of the Chinese population and communicate with the Senate. Only important issues would reach Canton. The English supercargoes (1777–1778) called themselves "foreigners" in Macau (G/12/62, fl. 27), affirming at an audience with the governor (1786): "as we are strangers in your city" (G/12/84, fl. 58, see also G/12/59, fl. 41, G/12/62, fl. 27, G/12/86, fl. 17). The Mandarinate, due to linguistic barriers and logistical questions, delegated jurisdiction over all foreigners in the enclave to the Portuguese, and in 1832 Anders Ljungstedt (*An Historical Sketch of the Portuguese Settlement in China*, 1992, p. 21) considered the foreigners to be an autonomous group in Macau (Portuguese vassals, Chinese and foreigners), finding the British community subordinate to the Portuguese authorities.

7. J. M. Braga, "A Seller of 'Sing-Songs': A Chapter in the Foreign Trade of China and Macau", *Journal of Oriental Studies*, vol. 6, nn. 1–2, 1961–1964, p. 107.

8. G/12/89 (1788), fl. 203.

9. Weng Eang Cheong, *The Hong Merchants of Canton*, 1997, p. 109, summarises the history of the Select Committee referring to the measures taken by the East India Company to establish a council of supercargoes that would remain in China during the trading seasons. In 1778, a small select committee was established with a president, three or four supercargoes and other employees, or "supercargoes below the select committee" [G/12/71 (1780–1781), fl. 59] to facilitate decision making. This administrative structure became the permanent representative body of the EIC in China until the end of the Company's monopoly in 1833–1834 (G/12/20, fls. 377–379v; Hosea B. Morse, *The Chronicles of the East India Company Trading to China 1635–1834*, vol. 2, 1926, pp. 38–49).

10. Anna Grimshaw, *The Ethnographer's Eye: Ways of Seeing in Modern Anthropology*, 2001, p. ix.

11. R. Lehan, *The City in Literature*, 1998, pp. 8–9, Kevin Lynch, *The Image of the City*, 2000, pp. 1–13.

Chapter 1 Anglo-Portuguese conflicts and the founding of the East India Company

1. Donald Lach, *Asia in the Making of Europe*, 1:1, 1994, pp. xvi–xix.
2. On early Anglo-Portuguese conflicts in Africa, see Rogério Miguel Puga, "'Scramble for Africa': As Viagens Inglesas à África Ocidental no Reinado de D. João III", in Roberto Carneiro and Artur Teodoro de Matos (eds.), *D. João III e o Império*, 2004, pp. 717–752.
3. John Bruce, *Annals of the Honorable East-India Company*, vol. 2, 1810, pp. 54–55, and Visconde de Santarém, *Quadro Elementar das Relações Políticas e Diplomáticas de Portugal*, 1865, vol. 15, p. 259.
4. Cf. Edgar Prestage, "The Anglo-Portuguese Alliance", *Transactions of the Historical Society*, 4th series, vol. 17, 1934, pp. 3, 12–23, and Charles R. Boxer, "Vicissitudes das Relações Anglo-Portuguesas no Século XVII", in *600 Anos de Aliança Anglo-Portuguesa: 600 Years of Anglo-Portuguese Alliance*, n.d., p. 26.
5. G/12/1, fl. 1, and Henri Cordier, *Histoire Générale de la Chine*, vol. 2, 1920, pp. 191–192.
6. M. Paske Smith, *Western Barbarians in Japan and Formosa in Tokugawa Days*, 1930, pp. 3–4.
7. See Rogério Miguel Puga, "Os Descobrimentos Portugueses em *The Principal Navigations* de Richard Hakluyt", *Anais de História de Além Mar*, n. 4, 2003, pp. 63–131.
8. The first account of China published in English is the *Treaty of China*, by the Portuguese author Galeote Pereira, translated from Italian by Richard Eden and Richard Willes and published by the latter in *History of Travayle in the West and East Indies*, as well as by Hakluyt (see Rogério Miguel Puga, "The Presence of the 'Portugals' in Macau and Japan in Richard Hakluyt's *Navigations*", *Bulletin of Portuguese/Japanese Studies*, vol. 5, December 2002, pp. 94–96).
9. Rogério Miguel Puga, "Macau in Samuel Purchas's *Hakuytus Posthumus, or Purchas His Pilgrimes* (1625)", *Review of Culture*, n. 28, October 2008, pp. 16–41.
10. Humphrey Gilbert, "A Discourse", in Richard Hakluyt, *Voyages*, vol. 5, pp. 92–130.
11. As we shall see, the Anglo-Portuguese alliance was used as an argument by successive governors of Macau and Goa viceroys to the benefit and favourable treatment of English in the city [*Arquivos de Macau (AM)*, 3rd series, vol. 10, n. 5, November 1968, p. 241].
12. See C. L. Kingsford, "The Taking of the *Madre de Dios*, anno 1592", in C. L. Laughton (ed.), *The Naval Miscellany II*, vol. 40, 1912, pp. 85–121.

13. Laurence Keymis Gent, "A Relation of the Second Voyage to Guiana, Performed and Written in the Yeere 1596", in Richard Hakluyt, *Voyages*, vol. 7, pp. 390–391.
14. On the Anglo-Spanish rivalry and the influence of the Portuguese voyages of exploration on Elizabethan literature, see Rogério Miguel Puga, "The 'Lusiads' at Sea and the Spaniards at War in Elizabethan Drama: Shakespeare and the Portuguese Discoveries", in Holger Klein and José Manuel González (eds.), *Shakespeare Yearbook: Shakespeare and Spain*, vol. 13, 2002, pp. 90–114.
15. On the foundation of the EIC and its early voyages to the East Indies, see John Keay, *The Honourable Company*, 1993, pp. 3–51; Philip Lawson, *The East India Company*, 1998, pp. 1–41; Anthony Wild, *The East India Company*, pp. 8–549; and P. J. Marshall, "The English in Asia to 1700", in Nicholas Canny (ed.), *The Oxford History of the British Empire*, vol. 1, 2001, pp. 264–285.
16. G. Birdwood and W. Foster, *The First Letter Book of the East India Company: 1600–1619*, 1893, p. 62.
17. G. Birdwood and W. Foster, *The First Letter Book of the East India Company*, p. 123.
18. On the Anglo-Dutch presence in Surat, see Maria Manuela Sobral Blanco, "O Estado Português da Índia: Da Rendição de Ormuz à Perda de Cochim (1622–1663)", vol. 1, 1992, pp. 423–434.
19. Sir G. Birdwood and W. Foster, *The First Letter Book of the East India Company*, pp. 219–220.

Chapter 2   The voyage east: The beginning of Anglo-Portuguese relations in the East Indies

1. On the Dutch attacks on Portuguese possessions in the Indian Ocean, see K. M. Mathew, "The Dutch Threat and the Security of the Carreira in India Waters", in Artur T. de Matos and Luís F. Thomaz (dir.), *As Relações entre a Índia Portuguesa, a Ásia do Sueste e o Extremo Oriente*, 1993, pp. 779–783; and Maria M. S. Blanco, "O Estado Português da Índia", vol. 1, pp. 393–451.
2. A. H. de Oliveira Marques, *História de Portugal*, vol. 2, 1997, p. 208.
3. Cf. William Finch, "Observations of William Finch", in Samuel Purchas, *Hakluytus*, vol. 4, p. 26.
4. Samuel Purchas, *Hakluytus*, vol. 4, p. 204.
5. François Pyrard de Laval, *Viagem de Francisco Pyrard de Laval*, vol. 2, 1944, p. 203.
6. Artur Teodoro de Matos (dir.), *Documentos Remetidos da Índia ou Livro das Monções (1625–1736)*, 2001, doc. 533, p. 265.
7. António Bocarro, *Década 13 da História da Índia*, 1876, p. 429.
8. Regarding the Anglo-Portuguese conflicts in Bantam and Surat, see Frederick Charles Danvers, *The Portuguese in India: Being a History of the Rise and Decline of*

Their Eastern Empire, vol. 2, 1966, pp. 152–395 and Holden Furber, *Rival Empires of Trade in the Orient 1600–1800*, 1976, pp. 38–78.

9. António Bocarro, *Década 13*, p. 336.

10. On the imprisoning of Englishmen in Goa and their transportation to Lisbon, see the Public Records Office (P.R.O.), *SP* 89/3, fls. 132–134, *SP* 89/3, fl. 144.

11. K. D. Bassett, "Early English Trade and Settlement in Asia, 1602–1690", in Anthony Disney (ed.), *An Expanding World*, vol. 4, 1995, pp. 134–135. On the three periods of Anglo-Dutch rivalry: [I) 1602–1684: aggression by the VOC, II) 1684–1760: commercial rivalry, III) 1760–1795: EIC power in Asia], see Femme S. Gaastra, "War, Competition and Collaboration", in H. V. Bowen et al. (eds.), *The Worlds of the East India Company*, pp. 50–68.

12. António Bocarro, *Década 13*, p. 303. In 1628, the governor of Goa Frei Luís de Brito e Meneses mentioned the great risk posed by the presence of English and Dutch corsairs in Asia (AN/TT, *Livros das Monções*, book 27, fls. 521–534v).

13. Hosea Ballou Morse, *The Chronicles*, vol. 1, p. 29.

14. Expression used in English sources to refer to the Portuguese Black Ship or *Nau do Trato* [Peter Pratt (ed.), *History of Japan Compiled from the Records of the English East India Company*, vol. 1, 1972, p. 153].

15. This chapter and the following summarise the Portuguese and English presences in Japan (1613–1623) and particularly the attempt by the EIC to establish direct trade with China from the archipelago, thus avoiding any Portuguese interference. On Anglo-Portuguese relations in Japan during the Hirado period, see Ludwig Riess, "History of the English Factory at Hirado (1613–1622)", *Transactions of the Asiatic Society of Japan*, vol. 26, 1898, pp. 1–114; and Derek Massarella, *A World Elsewhere: Europe's Encounter with Japan in the Sixteenth and Seventeenth Centuries*, 1990, pp. 58–328.

16. For contextual background to the Portuguese presence in Japan, I have drawn greatly on the works of Charles R. Boxer, *The Christian Century in Japan, 1549–1650*, 1967; João Paulo Oliveira e Costa, "O Cristianismo no Japão e o Episcopado de D. Luís Cerqueira", 1998 and "Japão", in A. H. de Oliveira Marques (dir.), *História dos Portugueses no Extremo Oriente*, 1:2, 2000, pp. 379–471, and Valdemar Coutinho, *O Fim da Presença Portuguesa no Japão*, 1999.

17. Expressions used, respectively, by Charles R. Boxer, *The Christian Century in Japan*, and João Paulo Oliveira e Costa, *Portugal and Japan: The Namban Century*, 1993.

18. Jorge Manuel Flores, "Macau: O Tempo da Euforia", in A. H. de Oliveira Marques (dir.), *História dos Portugueses no Extremo Oriente*, vol. 1, book 2, 2000, p. 187.

19. Valdemar Coutinho, *O Fim da Presença*, pp. 17, 21–23, 29.

20. João Paulo Oliveira e Costa, *Portugal and Japan*, pp. 71–73.

21. On the vessel's arrival in Japan and its cargo, see Diogo do Couto, *Cinco Livros da Década Doze da História da Índia*, book 5, ch. 2, 1645 [1596–1600], pp. 215–218.

22. João Paulo Oliveira e Costa, "O Cristianismo", vol. 2, pp. 765–772, and V. Coutinho, *O Fim da Presença*, pp. 30–32.

23. Literally "the ginger men", north Europeans with a physical appearance differing to the Portuguese.

24. Anthony Farrington, *The English Factory in Japan, 1613–1623*, 1991, p. 247.

25. On Iberian conflicts in Japan, see João Paulo Oliveira e Costa, "A Rivalidade Luso-Espanhola no Extremo Oriente e a Querela Missionológica no Japão", in Artur Teodoro de Matos and Roberto Carneiro (dirs.), *O Século Cristão do Japão*, 1994, pp. 477–524.

26. Anthony Farrington, *The English Factory in Japan*, vol. 1, doc. 24, p. 125.

27. Anthony Farrington, *The English Factory in Japan*, docs. 29, 31, pp. 138, 142, in which the English factor describes trade operations with the Goan "George Droit [Jorge Durois] the Portiges [Portuguese]".

28. Anthony Farrington, *The English Factory in Japan*, doc. 29, p. 138.

29. Anthony Farrington, *The English Factory in Japan*, doc. 82, p. 246.

30. Anthony Farrington, *The English Factory in Japan*, docs. 75, 83, 84, 85, pp. 227, 250, 252, 256–260.

31. Giles Milton, *Samurai William: The Adventurer Who Unlocked Japan*, 2003, pp. 297, 299.

32. G/12/9, fls. 1–2, 13–44.

33. M. Paske-Smith, *Western Barbarians in Japan*, pp. 29–35, defines three periods for English trading activities in Japan: first period (1613–1616): easy trade due to the privileges granted by the Japanese authorities; second period (1617–1619): period of Dutch attacks during which no English ship reached Japan (unless seized by the Dutch); third period: the Anglo-Dutch alliance, the formation of the Defence Fleet (1620), and the joint attacks on Iberian interests in Japan until 1622, when London decided to close the Hirado factory.

34. See Peter Pratt (ed.), *History of Japan*, vol. 1, pp. 327–375, doc. 416; Anthony Farrington, *The English Factory in Japan*, vol. 2, pp. 1173–1188; and docs. 419, 421–422, and 424.

35. Anthony Farrington, *The English Factory in Japan*, vol. 2, doc. 337, p. 829.

36. Anthony Farrington, *The English Factory in Japan*, vol. 2, doc. 364, p. 887.

37. In his correspondence to London in 1621, Richard Cocks, *Diary of Richard Cocks*, vol. 2, 1899, p. 333, reports: "I am afeard that their [Dutch] attempt against Amacon will cause both them and us to be driven out of Japon [...]. Yet our China frendes still tell us we may have trade into China".

38. Referred to in EIC documentation by his Christian name "Andrea Dittis" and as "China Captain".
39. Anthony Farrington, *The English Factory in Japan*, vol. 1, p. 381.
40. Anthony Farrington, *The English Factory in Japan*, vol. 2, p. 563.
41. English sources refer to him as *Captain Whaw* or *Whow* (Farrington, *The English Factory*, doc. 267).
42. Anthony Farrington, *The English Factory in Japan*, doc. 75, pp. 224–228.
43. Anthony Farrington, *The English Factory in Japan*, p. 3.
44. Anthony Farrington, *The English Factory in Japan*, vol. 1, doc. 229, p. 556.
45. Anthony Farrington, *The English Factory in Japan*, doc. 267, pp. 661–662.
46. Anthony Farrington, *The English Factory in Japan*, vol. 2, doc. 351, p. 852.
47. M. Paske-Smith, *Western Barbarians in Japan*, p. 28. In 1618, the Bantam factor, George Ball, advised London to follow the Dutch and attack Chinese boats to have access to goods, as the Chinese refused to trade with foreigners, so Li Tan's promises could only be false (cf. doc. 266 in Anthony Farrington, *The English Factory in Japan*, vol. 1, p. 655). In 1615, Richard Wickham described Dutch attacks on Chinese junks as an activity that provided 100% profit (Anthony Farrington, *The English Factory in Japan*, vol. 1, doc. 125, p. 327).
48. G/12, 15, fls., 23v–24, 40–42.
49. Anthony Farrington, *The English Factory in Japan*, vol. 2, doc. 229, p. 860.
50. Anthony Farrington, *The English Factory in Japan*, vol. 1, doc. 234, p. 583.
51. Anthony Farrington, *The English Factory in Japan*, docs. 133, 229, 269, pp. 341, 564, 677.
52. Anthony Farrington, *The English Factory in Japan*, doc. 234, p. 583.
53. The Hirado Factory documentation contains countless references to Portuguese activities in Japan, to the Black Ship, the Dutch rivalry, commercial espionage and the taking of Portuguese goods and vessels by the English: W. Nöel Sainsbury (ed.), *Calendar of State Papers, Colonial Series, East Indies, China and Japan, 1513–1617*, 1862, pp. 350–351, 353, 438, 450; and Anthony Farrington, *The English Factory in Japan*, vol. 1, pp. 72, 200, 202, 212, 242, 250, 252, 256–261, 263, 849–856, 863, 883, 895–898, 997–1028. Note the extent of variation in the spelling of the toponym Macau (at the time still uncommon in English), even within the same document: "Amakan", "Maccaw", "Macow", "Macaur", "Amakon", "Amacau" (vol. 1, pp. 68, 72, 86, 208, 227, 246–247), "Macawe", "Macowe", "Amacon", "Amakow", "Mackeaue", and "Mackcawe" (vol. 2, pp. 861, 882, 886, 890–891, 989, 1001).
54. Anthony Farrington, *The English Factory in Japan*, vol. 2, pp. 851–852.
55. Anthony Farrington, *The English Factory in Japan*, pp. 891, 893–894, 895–898.
56. AHU, *Macau*, box 8, doc. 6, AN/TT, *Colecção de São Vicente*, cod. 19, doc. 156, and Frei Álvaro do Rosário, "Ataque dos Holandeses a Macau em 1622", *Boletim*

da Agência Geral das Colónias, n. 38, 1928, pp. 17–30. EIC documents also mentioned the defeat of the Dutch in Macau [W. Nöel Sainsbury (ed.), *Calendar of State Papers, Colonial Series, East Indies, China and Japan, 1622–1624*, 1878, docs. 70 and 146, pp. 31, 65–66; Sir William Foster (ed.), *The English Factories in India: 1622–1623*, 1908, pp. 210, 225–226; and Peter Pratt (ed.), *History of Japan*, vol. 1, pp. 446–447].

57. Richard Cocks, *Diary of Richard Cocks*, 1883, vol. 2, p. 332.
58. Frei Sebastião Manrique, *Itinerário*, vol. 2, 1946, p. 144.
59. AN/TT, S. Vicente Collection, *cod.* 19, doc. 154.
60. Anthony Farrington, *The English Factory in Japan*, vol. 2, doc. 363, pp. 882–885, doc. 379, p. 922.
61. The ship's log contains an extensive account of all the problems raised by the Japanese authorities to ensure that the crew of the *Return* left Japan, with one such reason being the Anglo-Portuguese alliance and the English king taking Catharine of Bragança as his bride [Engelbert Kaempfer, *The History of Japan*, vol. 3, 1906, pp. 342–357; G/12/16 (1614–1703), fls. 60–66].
62. João Paulo Oliveira e Costa, "O Cristianismo no Japão", vol. 2, p. 764.
63. William Hickey, *Memoirs of William Hickey (1749–1775)*, vol. 1, 1913, pp. 169–197.
64. G/12/59, fl. 123.
65. As to Portuguese diplomatic strategies in 1641–1642, and 1654, see Eduardo Brasão, *A Diplomacia Portuguesa nos Séculos XVII e XVIII*, vol. 1, 1979, pp. 46–51, and Luís da Cunha Gonçalves, "A Restauração de 1640 no Oriente", *Boletim da Segunda Classe da Academia das Ciências*, vol. 9, 1915, pp. 396–404.
66. In a letter to the viceroy of India, Phillip II referred to the articles, especially the ninth, of the Anglo–Portuguese peace treaty of 1604, strengthened by that of 1630 [Júlio Firmino Biker (ed.), *Colecção de Tratados e Concertos de Pazes que o Estado da Índia Portugesa Fez*, book 1, 1995, p. 262, book 2, pp. 37–38].
67. G/12/10, fls. 67–80, Júlio Firmino Biker (ed.), *Colecção de Tratados*, pp. 239–261. The thirty-four articles of the 1630 treaty sought to improve ties of friendship between the two nations, strengthen the free trade and protect their Asian domains against the Dutch (chs. 1–4, 7–8, 11–12).
68. The proposal was initially conveyed to Goa by two Jesuit informers loyal to the viceroy who were in Surat, António Pereira and Paulo Reimão [National Library of Portugal, *Fundo Geral*, cod. 7640; see also Sir William Foster (ed.), *The English Factories in India 1630–1633*, pp. 220–22]. In August 1633, Joseph Hopkinson and the Council of Surat informed Father Paulo Reimão that once Portugal and England joined forces "we would be lords of all India and neither Moor nor Dutch

would be able to withstand" [Panduronga S. Pissurlencar, *Assentos do Conselho do Estado*, vol. 1 (*1618–1633*), 1953, p. 481].

69. "Exchange Made between the Viceroy, the Count of Linhares and Guilherme Methewold", in Júlio Firmino Biker (ed.), *Colecção de Tratados*, book 2, pp. 50–51 (English version pp. 52–53).
70. Júlio Firmino Biker (ed.), *Colecção de Tratados*, book 2, pp. 263–264.
71. Panduronga Sacarama Sinai Pissurlencar, *Assentos*, vol. 2, 1954, pp. 3–5.
72. Sir Wiliam Foster (ed.), *The English Factories in India 1634–1636*, 1911, pp. 15–17, 79–80, 96.
73. G/12/10, fls. 69–74, José Ferreira Borges de Castro (org.), *Colecção dos Tratados, Convenções, Contratos e Actos Públicos Celebrados ente a Coroa de Portugal e as Mais Potências desde 1640 até ao Presente*, vol. 1, 1856, pp. 102–103, Montalto Jesus, *Historic Macau*, 1902, pp. 95–96, and A. R. Disney, *Twilight of the Pepper Empire*, 1978, pp. 148–154.
74. The "Relação Breve, Geral das Principaes Couzas que Sucederão em a India o Anno de 1633", National Library of Portugal, *Fundo Geral*, cod. 7640, p. 60, lists the advantages of the peace agreement to be signed with England, especially the increase in trade and customs duties, as well as the weakening of the Dutch enemies.
75. Letter from the viceroy (1636) on the ceasefire with the English stating that it should be maintained due to the "many enemies" and the difficult situation faced by the Portuguese empire (AN/TT, *Livros das Monções*, book 33, pp. 247–247v).
76. G/12/10, fl. 98 and José Ferreira Borges de Castro (org.), *Colecção dos Tratados*, pp. 82–101; Edgar Prestage, *The Diplomatic Relations of Portugal with France, England, and Holland from 1640 to 1668*, 1925, pp. 99–104; and D. K. Bassett, "Early English Trade and Settlement in Asia, 1602–1690", pp. 134–136.
77. Júlio Firmino Biker (ed.), *Colecção de Tratados*, book 1, pp. 264–266.
78. G. V. Scammell, "England, Portugal and the *Estado da Índia c.*1500–1635", *Modern Asian Studies*, vol. 16, 1982, pp. 177–192, summarises Anglo-Portuguese conflicts through to the Convention of Goa.
79. Maria Manuela Sobral Blanco, "O Estado Português da Índia", vol. 1, pp. 540–542.
80. On the context leading to the Anglo-Portuguese *entente cordiale* against the VOC in the seventeenth century, see G. R. Crone, *The Discovery of the East*, 1972, pp. 120–147, and Marcus P. M. Vink, "The Entente Cordiale: The Dutch East India Company and the Portuguese Shipping through the Straits of Malacca, 1641–1663", *Revista de Cultura*, vol. 1, nn. 13–14, 1991, pp. 289–309. The latter author states that the Dutch in Batavia were preparing for possible joint attacks from their Portuguese and English enemies. The study concludes that the Anglo-Portuguese *entente cordiale* was harmful in the long term to the Portuguese as while the English

did weaken the Dutch naval blockades and transport Portuguese goods, but they were not able to protect Portuguese possessions in Asia.

81. See Jorge Manuel Flores, "Macau: O Tempo da Euforia", p. 179.

82. John Francis Careri, *A Voyage Round the World in Six Parts*, 1752, p. 275.

Chapter 3　The arrival of the English in Macau

1. AN/TT, *Livros das Monções*, book 33, fl. 248, book 44, fls. 426–427, book 45, fls. 350–351, and Sir William Foster (ed.), *The English Factories in India 1634–1636*, pp. 103–104, 150, 177–178, 189–190, 226–230, which details under "Consultation Held in Surat", pp. 102–103: "an English ship 'should be sent from Goa to Macau in China for freight goods [...]. The voiadge in itselfe was generally approved [...] were it but *to experience the trade in those parts, which hath ever bene desired*'" (my emphasis; see G/12/1, fl. 24).

2. Sir William Foster, *The English Factories in India 1634–1636*, p. 228, and G/12/10, fls. 86–88.

3. Júlio Firmino Biker (ed.), *Colecção de Tratados*, book 1, p. 266.

4. *Arquivo Histórico de Goa* (AHG), *Filmoteca Ultramarina Portuguesa* (FUP), *Livro dos Segredos*, no. 1, fls. 6–7.

5. Júlio Firmino Biker (ed.), *Colecção de Tratados*, book 1, p. 267.

6. Sir William Foster, *The English Factories in India 1634–1636*, pp. 105–106.

7. G/12/10, fls. 81–84.

8. Sir William Foster (ed.), *The English Factories in India 1634–1636*, p. 106.

9. In 1794, Aeneas Anderson (*A Narrative of the British Embassy to China*, 1795, p. 392), visited Macau as part of the first English embassy to China and criticised the Catholics of Macau for obliging the English who passed away in China to be buried outside of the city alongside the Chinese as "the papists have particular places of internment for those who depart this life in the faith of their church".

10. Padre Manuel Teixeira, *Macau e a Sua Diocese*, vol. 2, 1940, pp. 260–262.

11. G/12/10, fl. 81.

12. AN/TT, *Livros das Monções*, book 34, fls. 64v–65. On the "intent" of the voyage and Manuel Bocarro's artillery to be transported to Goa, see the instructions given to Manuel Ramos, administrator of the Japan voyage, which mentioned the peace with the English "in conformity with the peace that his majesty made with their King" (fls. 72–72v).

13. AN/TT, *Livros das Monções*, fl. 63v.

14. This idea was repeated at the end of the letter (AN/TT, *Livros das Monções*, book 34, fl. 66) and in the instructions given to Manuel Ramos (fl. 73 and book 35, fl. 263).

15. AN/TT, *Livros das Monções*, book 34, fl. 64, book 35, fl. 263.
16. Counsel given both in the letter sent to the captain-general of Macau and in another one addressed to Manuel Ramos, dated May 3, 1635 (fl. 73v).
17. AN/TT, *Livros das Monções*, book 35, fl. 243.
18. AN/TT, *Livros das Monções*, book 35, fl. 243.
19. AN/TT, *Livros das Monções*, book 35, fls. 244–244v.
20. For details of the vessel's route from Downs, via Surat, to Macau, see Anthony Farrington, *East India Company Ships, 1600–1833*, 1999, p. 386.
21. Letter from Manuel Ramos to the Viceroy of India (20-10-1635): AN/TT, *Livros das Monções*, book 35, fl. 253v.
22. Letter from the viceroy (18–02–1636): AN/TT, *Livros das Monções*, book 33, fl. 247v.
23. Letter from Manuel Ramos to the viceroy (20–10–1635): AN/TT, *Livros das Monções*, book 35, fl. 251.
24. Sir William Foster (ed.), *The English Factories in India 1634–1636*, p. 275.
25. AN/TT, *Livros das Monções*, book 33, fl. 247v.
26. Júlio Firmino Biker (ed.), *Colecção de Tratados*, book 1, p. 268.
27. AN/TT, *Livros das Monções*, book 33, fl. 253. In another letter Manuel Ramos lists some of the Portuguese passengers carried to and from Macau (fls. 259v–260).
28. Peter Mundy, *The Travels*, 1907–1936, vol. 3, part 2, p. 484.
29. Henry Charles Sirr, *China and the Chinese*, vol. 1, p. 161.
30. AN/TT, *Livros das Monções*, book 33, fl. 261.
31. Anders Ljungstedt, *An Historical Sketch*, p. 28.
32. "Henry Bornford at Surat to the Company, April 29, 1636", in Sir William Foster, *The English Factories in India 1634–1636*, p. 226, see also Henri Cordier, *Histoire Générale de la Chine*, 2, p. 211.
33. "Henry Bornford at Surat", p. 227.
34. "Henry Bornford at Surat", p. 227.
35. "Henry Bornford at Surat", pp. 229–230.
36. AN/TT, *Livros das Monções*, book 33, fl. 248.
37. AN/TT, *Livros das Monções*, book 33, fl. 248.
38. AN/TT, *Livros das Monções*, book 35, fl. 267.
39. AN/TT, *Livros das Monções*, book 33, fl. 248.
40. AN/TT, *Livros das Monções*, book 33, fl. 248.
41. AHG, FUP, *Livro dos Segredos*, n. 1, fl. 11. Nevertheless, in 1639 Pedro da Silva told William Fromlin, Methwold's successor, that he would send someone to discuss with him the charters agreed both for Malacca and China (fl. 30).

42. In May 1639, Pedro da Silva warned the Danish traders that they could only negotiate with China after permission from the captain-general of Macau (AHG, FUP, *Livro dos Segredos*, fls. 31, 31v, 33).

43. AHG, FUP, *Livro dos Segredos*, fl. 583, n. 399.

44. "Copia do Conçelho sobre o Comerçio dos Ingleses", in P. S. S. Pissurlencar (ed.), *Assentos*, vol. 2, 1954, pp. 115–116.

45. G/12/1, fl. 58. Pedro da Silva informed Surat that Portuguese ports would not trade with English vessels and that these were only authorised to anchor for shelter or to take on supplies (Sir William Foster, *The English Factories in India 1634–1636*, pp. 152, 159). In another English document dated 1639, António Teles de Meneses, the governor of India who succeeded Pedro da Silva, was considered friendlier towards English interests (G/12/1, fl. 59).

46. G/12/1, fl. 60, and G/12/10, fls. 82–84.

47. Ethel Bruce Sainsbury and William Foster (eds.), *A Calendar of the Court Minutes of the East India Company 1635–1639*, 1907, pp. 120–121.

48. In December 1635, Charles I granted a charter establishing the William Courteen Association, which was the first main competitor of the EIC in Asia. The interloping company owned by the London merchant Sir William Courteen (1600–1649) held the right to trade for five years at any Asian port in which there was no EIC factory already established. The Association was poorly managed and collapsed around 1649, but before that it sent several ships to Portuguese ports in Asia, including Macau, as we shall see.

49. G/12/10, fls. 107–110; AHU, *Macau*, box 1, doc. 42; AN/TT, *Livros das Monções*, book 48, fls. 287v, 294v; AHG, FUP, *Livro dos Segredos*, n. 1, fl. 67.

50. AN/TT, *Livros das Monções*, book 48, fl. 287v, book 50, fl. 124v. On the several Portuguese chartering of English ships, see Maria Manuela Sobral Blanco, "O Estado Português da Índia", pp. 552, 585 (footnotes 418–421), 586 (footnotes 422–424), which summarises this Portuguese strategy to outflank the Dutch blockade. The author states that in 1644 the vessels *Hind*, from Swahili (Surat factory), and *William*, to which I shall later refer to, belonging respectively to the EIC and the Courteen Association, went to Macau in the service of the Portuguese Crown with munitions and gunpowder, which would be exchanged for cinnamon.

51. AN/TT, *Livros das Monções*, book 33, fl. 249.

52. G/12/68, fl. 6; G/12/89, fl. 65; R/10/6, fl. 192; Ethel Bruce Sainsbury and William Foster (eds.), *A Calendar of the Court Minutes Etc. of the East India Company 1640–1643*, 1909, p. 151; and Sir William Foster (ed.), *The English Factories in India 1642–1645*, 1913, p. 36.

53. Count Linhares, *Diário do 3.º Conde de Linhares, Vice-Rei da Índia*, 1943, p. 267.

54. On the voyage, see Charles R. Boxer, *Macau na Época da Restauração/Macau Three Hundred Years Ago*, 1993, pp. 49–75; Rogério Miguel Puga, "Images and Representations of Japan and Macau in Peter Mundy's *Travels* (1637)", *Bulletin of Portuguese/Japanese Studies*, vol. 1, December 2000, pp. 97–109; and (in Portuguese) "A Dimensão da Alteridade em *The Travels* de Peter Mundy (1637): Contribuição para o Estudo das Relações Anglo-Portuguesas no Extremo Oriente", *Revista de Cultura*, n. 3, July 2002, pp. 136–152.
55. G/12/10, fl. 66.
56. G/12/10, fl. 89.
57. G/12/10, fl. 90. See fls. 91–92 for an example of a charter contract for English vessels to sail between Goa, Malacca and Macau (1639), with point 6 stipulating one of the obligations of the ship: "To bring from Macau, on account of Royal Goods, as Ballast, 3000 *Quintals* weight, namely in copper, ordnance, or shot. If a second vessel proceed, she was also to bring as much artillery, copper, and shot, with other goods on account of individual merchants as she can. To be paid for as those brought on ship *London* were". Point 9 sets out that the safe place for the boat to anchor in China will be established by Macau, on the order of the viceroy. The following point warned that the possible unruly behaviour of the crew, "not accustomed to the country", may lead to a violent response from the Chinese, therefore only the factors should disembark. Point 11 forbids the crew from carrying any passengers besides those stipulated prior to departure, "according to the amity which ought to subsist between both nations".
58. G/12/10, fl. 98.
59. G/12/10, fls. 99–101.
60. Regarding this episode, I make particular use of the Portuguese sources, given that the English sources were already considered in the aforementioned studies (see G/12/12 fls. 9–75, G/12/16, fls. 1–33).
61. Patrícia Drumond Borges Ferreira, *As Relações Luso-Britânicas na China Meridional (Século XVII)*, 2002, pp. 76–105.
62. AN/TT, *Livros das Monções*, book 41, fls. 191–191v (27-12-1637).
63. AN/TT, *Livros das Monções*, book 43, fls. 256–257.
64. Peter Mundy, *Travels*, vol. 3, pp. 141–142. See also G/40/1, fls. 32, 60. Frobisher's servant ended up staying in Macau and marrying a Portuguese man. On the later complaints presented by the widow of Frobisher to the EIC in 1626 regarding her stay in Macau, see W. Nöel Sainsbury (ed.), *Calendar of State Papers, Colonial Series, East Indies, China and Persia, 1625–1629*, 1884, doc. 369, p. 256.
65. Peter Mundy, *Travels*, vol. 3, pp. 242–243.
66. Rogério Miguel Puga, "Images and Representations", pp. 97–109; and "A Dimensão", pp. 136–152.

67. Peter Mundy, *Travels*, vol. 3, pp. 428–531; and Maria Manuel Sobral Blanco, "O Estado Português da Índia", vol. 2, pp. 372–374.
68. AN/TT, *Livros das Monções*, book 41, fl. 200, repeated in book 43, fls. 258–258v.
69. AN/TT, *Livros das Monções*, book 41, fl. 202, repeated in book 43, fl. 259.
70. AN/TT, *Livros das Monções*, book 43, fls. 258, 269–270; book 41, fl. 211.
71. AN/TT, *Livros das Monções*, book 34, fls. 63v–65.
72. AN/TT, *Livros das Monções*, book 35, fls. 242–243.
73. See the consultations of the Senate (1645) and of the Overseas Council (1647) on the prohibition of English vessels entering the enclave even when in the service of Portugal (AHU, *Macau*, box 1, doc. 48).
74. An idea repeated, as well as the argument over the losses caused by the *London*'s visit to Macau, in a long letter from the city to Weddell, saying that the English come to "trade [...], something that [the Portuguese] could not allow [...], out of great respect and for being on the land of the king of China, a person so conscientious guarding his lands" (AN/TT, *Livros das Monções*, book 43, fl. 268).
75. AN/TT, *Livros das Monções*, book 41, fl. 201; see also G/12/1, fl. 30.
76. PRO, *FO* 233/189, fl. 37.
77. The way in which the Mandarin referred to the English on their arrival in Canton (AN/TT, *Livros das Monções*, book 43, fl. 261) and which may also be translated as "ginger barbarians".
78. AN/TT, *Livros das Monções*, book 43, fls. 260v–262.
79. See the long letter that the captain-general of Macau wrote to the king of England three days prior to the fleet's departure on 24 December, detailing the release of six Englishmen imprisoned in Canton during their visit, as well as the courtesy with which the Portuguese received the subjects of Charles I (AN/TT, *Livros das Monções*, book 41, fls. 220–227).
80. AN/TT, *Livros das Monções*, book 43, fl. 268.
81. AN/TT, *Livros das Monções*, book 41, fls. 213–213v, also copied in book 43, fls. 264–264v.
82. W. E. Soothill, *China and England*, 1928, pp. 4–7; Earl H. Pritchard, *Anglo-Chinese Relations*, pp. 54–55; and Sir William Foster, *England's Quest for Eastern Trade*, pp. 324–335.
83. Peter Mundy, *Travels*, vol. 3, pp. 282–284.
84. AN/TT, *Livros das Monções*, book 43, fl. 260v, also copied on fl. 269.
85. AN/TT, *Livros das Monções*, book 43, fl. 267v, also copied on fl. 259.
86. AN/TT, *Livros das Monções*, book 43, fls. 267v–268, also copied on fl. 259v.
87. AN/TT, *Livros das Monções*, book 43, fls. 260/268, argument also mentioned by Peter Mundy, *Travels*, vol. 3, pp. 222–223.
88. AN/TT, *Livros das Monções*, book 41, fl. 212, also copied on book 43, fl. 263v.

89. AN/TT, *Livros das Monções*, book 41, fls. 213–213v.
90. AN/TT, *Livros das Monções*, book 41, fls. 220–220v, 267v–268.
91. AN/TT, *Livros das Monções*, book 41, fls. 220v–221.
92. AN/TT, *Livros das Monções*, book 41, fl. 221.
93. AN/TT, *Livros das Monções*, book 41, fl. 221v.
94. AN/TT, *Livros das Monções*, book 41, fls. 238–241v.
95. AN/TT, *Livros das Monções*, book 41, fl. 220.
96. AN/TT, *Livros das Monções*, book 43, fl. 265 and G/12/1, fls. 30–58.
97. AN/TT, *Livros das Monções*, book 43, fls. 193v–194v.
98. AN/TTT, *Livros das Monções*, book 43, fl. 267v.
99. AN/TT, *Livros das Monções*, book 43, fls. 267–267v.
100. AN/TT, *Livros das Monções*, book43, fl. 264v.
101. AN/TT, *Livros das Monções*, book 43, fls. 18v–19v.
102. AN/TT, *Livros das Monções*, book 43, fls. 20v–21, 37–38, 41–41v.
103. Jorge Manuel Flores, "Macau e o Comércio da Baía de Cantão (Séculos XVI e XVII)", in Artur Teodoro de Matos and Luís Filipe F. Reis Thomaz (dir.), *As Relações entre a Índia Portuguesa, a Ásia do Sueste e o Extremo Oriente*, 1993, pp. 21–48.
104. Jin Guoping and Wu Zhiliang (eds.), *Correspondência Oficial*, vol. 1, 2000, doc. 130, p. 278.
105. Earl H. Pritchard, *Anglo-Chinese Relations*, pp. 16–41.
106. John Francis Gemelli Careri, *A Voyage Round the World in Six Parts*, p. iv.
107. A. J. Sargent, *Anglo-Chinese Commerce*, pp. 4–5.
108. W. E. Soothill, *China and England*, 1928, pp. 4–7; Earl H. Pritchard, *Anglo-Chinese Relations*, pp. 54–55; and Sir William Foster, *England's Quest for Eastern Trade*, pp. 324–335.
109. D. K. Bassett, "The Trade of the English East India Company in the Far East, 1623–84", in Om Prakash (ed.), *An Expanding World: The European Impact on World Economy 1450–1800*, vol. 10, 1997, pp. 213 (n. 1), 214–218.
110. D. K. Bassett, "The Trade of the English East India Company", pp. 213–214, 222.
111. Sir William Foster (ed.), *The English Factories in India 1634–1636*, 1911, p. 103.
112. Sir William Foster (ed.), *The English Factories in India 1637–1641*, pp. 131–132.
113. Sir William Foster (ed.), *The English Factories in India 1637–1641*, p. 303.
114. AN/TT, *Livros das Monções*, book 50, fls. 120–122.
115. *AM*, 3rd series, vol. 2, n. 2, August 1964, p. 129.
116. AHU, *Cartas Régias*, n. 208, fls. 46 and 104 (see Maria Manuela Sobral Blanco, "O Estado Português da Índia", vol. 1, p. 544).
117. G/12/1, fl. 61.

118. G/12/1, fls. 62–65, G/12/10, fls. 93, 101–104, and Sir William Foster (ed.), *The English Factories in India 1642–1645*, 1913, p. 180.

119. Kingsley Bolton, *Chinese Englishes: A Sociolinguistic History*, 2003, p. 146.

120. Sir William Foster (ed.), *The English Factories in India 1642–1645*, p. 212, and G/12/10, fl. 101.

121. G/12/10, fl. 102, and AHG, FUP, *Livro dos Segredos*, n. 1, fls. 66–66v, 71–72v.

122. AHG, FUP, *Livro dos Segredos*, n. 1, fl. 67.

123. Maria Manuela Sobral Blanco, "O Estado Português da Índia", vol. 1, p. 585, n. 419 [*Reg. e Inst.*, 4, fl. 66 (05–05–1643)].

124. G/12/1, fls. 62–63, G/12/19, fls. 103–104.

125. G/12/1, fls. 62–63, and G/121/10, fl. 104.

126. Cf. John E. Wills Jr., "The Survival of Macau, 1640–1729", in Jorge M. dos Santos Alves (coord.), *Portugal e a China*, 1999, pp. 111–124.

127. Earl H. Pritchard, *Anglo-Chinese Relations*, p. 57.

128. Sir William Foster (ed.), *The English Factories in India: 1646–1650*, 1914, pp. 8–9; and G/12/10, fl. 106, my emphasis.

129. G/12/10, fl. 111.

130. Ethel Bruce Sainsbury and William Foster (eds.), *A Calendar of the Court Minutes Etc. of the East India Company 1644–1649*, 1912, p. 188.

131. G/12/10, fls. 113–114.

132. G/12/10, fl. 114.

133. R/10/5 (1761–1769), fl. 42.

134. Ethel Bruce Sainsbury and William Foster (eds.), *A Calendar of the Court Minutes Etc. of the East India Company 1644–1649*, p. 365.

135. AHU, *Macau*, box 1, annex 2 of doc. 48.

136. AN/TT, *Livros das Monções*, book 57, fl. 99.

137. G/12/1, fl. 63.

138. G/12/1, fl. 64: "The Trade of China is so much declined, by reason of the Portugalls poverty and troubles in that vast kingdom".

139. G/12/1, fl. 64.

140. G/12/10, fl. 116; José Ferreira Borges de Castro (org.), *Colecção dos Tratados*, pp. 162–167, 168–203.

141. At war with Spain, Portugal signed the Treaty of Peace and Alliance with England in Westminster (10–06–1654). Its twenty-eight articles mainly favoured English trade, while the EIC directors hoped that Cromwell obtained Bombay or Bassein through a diplomatic treaty.

142. Conde de Sarzedas, *Diário do Conde de Sarzedas, Vice-Rei do Estado da Índia*, 2001, pp. 123–132.

143. G/12/1, fl. 65, G/12/10, fls. 121–121, 124.

144. G/12/10, fls. 133, 135.
145. See G/12/10, fls. 127–128.
146. G/12/10, fl. 134.
147. G/12/10, fls. 137–140.
148. G/12/1, fl. 66.
149. G/12/10, fl. 141 and G/12/13, fl. 76.
150. G/12/1, fl. 70.
151. G/12/1, fls. 68–78.
152. G/12/10, fl. 142.
153. G/12/1, fl. 78 and G/12/10, fl. 142.
154. G/12/1, fl. 75
155. G/12/1, fls. 66a, 68–77.
156. G/12/1, fl. 78.
157. George B. Souza, "Commerce and Capital: Portuguese Maritime Losses in the South China Sea, 1600–1754", in Artur Teodoro de Matos and Luís Filipe Thomaz (eds.), *As Relações entre a Índia Portuguesa, a Ásia do Sueste e o Extremo Oriente*, 1993, pp. 321–329.
158. AHU, *Macau*, box 2, doc. 5.
159. AHU, *Macau*, box 2, docs. 5 and 9.
160. *AM*, 3rd series, vol. 4, n. 3, 1965, pp. 130–131; vol. 8, n. 2, 1967, pp. 81–85; vol. 10, n. 2, 1968, pp. 85–86; vol. 17, nn. 3–4, 1972, pp. 159–166, 186–187; AHU, *Macau*, box 13, doc. 17, box 20, docs. 33, 38, box 31, doc. 30; and Carl T. Smith and Paul A. Van Dyke, "Armenian Footprints in Macau", and "Four Armenian Families", *Review of Culture*, n. 8, October 2003, pp. 20–39, and 40–50, respectively.
161. PRO, *SP* 89/9, fl. 77, G/12/13, fls. 89–90.
162. PRO, *SP* 89/9, fl. 186v, *SP* 89/10, fl. 28.
163. Sir William Foster (ed.), *The English Factories in India 1634–1636*, p. 211.
164. BA, *Ms. Av.* 54-X-19, n. 19, PRO, *SP/89/10*, fl. 10.
165. Joaquim Veríssimo Serrão, *História de Portugal*, vol. 5, pp. 59, 87.
166. Vitorino Magalhães Godinho, *Ensaios sobre História de Portugal II*, 1978, p. 413.
167. PRO, *SP* 89/17, fl. 339.
168. PRO, *SP* 89/3, fl. 187, *SP* 89/12, fl. 32, *SP* 89/28, fls. 47, 105, *SP* 89/31, fl. 200, *SP* 89/50, fl. 82, *SP* 89/67, fl. 120, and *SP* 89/80, fl. 40.
169. Júlio Firmino Biker (ed.), *Colecção de Tratados*, vol. 2, pp. 250–275.
170. PRO, *SP* 89/4, fl. 177.
171. Adriano José Ernesto, "A Cessão de Bombaim à Inglaterra", 1952, *passim*.
172. Júlio Firmino Biker (ed.), *Colecção de Tratados*, tomo 3, Sir William Foster (ed.), *The English Factories in India 1665–1667*, 1925, pp. 47, 293, 308; *Arquivo das Colónias*, vol. 5: n. 26, 1929, pp. 7–30, n. 27, 1930, pp. 13–30, n. 33, pp. 295–314,

n. 33, pp. 13–30, nn. 34 and 38, 1931, pp. 445–477; and Pedro Nobre, "A Entrega de Bombaím à Grã-Bretanha e as suas Consequências Políticas e Sociais no Estado da Índia (1661–1668)", 2008.

173. D. K. Bassett, "Early English Trade and Settlement in Asia, 1602–1690", pp. 128–129.

174. Júlio F. Biker (ed.), *Colecção de Tratados*, pp. 278–285 (ch. 11 and the secret article).

175. José Ferreira Borges de Castro, *Colecção dos Tratados*, vol. 1, p. 260.

176. G/12/1, fls. 144–147, G/12/10, fls. 161–163, G/12/13, fl. 288, G/12/16, fls. 60–66, and G/12/2, fl. 153.

177. Acácio Fernando de Sousa, "Do Japão a Macau: O Comércio em Tempos de Proibições", *Revista de Cultura*, n. 17, 1993, pp. 35–39.

178. Acácio Fernando de Sousa, "Do Japão a Macau", pp. 38–39, G/12/1, fl. 144; and Charles R. Boxer, *Jan Compagnie in Japan, 1672–1674*, pp. 139–146, 161–167.

179. Anonymous, "Treslado da ordem que se fez em caza do capitão geral António Barboza Lobro [*sic*] sobre o conteudo nelle" [1673], in Acácio Fernando de Sousa, "Do Japão a Macau", pp. 38–39, translated in G/12/10, fl. 162.

180. Anonymous, "Treslado", p. 38.

181. G/12/1, fl. 146.

182. G/12/10, fls. 161–162.

183. G/12/19, fl. 209, G/12/51, fl. 31, G/12/14, fls. 1–40, 161–179.

184. G/12/57, fl. 162.

185. *AM*, 3rd series, vol. 7, n. 6, June 1967, p. 316.

186. G/12/10, fls. 162–163.

187. Anonymous, "Treslado", p. 39.

188. G/12/1, fl. 148.

189. Patrícia Drumond Borges Ferreira, *As Relações Luso-Britânicas*, p. 118.

190. John Bruce, *Annals*, vol. 2, p. 350, and note in G/12/1, fl. 144.

191. K. D. Bassett, "The Trade of the English East India Company", p. 232.

192. On the legislative measures that granted British vessels the monopoly of Britain's colonial trade, as a measure against Dutch competition, in 1650 (forbidding foreign ships to trade in British dominions), in 1651 (goods from British colonies could only be transported by British vessels, and their crews needed to be 75% British), and in 1660 (when the Navigation Act decreed that some "colonial" commodities could only be transported to England), see Larry Sawers, "The Navigation Acts Revisited", *Economic History Review*, 2nd series, vol. 40, 1992, pp. 262–284.

193. G/12/2, fl. 247.

194. G/12/2, fl. 232.

195. G/12/2, fls. 249–250.

196. G/12/2, fls. 254, 281.

197. On the China Trade development, see Earl H. Pritchard, *Anglo-Chinese Relations*, pp. 70–74; Michael Greenberg, *British Trade and the Opening of China, 1800–42*, 1951, pp. 1–17; J. H. Parry, *Trade & Dominion*, p. 83; Trea Wiltshire, *Encounters with Asia: Merchants, Missionaries and Mandarins*, 1995, pp. 10–24; and Paul A. Van Dyke, *The Canton Trade: Life and Enterprise on the China Coast, 1700–1845*, 2005.

198. On the British voyages to Amoy, Tonkin and Formosa, and trade in those locations sometimes with the help of Portuguese interpreters, see G/12/1, fls. 79–82, 88–135, G/12/2, fls. 172–245, 251–298, G/12/3, 4, G/12/16 (1614–1703), fls. 90–277, G/12/17 (1672–1697); and Hosea Ballou Morse, *The Chronicles*, vol. 1, pp. 44–65, 127–134, 220–229.

199. G/12/3, fls. 324–325, and G/12/11, fl. 36.

200. G/12/6, fls. 823–824.

201. Roderich Ptak, "Early Sino-Portuguese Relations up to the Foundation of Macau", *Mare Liberum*, n. 4, December 1992, pp. 293–294, reminds us that China was a market that did not function as a whole, being composed of macro-regions, as proved by the establishment of the Portuguese in Sanchuan and Lampacau before Macau.

202. G/12/2, fls. 299–306, G/12/16, vol. 1, fls. 67–79.

203. *Records of St. George: Diary and Consultation Book of 1686*, 1913, p. 64.

204. G/12/2, fl. 301.

205. G/12/2, fls. 303–304, 306.

206. G/12/3, (1682), fl. 307, G/12/13, fls. 122, 134. Taipa Quebrada was an anchorage in Taipa island that at the time was formed by two small islands, Taipa Grande (or Taipa Quebrada), and Taipa Pequena, initially separated by a narrow channel.

207. G/12/26, fls. 3–3v.

208. G/12/2, fl. 314.

209. G/12/2, fls. 311–320.

210. G/12/2, fl. 306, G/12/3, fls. 315–316.

211. G/12/2, fls. 326–349.

212. Cf. D. K. Bassett, "The Trade of the English East India Company", p. 235.

213. *Records of St. George: Despatches from England 1681–1686*, 1916, p. 204.

214. AHU, *Macau*, box 2, docs. 3 and 5.

215. AHU, *Macau*, box 2, doc. 2.

216. *Records of St. George: Despatches from England 1681–1686*, p. 204.

217. *Records of St. George: Diary and Consultation Book of 1688*, 1916, p. 75.

218. G/12/4, fls. 486–493, G/12/16, vol. 2, fls. 255–266, and *Records of St. George: Diary and Consultation Book of 1689*, 1916, pp. 38, 62–63.

219. George Bryan Souza, *A Sobrevivência do Império Português: Os Portugueses na China (1630–1754)*, 1991, p. 264.
220. G/12/8, fl. 1303.
221. *AM*, 3rd series, vol. 5, n. 4, April 1966, p. 235.
222. George Bryan Souza, *A Sobrevivência do Império Português*, p. 265.
223. Anonymous, "Descrição da Cidade de Macau ou a Cidade de Macau Reivindicada" [c.1693], in Artur Teodoro de Matos, "Uma Memória Seiscentista", *Macau*, December 1999, n. 92, p. 198.
224. G/12/79, part 3, fls. 41 and 49.

Chapter 4   The beginning of regular East India Company trade with China

1.   J. H. Parry, *Trade & Dominion: The European Overseas Empires in the Eighteenth Century*, 2000, pp. 83–84.
2.   Roderich Ptak, "A China Meridional e o Comércio Marítimo no Este e no Sudeste da Ásia entre 1600 e 1750", *Povos e Culturas*, n. 5, 1996, p. 212.
3.   Susana Münch Miranda, "Os Circuitos Económicos", in A. H. de Oliveira Marques (dir.), *História dos Portugueses no Extremo Oriente*, vol. 2, pp. 261–283.
4.   Frei José de Jesus Maria, *Ásia Sínica e Japónica*, vol. 2, pp. 231.
5.   Charles Boxer, *Fidalgos no Extremo Oriente*, 1990, p. 269.
6.   *AM*, vol. 1, n. 1, June 1929, p. 25.
7.   Padre Manuel Teixeira, *Macau no Século XVIII*, p. 478.
8.   G/12/5, fl. 647.
9.   G/12/5, fl. 651.
10. The term "hopu" designated both the Chinese customs house that received taxes from foreign ships, and the superintendent of the Chinese maritime custom who supervised trade and received custom's taxes in Macau, since 1684, as well as in Canton (see Count Lapérouse, *Voyage de Lapérouse*, 1970, p. 207; António Feliciano M. Pereira, *As Alfândegas Chinesas de Macau*, 1870; and Weng Eang Cheong, *The Hong Merchants of Canton*, pp. 193–213, 230–233).
11. G/12/5, fl. 654.
12. G/12/5, fls. 645–756.
13. G/12/5, fls. 654–655.
14. Necessary permit for any ship arriving at Macau (G/12/76, fl. 21).
15. G/12/6, fls. 785–804.
16. On the British activity, namely Catchpole's, in Chusan, Amoy and Pulo Condor (1699–1759), see G/12/6, fls. 793–921; G/12/14, G/12/16, G/12/17, G/12/16, fls. 267–277.
17. G/12/6, fls. 845–851.

18. G/12/6 (1699–1700), fls. 821–877.
19. Hosea Ballou Morse, *The Chronicles*, vol. 1, pp. 112–113.
20. Macau was, from an early stage, origin and destiny of correspondence between British residents and Western ships approaching China, so that the crews' arrivals could be prepared [G/12/32 (1731), fl. 16].
21. R/10/5 (17161–1769), fls. 1, 16–19, 52, R/10/6, fl. 119, R/10/11 (1780–1781) part 2, fls. 37–38.
22. G/12/78 (1783–1784), fl. 29.
23. G/12/82 (1785–1786), fl. 21; and Jin Guoping and Wu Zhiliang (eds.), *Correspondência Oficial*, vol. 1, docs. 228–229.
24. R/10/13, fls. 201–202; G/12/6, fl. 821, *Records of St. George: Letters to Fort St. George 1684–1685*, vol. 3, 1917, pp. 42–43; Alexander Hamilton, *A New Account of the East Indies*, vol. 2, 1930, p. 118.
25. G/12/27, fl. 7; G/12/28, fls. 7, 53; G/12/29, fls. 17–18; G/12/90, fl. 7.
26. G/12/98, fl. 13.
27. G/12/40, fl. 75; G/12/41, fl. 45 (1735–1737).
28. *Records of St. George: Despatches from England 1744–47*, 1931, p. 24.
29. G/12/27, fl. 19; G/12/86, fl. 10.
30. G/12/25, fl. 3; G/12/27, fls. 30 and 57; G/12/29, fl. 73; G/12/44, fl. 58; G/12/50, fl. 4: the sentence "arrived at Macau and went ashore for advices/intelligence" is recurrent in the EIC documentation.
31. G/12/46, fl. 18.
32. G/12/33, fl. 51; G/12/58, fl. 9; G/12/59, fl. 90; G/12/89, fl. 85; G/12/105, fls. 73, 79; G/12/112, fl. 18.
33. G/12/76 (1782–1783), fl. 91.
34. G/12/19, fl. 187; G/12/66, fl. 17.
35. G/12/112, fls. 19–20. See Jane Kilpatrick, *Gifts from the Gardens of China*, 2007, pp. 9–11, 76, 80, 108, 168, 210, 214, 219.
36. AHU, *Macau*, box 8, doc. 31.
37. R/10/13 (1783), fls. 154–155.
38. *AM*, 3rd series, vol. 16, n. 3, September 1971, p. 135; 4th series, vol. 8:1, January–June 1988 (1989), p. 101; AHU, *Macau*, box 7, doc. 32.
39. António M. Martins do Vale, *Os Portugueses em Macau (1750–1800)*, 1997, p. 38.
40. Júlio Firmino Biker (ed.), *Colecção de Tratados*, vol. 3, pp. 242–244.
41. Practice that lasts throughout the eighteenth century; see AHU, *Macau*, box 14, doc. 16.
42. *AM*, 3rd series, vol. 6, n. 1, 1966, pp. 41, 44.
43. *AM*, 3rd series, n. 3, September 1966, p. 120.
44. *AM*, 3rd series, vol. 7, n. 4, April 1967, p. 177.

45. *AM*, 3rd series, vol. 7, n. 4, April 1967, p. 177.

46. See António M. Martins do Vale, *Os Portugueses em Macau (1750–1800)*, pp. 35–47.

47. *AM*, 1st series, vol. 1, n. 7, 1929, pp. 397–400; 3rd series, vol. 8, 1967, p. 28, vol. 17, n. 1, 1972, p. 30.

48. Charles Boxer, *Fidalgos no Extremo Oriente*, p. 270.

49. AHU, *Macau*, box 62, docs. 27 and 35; box 63, doc. 5; box 64, doc. 12.

50. *AM*, 3rd series, vol. 7, n. 5, May 1967, pp. 248–249.

51. Earl H. Pritchard, *Britain and the China Trade*, p. 115, and Paul A. Van Dyke, *The Canton Trade*, pp. 5–33, 95–115, 137–141, 161–176.

Chapter 5 The gradual growth of the British presence in Macau in the early eighteenth century

1. Cf. Alexander Hamilton, *A New Account of the East Indies*, pp. 116–125. In 1702, the EIC sent two ships to Canton, the *Fleet* that anchored in Macau in August together with the *Halifax*. The crews immediately travelled to Canton to discuss the prices of merchandise with their Chinese partners (G/12/6, fls. 875–880; G/12/7, fls. 1093–1094; G/12/16, fl. 41).

2. Charles Lockyer, *An Account of the Trade in India*, 1711.

3. Charles Lockyer, *An Account*, pp. 97–188.

4. Charles Lockyer, *An Account*, p. 100.

5. Cf. Hosea Ballou Morse, *The Chronicles*, vol. 1, p. 136.

6. G/12/7, fls. 1015–1016, 1022 (log of the *Kent*: fls. 1020–1061).

7. G/12/6 (1615–1703), fls. 868–869. According to the "Abstract Letter Diary" of Commander Burges and John Hillar, chief-supercargo of the fleet's frigate, the vessels arrived at Macau on 26 August 1702. After a few days in Macau, and desiring to buy silk, the crew travelled to Canton and, in within days, contacted the most important Chinese traders. The French embassy led by the Jesuit priest Bouvet in 1698 also spent little time in Macau before leaving for Canton (cf. Gio Ghirardini, *Relation du Voyage Fait à la Chine sur le Vaisseau l' Amphitrite, en l' Année 1689*, 1700, p. 68).

8. G/12/8, fl. 1415.

9. Hosea Ballou Morse, *The International Relations of the Chinese Empire*, vol. 1, 1910, pp. 51–53, 64. In June 1727, and according to the crew of the *Prince Augustus*, the ancient Ton Hunqua hong or warehouse is already known as "English factory" (G/12/26, fl. 4).

10. G/12/11, fls. 51–53.

11. In 1717–1718 the *Carnarvon* stayed in Macau and its crew tried to find out if they could go up to Canton (G/12/8, fl. 1349). The ship's diary (fls. 1349–1352) lists the nine articles that the British insisted on seeing respected by the Chinese: (1) free trade with any Chinese; (2) freedom to employ Chinese; unruly British are not judged by the Chinese authorities but by the EIC; (3) freedom to buy provisions for the factory and the ships; (4) the end of tax payment for goods consumed in the factory; (5) freedom to camp and restore ships; (6, 7) and for the supercargoes and their luggage to go through customs without being searched; (8, 9) the hopu should defend the British from popular violence and from the growing demands of the Mandarinate, and should be rigorous when measuring the ships.

12. G/12/26 (1726–1728), fl. 1; G/12/8 (1723), fl. 1402.

13. G/12/24, fl. 39; G/12/92, fls. 452, 458; G/12/96, fl. 43, George Mortimer, *Observations and Remarks Made during a Voyage*, 1791, p. 70; *AM*, 3rd series, vol. 7, n. 5, 1967, p. 249; and Paul Van Dyke, *The Canton Trade*, pp. 19, 35–47.

14. In 1792 the hopu demanded a British ship anchor near Macau to enter the Pearl River delta to be measured, otherwise it should continue its voyage [R/10/20, fl. 171; see Jin Guoping and Wu Zhiliang (eds.), *Correspondência Oficial*, vol. 2, docs. 183 and 184, pp. 314–315, 316–317].

15. G/12/8, fl. 1429.

16. G/12/8, fls. 1336–1339; *Records of St. George: Public Despatches to England 1719*, 1929, p. 11.

17. G/12/92, fls. 201–208; and Alain Peyrefitte, *O Império Imóvel*, 1995, pp. 149–150.

18. Hosea Ballou Morse, *The Chronicles*, vol. 1, pp. 155–156.

19. Hosea Ballou Morse, *The Chronicles*, vol. 1, pp. 158, 197; vol. 2, p. 51; and R/10/10, fl. 138.

Chapter 6   Macau as a centre for Chinese control over the European "barbarians"

1. *AM*, 3rd series, vol. 9, n. 3, March 1968, p. 121. See also Bento da França, *Subsídios para a História de Macau*, 1888, p. 104; and Artur Levy Gomes, *Esboço da História de Macau*, 1957, p. 216.

2. The EIC documentation describes a few episodes dealing with Sino-Portuguese relations. In 1785 the supercargoes informed London that a Chinese who had hidden Catholic missionaries in China ran away to a convent in Macau. The Mandarins demanded that the city deliver him, but Macau refused to do so and the hong merchants were heavily fined (G/12/79, part 2, fl. 174).

3. António Vale, "Macau: Os Eventos Políticos. 2", in A. H. de Oliveira Marques (dir.), *História dos Portugueses no Extremo Oriente*, vol. 2, pp. 182–183.

4. G/12/11, fls. 57–58. Weng Eang Cheong, *The Hong Merchants of Canton*, pp. 12–13, reinterprets Morse, Cordier and Pritchard's conclusions, and defends that the formation of the co-hong in the beginning of the eighteenth century was the official Chinese reaction to the growing of the foreign trade in Canton.

5. Each of the hongs does business individually but the group is responsible for all the questions related to the safety of the foreign crews in China, and that is why they are called "security merchants" (see Ann Bolbach White, "The Hong Merchants of Canton", 1967; and Anthony Kuo-tung Ch'en, *The Insolvency of the Chinese Hong Merchants, 1760–1834*, 1990).

6. On the regulations, see Hosea Ballou Morse, *The International Relations of the Chinese Empire*, vol. 1, pp. 5–6, 69–70, and Maurice Collis, *Foreign Mud*, 1956, pp. 14–15.

7. G/12/30–31, and the Diary of James Naish, who in 1730–1731 became the first supercargo to stay in China all year long to do business (G/12/21, fls. B-29; G/12/32).

8. G/12/8, fl. 1402.

9. G/12/8, fl. 1415, doc. repeated in G/12/21, fl. 38.

10. G/12/8, fl. 1421. The document mentions the case of Governor Cristóvão de Severim Melo, considered a tyrant by the Senate. He is deposed and substituted by his predecessor António da Silva Telo e Meneses in 1723.

11. *AM*, 1st series, vol. 1, n. 5, October 1929, pp. 253–269; vol. 6, 1966, pp. 308–317.

12. AHU, *Macau*, box 8, doc. 6.

13. See Ângela Guimarães, *Uma Relação Especial: Macau e as Relações Luso-Chinesas (1780–1844)*, 2000, p. 16.

14. Hosea Ballou Morse, *The Chronicles*, vol. 1, p. 218.

15. *AM*, 3rd series, vol. 9, n. 4, April 1968, pp. 214–215.

16. M. Múrias (ed.), *Instrução para o Bispo de Pequim e outros Documentos para a História de Macau*, 1988, pp. 257–259; *AM*, 3rd series, vol. 15, n. 5, 1971, pp. 244, 253–254, and n. 6, 1971, pp. 326–327.

Chapter 7   The visit of the *Centurion*

1. G/12/11, fls. 82–89.

2. See Lawrence Stone (ed.), *An Imperial State at War: Britain from 1689 to 1815*, 1993; and Michael Duffy, "World-Wide War and British Expansion, 1793–1815", in P. J. Marshall (ed.), *The Oxford History of the British Empire*, vol. 2: *The Eighteenth Century*, 2001, pp. 184–207.

3. Glyndwr Williams (ed.), *Documents Relating to Anson's Voyage Round the World 1740–1744*, 1967, p. 136.

4. Boyle Somerville, *Commodore Anson's Voyage into the South Seas and around the World*, 1934, p. 194. Macau was, once more, a place where crews could rest and gather information about China for their own immediate use and to be published in Great Britain.

5. Tcheong-Ü-Lâm e Ian-Kuong-Iâm, *Ou-Mun Kei-Leok: Monografia de Macau* [1751], 1979, pp. 287–288.

6. In late 1742 the supercargoes also informed London that they had advised the commodore to try to obtain permission from the Chinese authorities through the Macau Senate [cf. Glyndwr Williams (ed.), *Documents*, p. 145].

7. For a description of Sumarez's stay in Macau, the initial negotiations with the governor, and their anchorage in Taipa with the help of a Portuguese pilot sent by the city, see Boyle Somerville, *Commodore Anson's Voyage*, pp. 198–199.

8. Cf. Richard Walter, *A Voyage Round the World, In the Years MDCCXL, I, II, III, IV, by George Anson*, 1748, pp. 470–471.

9. In December 1742 Anson writes to James Naish: "the Portuguese have not the least power" [Glyndwr Williams (ed.), *Documents*, pp. 152–153].

10. The Portuguese disliked the fact that the Chinese helped Anson (BA, *Jesuítas na Ásia*, cod. 49-V-29, fls. 112–113).

11. The *"nau de prata"*, commanded by the Portuguese Jerónimo Monteiro, was carrying great quantities of silver from Manila to Mexico (Richard Walter, *A Voyage*, pp. 499–509; and B. Somerville, *Commodore Anson's Voyage*, pp. 216–235).

12. "Lawrence Millechamp's Journal, April 1743–June 1744", in Glyndwr Williams (ed.), *Documents*, p. 189.

13. According to Christopher Loyd, "Introduction", in Philip Sumarez, *Log of the Centurion Based on the Original Papers of Captain Philip Sumarez*, 1973, p. 10, the work was not written by Walter, but by Benjamin Robins, professional pamphleteer who was supervised by Anson.

14. Cf. Austin Coates, *Macau and the British*, p. 54. In 1742 Philip Sumarez (*Log*, p. 203), Anson's first lieutenant, said that the governor of Macau did not have any power to solve the problems related to the presence of the *Centurion* and was a puppet in the hands of the Chinese.

15. Richard Walter, *A Voyage*, pp. 469–470.

16. See João de Pina Cabral and N. Lourenço, *Em Terra de Tufões: Dinâmicas da Etnicidade Macaense*, 1993, p. 11, and Wu Zhiliang, *Segredos da Sobrevivência: História Política de Macau*, 1999, pp. 14–17.

17. On the reasons of the Portuguese permanent stay in Macau (a tacit agreement between Portuguese and Chinese for the benefit of both: payment of rent, military power in Macau), see Tcheong-Ü-Lâm and Ian-Kuong-Iâm, *Ou-Mun Kei-Leok*, pp.

103–104; and Benjamim Videira Pires, "O "Foro do Chão" de Macau", *Boletim do Instituto Luís de Camões*, vol. 1, n. 4, March 1967, pp. 319–334.

18. Silva Rego, *A Presença Portuguesa em Macau*, 1947, p. 17; and João P. Cabral and N. Lourenço, *Em Terra de Tufões*, p. 24.

19. John Campbell (ed.), *Navigantium atque Itinerantium Bibliotecha*, vol. 1, 1744, pp. 364–365.

20. Jonas Hanway, *A Review of the Proposed Naturalization of the Jews*, 1753, pp. 97–98; and Entick, *A New Naval History*, 1757, p. i.

Chapter 8   British relations and conflicts with the Portuguese and Chinese authorities in the second half of the eighteenth century

1.   AHU, *Macau*, box 21, doc. 18.

2.   *AM*, 3rd series, vol. 10, n. 1, pp. 99, 118; n. 4, 1968, pp. 192, 222, 233; n. 6, 1968, p. 314; vol. 16, n. 4, 1971, p. 246, and n. 6, 1971, p. 325.

3.   Earl H. Pritchard, *Britain and the China Trade*, p. 126; James Bromley Eames, *The English in China*, 1974, p. 78. See also William Milburn, *Oriental Commerce*, vol. 1, 1813, pp. xlv–xlviii. Due to economic interests and conflicts in Europe, the British tried to avoid European commercial competition in China, and in 1781 they threatened the Chinese that if they found Dutch junks they would take them, while the Select Committee suspected that the latter traded tea using Macau ships (R/10/11, fls. 93–94, 109). A year later the supercargoes listed as their possible China Trade rivals the Swedish, the Danes and the Portuguese (R/10/12, fl. 149; G/12/76, fl. 135), and described the movement of Portuguese and other European ships [R/10/10 (1779–1780), fl. 163 and part 2, fl. 159; R/10/11 (1780–1781), fls. 100–111; R/10/12 (1782), fl. 109; R/10/13 (1783), fl. 25; R/10/14 (1784–1785), fls. 4, 15, 26; R/10/17 (1788–1789), fl. 71; R/10/18 (1789–1790), part 2, fl. 3; R/10/19 (1791), fl. 8; G/12/32 (1731), fls. 2, 13; and G/12/72 (1781), fl. 32].

4.   Earl H. Pritchard, *Britain and the China Trade*, p. 118, considers the period between 1750 and 1800 to be so important that he calls it "the crucial years in early Anglo-Chinese relations", characterized by the strong trade growth and by the peaceful efforts to open China to the Western trade, especially through (the failed) Lord Macartney's embassy. Paul A. Van Dyke, *The Canton Trade*, pp. 10–29, 161–167 shows that, although the foreign traders are restricted to Canton in 1757, the China Trade system was formed around 1720 and remained unchanged until 1842.

5.   AHU, *Macau*, box 63, doc. 33

6.   *AM*, 3rd series, vol. 9, n. 4, April 1968, pp. 209–210.

7.   *AM*, 3rd series, vol. 16, n. 3, September 1971, p. 135.

8. Alain Peyrefitte, *Un Choc de Cultures*, p. lxxxv. In 1760 a British vessel anchored in Taipa, recruited several Portuguese from Macau, and its crew got involved in several conflicts, namely the kidnapping of slaves owned by Macau residents. The Senate asked the judge to investigate if any resident of Macau was passing information about the city on to the British. Espionage was therefore implicit in the request, and this practice favoured the British and made the defence of the city's interests harder (*AM*, 3rd series, vol. 7, n. 5, May 1967, pp. 256–257).

9. For a contemporary description of the British factory and the Chinese surveillance in Canton, see the anonymous narrative *A Voyage to the East Indies in 1747 and 1748*, 1762, pp. 223–225.

10. AHU, *Macau*, box 11, doc. 10.

11. For a summary of the documents, see Hosea Ballou Morse, *The International Relations*, pp. 69–71; Earl H. Pritchard, *Britain and the China Trade*, pp. 133–134, and James Bromley Eames, *The English in China*, p. 89.

12. Guo Deyan, "The Study of Parsee Merchants in Canton, Hong Kong and Macau", *Review of Culture*, n. 8, October 2003, pp. 51–69; Madhavi Thampi, "Parsis in the China Trade", *Review of Culture*, n. 10, April 2004, pp. 16–25; and Carl T. Smith, "Parsee Merchants in the Pearl River Delta", *Review of Culture*, n. 10, pp. 36–49.

13. See Carl T. Smith and Paul A. Van Dyke, "Armenian Footprints in Macau", pp. 20–39.

14. From Macau the supercargoes informed London about the movement of European ships [R/10/5 (1761–1769), fl. 70; G/12/32 (1731), fl. 15]. On French trade in China since 1698, see AHU, *Macau*, box 18, doc. 11; *AM*, 3rd series, vol. 4, n. 3, 1965, pp. 130–131; n. 5, 1965, pp. 315–330; vol. 10, n. 5, 1968, pp. 240–241; vol. 16, n. 3, 1971, pp. 135–136, n. 4, 1971, pp. 214–215, 241–242; vol. 23, n. 3, 1975, pp. 126–131; and Claudius Madrolle, *Les Premiers Voyages Français à la Chine. La Compagnie de Chine (1698–1719)*, 1901; Padre Manuel Teixeira, *Macau no Século XVIII*, pp. 14–15, 205–213, 594; and Catherine Manning, *Fortunes à Faire: The French in Asian Trade, 1719–48*, 1996.

15. See Trea Wiltshire, *Encounters with Asia*, pp. 74–76.

16. R/10/5 (1761–1769), fl. 59; R/10/11 (1780–1781), fl. 200.

17. R/10/5, (1761–1769), fls. 41–42, 47–49, 56, 61, 85, 107; R/10/6 (1763–1769), fls. 71–72v., 81v.–82v.; R/10/13 (1783), fl. 191; G/12/79 (1784–1785), part 3 (1785), fl. 46; *AM*, 3rd series, vol. 7, n. 1, 1961, p. 150 (British supercargoes borrowed money from the Jesuits).

18. R/10/10 (1779–1780), part 1, fls. 21–55, part 2, fls. 14–216; G/12/18 (1753–1787), fls. 91–112; G/12/68 (1779–1780), fls. 4–200; G/12/70 (1780), fls. 57, 61, 91, 102–103; G/12/91 (1787–1792), part 2.

19. G/12/68 (1779–1780), fls. 135–141, doc. also copied in G/12/70, fls. 73–81.

20. The headquarters of the EIC was formed by four houses on the Praia Grande, close to the Governor's Palace, which stretched up the hill towards the church of São Lourenço [see George Chinnery's painting (1836) in Patrick Conner, *George Chinnery 1774–1852: Artist of India and the China Coast*, 1993, p. 189, plate 118].
21. On the Casa *Garden*, see Rogério Beltrão Coelho, *Casa Garden*, 1991.
22. In 1795 the supercargo Thomas Kuyck Van Mierop left his house in Macau to his Macanese wife Marta da Silva (cf. will of Thomas Van Mierop, Public Record Office, The Family Records Centre, London, *Wills*, PROB11/1267, fl. 56). See Rogério Miguel Puga, "A Vida e o Legado de Marta da Silva van Mierop", *Review of Culture*, n. 22, April 2007, pp. 40–51.
23. G/12/58, fl. 11.
24. G/12/58, fls. 11–15.
25. G/12/59, fls. 26–43; G/12/60, doc. 13.
26. *AM*, 3rd series, vol. 17, n. 1, January 1972, p. 35. In 1783, the Select Committee got involved in a legal dispute with Simão Vicente de Araújo Rosa, a prominent Senate member and owner of the Casa Garden, then rented to the EIC. The Macanese raised the rent and disrespected the contracted signed years before. The supercargoes won the case in court and were able to stay until the end of the date defined by the contract. The judge praised the "the respectable society which [... the Select Committee] compose[d] in th[at] part of the world [...] and the firm alliance observed between their Britannic and most faithful majesties" (R/10/13, fls. 179–181; G/12/77, fls. 123–126). The Anglo-Portuguese Alliance was therefore an argument for a good relationship used by the Portuguese and British in Macau throughout the centuries, as we can see from another dispute between the Committee and the governor after Samuel Peach was physically attacked by the guards [R/10/16 (1787–1788), fls. 15, 22; G/12/86, fls. 15–16]. The supercargoes complained to the viceroy of Goa, who replied that "the good friendship that happily subsists between both our Nations requires that amongst their subjects dissentions of any kind should not happen" and said that the governor, unlike the Senate, did not have any civil or criminal jurisdiction [fl. 83; see R/10/17 (1788–1789), fls. 82–84].
27. AHU, *Macau*, box 17, doc. 66, fl. 4.
28. AHU, *Macau*, box 21, doc. 37, fl. 4.
29. AHU, *Macau*, box 21, doc. 37, fl. 3.
30. Padre Manuel Teixeira, *Macau no Século XVIII*, p. 679.
31. *AM*, 3rd series, vol. 16, n. 4, 1971, pp. 204–209.
32. Syed H. Askari (ed.), *Fort William-India House Correspondence*, vol. 16: *1787–1791*, 1976, p. 143.
33. AHU, *Macau*, box 20, doc. 36.

34. Jin Guoping and Wu Zhiliang (eds.), *Correspondência Oficial*, vol. 1, docs. 5, 49, 84, 100, 133–140, 144–150, 206–210, 228–229; vol. 2, docs. 132, 166–168, 183–187, 232–234, 241.
35. Jin Guoping and Wu Zhiliang (eds.), *Correspondência Oficial*, vol. 1, docs. 100, 133, 138, 183, 206, 209.
36. Jin Guoping and Wu Zhiliang (eds.), *Correspondência Oficial*, vol. 1, doc. 143. Macau negotiated locally with the Chinese authorities, while Lisbon, respecting the ancient Anglo-Portuguese Alliance, allowed the entry and stay of British traders in the Portuguese colonies, as was the case with the ratification of the treaty between Queen Maria I and King George III in 1793 [José Ferreira Borges de Castro (org.), *Colecção dos Tratados*, vol. 4, 1857, pp. 18–25].
37. The Macau lorcha was a hybrid sailing vessel having a Chinese junk rig on a Portuguese (European) hull; it was faster than the normal Chinese junk because of its hull style.
38. Jin Guoping and Wu Zhiliang (eds.), *Correspondência Oficial*, vol. 2, docs. 183, 186.
39. The Commutation Act (20–08–1784) safeguarded the British tea trade profits by lowering the taxes paid by British importers, putting an end to the smuggling of tea carried out by foreign merchants [Patrick Tuck, "Introduction: Sir George Thomas Staunton and the Failure of the Amherst Embassy of 1816", in Patrick Tuck (ed.), *Britain and the China Trade 1635–1842*, vol. 10, 2000, p. x]. The amount of tea sold in Great Britain doubled in the 1780s (see Earl H. Pritchard, *Britain and the China Trade*, pp. 212–220).
40. H. B. Morse, *The Chronicles*, vol. 2, p. 86 [identical decisions in 1762–1767 (G/12/11, fls. 113–124)].
41. G/12/18, fls. 43–54.
42. The behaviour of the supercargoes also affected Sino-Portuguese relations. In September 1781 the governor of Macau informed the president of the Select Committee that the Mandarinate had ordered him to arrest some British supercargoes but he had ignored the order (G/12/72, fl. 105).
43. R/10/11 (1780–1781), part 2, fl. 109; G/12/19, fls. 181–185, 188–204, 219–228, 253–274; and G/12/72 (1781), fl. 32.
44. R/10/11, part 2, fl. 109; and G/12/72, fls. 87–90, 97–98, 104, 138–139.
45. *AM*, 3rd series, vol. 16, n. 4, October 1971, p. 246; AHU, *Macau*, box 14, docs. 10, 11.
46. R/10/11 (1780–1781), part 2, fl. 110. McClary was released in July and took a Dutch ship in Whampoa. The Committee visited Macau and was criticised by the Mandarinate, who demanded McClary's imprisonment. The latter also took Chinese junks (G/12/76, 1782–1783, part 2, fl. 198), leading the Portuguese and

Dutch to complain to the British presidency of Fort William [G/12/77 (1783), fls. 87–88]. The supercargoes criticised McClary's behaviour (fls. 113–129), and the latter intended to attack Macau ships to punish the Senate for forcing him to compensate the owners of the ships he had already stolen (G/12/73, fls. 3–4). In 1786 the problems caused by independent traders made George Smith suggest that the president of the Select Committee should also be nominated British consul so that he could control all country ships (G/12/19, fls. 173–183). In that same year, the EIC published its regulations concerning the control of independent traders in China (G/12/20, fls. 429–33). On the repercussions of MacClary's piracy in Macau and in Fort William, see G/12/77 (1783), fls. 92–94, 97, B. A. Saletore (ed.), *Fort William-India House Correspondences*, vol. 9: *1782–85*, 1959, pp. 362–363, 390, 396, pp. 76, 480–481, and *AM*, 3rd series, vol. 10, n. 6, Dec. 1968, p. 293.

47. R/10/11, part 2, fls. 106–107.
48. R/10/11 (1780–1781), part 2, fls. 107–108; G/12/58, fls. 186–202; G/12/69, fls. 50–61; G/12/73 (1781–1782), fls. 37–38; and G/12/94, fls. 115–116 (1788–1789).
49. R/10/11, fls. 57–58; G/12/76, fls. 64–65; R/10/11, fls. 58–59; G/12/76, fls. 57–69, 111–113, 158–159; R/10/12, fls. 25, 29; and R/10/13, fl. 2. In 1782 the governor wrote to the Committee on behalf of Simão da Rosa and António Botelho, requesting that the Committee complained to the Bengal Council so that nothing could disturb the harmony between the two allied European nations (R/10/12, fls. 60–63). Fort St. George told the governor of Macau that the British would do all that they could to punish and stop McClary (fls. 113–119).
50. *AM*, 3rd series, vol. 4, n. 3, 1965, pp. 166–169–175, 184–186.
51. R/10/14, fls. 90–107; R/10/15, fl. 38; G/12/11, fls. 136–141a; G/12/ 18, fls. 49–83 (also copied in G/12/20, fls. 413–427v); and G/12/79, fls. 102–103, 118–156, 169–172.
52. When visiting Macau in January 1787 Count Lapérouse mentioned this incident but did not identify it, presenting it as an example of the difficulties that the foreign traders faced due to the Chinese impositions (Count Lapérouse, *Voyage de Lapérouse*, pp. 201–202).
53. The *Empress of China* left New York and arrived at Macau in August 1784 (G/12/79, fl. 116), returning to the US in September of the following year. On the early North American presence in Macau, see Jacques M. Downs, *The Golden Ghetto: The American Commercial Community at Canton and the Shaping of American China Policy, 1784–1844*, 1997, and Rogério Miguel Puga, "O Primeiro Olhar Norte-Americano sobre Macau: Os Diários de Samuel Shaw (1754–1794)", in Ana Gabriela Macedo *et alii* (org.), *Intertextual Dialogues, Travel & Routes*, *Actas do "XXVI Encontro da APEAA*, 2007, pp. 227–251.

54. E. J. Eitel, *Europe in China: The History of HongKong from the Beginning to the Year 1882*, 1895, wrongly identifies the first English woman to visit Macau as Mrs. McClannon, but, as I said before, the pioneers were the maid and wife of Richard Frobisher, in 1620.

55. "Natural Curiosity", *Caledonian Mercury* (Edinburgh), n. 12312, 21–08–1800, p. 3; and *Trewman's Exeter Flying Post*, n. 1923, 21–08–1800, p. 3.

56. *AM*, 3rd series, vol. 10, n. 5, November 1968, p. 240; vol. 14, n. 4, October 1970, pp. 218–219; vol. 16, n. 4, October 1971, p. 246.

57. *AM*, 3rd series, vol. 16, n. 4, October 1971, p. 219.

58. Hosea Ballou Morse, *The Chronicles*, vol. 1, p. 67.

59. G/12/49, fl. 7.

60. Susan Reed Stifler, "The Language Students of the East India Company Canton Factory", *Journal of the North China Branch of the Royal Asiatic Society*, vol. 69, 1938, pp. 48, 54; J. L. Cranmer-Byng, "The First English Sinologists: Sir George Staunton and the Reverend Robert Morrison", in F. S. Drake (ed.), *Symposium on Historical, Archaeological and Linguistic Studies on Southern China, South-East Asia and the Hong Kong Region*, 1967, p. 248; and G/12/110, fl. 52 (1795).

61. G/12/11, fls. 100–112.

62. The first translation of a Chinese literary work into English, *Han Kiou Choaan/The Fortunate Union: A Chinese Novel*, was made by the supercargo James Wilkinson (c.1719) from a previous Portuguese translation (cf. Susan Reed Stifler, "The Language Students", p. 47).

63. The Committee sent literary works to London and founded the already mentioned library of the British factory (British Library) in 1806. When the EIC ended its activity in China, the library had 4,000 volumes.

64. The foreigners' daily life in ships and at home depended to a great extent on the action of the comprador, the "bicultural middleman" between Chinese and Westerners (see Yen-Ping Hao, *The Compradore in Nineteenth Century China: Bridge between East and West*, 1970, pp. 1–77, 154–223).

65. Harriett Low, *Lights and Shadows*, vol. 1, pp. 77, 192, 318; vol. 2, pp. 571, 608–609.

Chapter 9 The "scramble for the use of Macau"

1. Expression used by J. M. Braga, "A Seller of 'Sing-Songs'", p. 85, when he mentions the clash of interests between the EIC, the country traders and the interlopers regarding the use of Macau as a support platform for the China Trade.

2. AHU, *Macau*, box 48, doc. 22 ; box 55, doc. 24 ; box 60, doc. 31.

3. *AM*, 3rd series, vol. 7, n. 6, June 1967, p. 316; vol. 8, n. 3, September 1967, pp. 121–126.

4. G/12/79, part 2, fls. 115, 172.

5. On the opium smuggling system between Bengal and other places and Canton carried out by the country traders, also through Macau (due to the fact that the supercargoes had been forbidden to smuggle opium), see David Edward Owen, *British Opium Policy in China and India*, 1934, pp. 1–54; D. Eyles, "The Abolition of the East India Company's Monopoly 1833", PhD thesis, 1955, pp. 4–6; and P. J. Marshall, "Private British Trade in the Indian Ocean Before 1800", in Om Prakash (ed.), *An Expanding World*, pp. 258–262.

6. G/12/79, part 2, fl. 171.

7. Opium that was sold in Fort William (Calcutta). For a survey of the British opium trade since 1757, also through Macau, see John Keay, *The Honourable Company*, pp. 359–360, 430–431; and Hunt Janin, *The India-China Opium Trade in the Nineteenth Century*, 1999.

8. There are numerous references to the opium smuggling through Macau in the second half of the eighteenth century in the EIC and Portuguese documentation [Morse, *The Chronicles*, vol. 2, pp. 282–343; P. C. Gupta (ed.), *Fort William-India House Correspondences*, vol. 13: *1796–1800*, 1959, p. 508; I. B. Banerjee (ed.), *Fort William-India House Correspondences*, vol. 11: *1789–92*, 1974, pp. 400, 441, 459–460; *AM*, 3rd series, vol. 10, n. 4, October 1968, pp. 192–193; AHU, *Macau*, box 11, doc. 5, fl. 1 (about Lintin see box 55, doc. 24, box 56, doc. 73, box 63, doc. 5)].

9. *AM*, 3rd series, vol. 8, n. 2, 1967, pp. 102–103; vol. 16, n. 5, 1971, pp. 135–136.

10. D. Eyles, "The Abolition of the East India Company's Monopoly 1833", p. 5. Regarding the problem of supplying silver to the EIC in Canton, see "Sketch of a Plan for Supplying the Hon'ble East India Company with Silver at Canton", 1786: G/12/18, (1753–1787), fls. 21–24.

11. *AM*, 3rd series, vol. 10, n. 4, October, p. 230; vol. 14, n. 4, October 1970, pp. 210–213; António M. Martins do Vale, *Os Portugueses em Macau (1750–1800)*, pp. 46–47. Every year the British brought to China, through Macau, around 200 chests of opium. In 1766, 1,000 chests were used to bribe the Chinese to allow the drug smuggling [P. J. Marshall, "Britain and China in the Late Eighteenth Century", in Robert A. Bickers (ed.), *Ritual & Diplomacy: The Macartney Mission to China (1792–1794)*, 1993, p. 18]. On the accusations between the Macau Senate and the governors concerning opium smuggling, see *AM*, 3rd series: vol. 6, n. 5, 1966, p. 255; vol. 7, nn. 5–6, 1967, pp. 249, 256–257, 286–287, 317; vol. 8, n. 1, 1967, pp. 252–255; vol. 10, nn. 2, 4, 1964, pp. 99, 192–193, 222–223.

12. Regarding the mutual interests and opium smuggling operations of both Portuguese and British (which even involved two governors bribed by the EIC), see António M. Martins do Vale, *Os Portugueses em Macau (1750–1800)*, pp. 207–209, 211.

13. *AM*, 3rd series, vol. 7, n. 6, June 1967, p. 302.

14. On the production of opium in India smuggled by the British using Portuguese ships from Macau that unload the drug in the enclave, see R/10/12 (1782), fls. 45–46, 50–51, 150, 180, 187–188; R/10/13 (1783), fls. 56–57; R/10/19 (1791), fls. 40–42, 76–66; G/12/76, fls. 41, 43, 136, 147–149; G/12/76, part 2, fls. 205, 234; G/12/77, fl. 59; Paul Wilson Howard, "Opium Suppression in Qing China: Responses to a Social Problem, 1729–1906", 1998, pp. 65–117; and Alfredo Gomes Dias, *Portugal, Macau e a Internacionalização da Questão do Ópio (1909–1925)*, 2004, pp. 26–35.

15. *AM*, 3rd series, vol. 7, n. 6, 1967, pp. 313, 318–319; vol. 8, n. 2, p. 102; n. 3, pp. 121–131.

16. Ângela Guimarães, "A Conjuntura Política antes de Hong Kong", in A. H. de Oliveira Marques (dir.), *História dos Portugueses no Extremo Oriente*, vol. 3, p. 20. For a list of the opium chests that officially entered Macau and the custom duties paid by the British between 1784–1838, see Fernando Figueiredo, "Os Vectores da Economia", in A. H. de Oliveira Marques (dir.), *História dos Portugueses no Extremo Oriente*, vol. 3, pp. 106–107.

17. Jin Guoping and Wu Zhiliang (eds.), *Correspondência Oficial*, vol. 1, doc. n. 43, p. 123; doc. 95, p. 230; doc. 107, p. 244.

18. *AM*, 3rd series, vol. 6, n. 4, 1966, pp. 186–187, n. 5, p. 255; vol. 7, n. 5, 1967, pp. 249, 256–257, n. 6, pp. 291, 313, 318; vol. 10, n. 2, 1968, pp. 99, 192–193, n. 4, pp. 222–223; vol. 14, nn. 3–4, 1970, pp. 162, 186–187; vol. 17, n. 2, 1972, p. 96, n. 3, pp. 133–135, 159–166; vol. 24, n. 3, 1970, p. 146; AHU, *Macau*, box 20, docs. 10–11, box 21, docs. 11–37.

19. G/12/86, fl. 11 (1787). Cheminant was released two days later and promised to leave Macau.

20. *AM*, 3rd series, vol. 17, n. 3, pp. 159–166.

21. On the powers of the *ouvidoria* (judge), extinct in 1740 because of the Senate's pressure, and reinstated in 1784, see António M. Martins do Vale, *Os Portugueses em Macau*, pp. 15–19.

22. See António M. Martins do Vale, *Os Portugueses em Macau*, pp. 59–67, *idem*, "Macau: Os Eventos Políticos. 2", pp. 164–170; and Cristina Seuanes Serafim, "Organização Política e Administrativa", in A. H. de Oliveira Marques (dir.), *História dos Portugueses no Extremo Oriente*, vol. 2, pp. 303–314.

23. Manuel Múrias (ed.), *Instruções para o Bispo de Pequim*, p. 56.

24. In the 1790s three British traders created their own company in Macau and used the name of a poor resident to whom they paid so that they could own ships and borrow money from the Senate (António M. Martins do Vale, *Os Portugueses em Macau*, p. 210).

25. The Portuguese ships used by the British were called "*embandeirados*" because they carried the Portuguese flag (Fernando Figueiredo, "Os Vectores da Economia", p. 101; *AM*, 3rd series, vol. 7, nn. 5–6, 1967, pp. 238–239, 249–250, 318; vol. 8, n. 3, 1967, pp. 121–132; vol. 14, n. 4, 1970, pp. 218–219; vol. 16, n. 4, 1971, pp. 209–210; AHU, *Macau*, box 15, doc. 19, box 17, doc. 66, box 18, doc. 34, box 20, docs. 10, 11, 35, 36, box 21, doc. 18). As the Portuguese governors were forbidden to trade, some of them, like Vasco Luís Carneiro de Sousa e Faro, also used the names of poor residents to do business. To enter the port of Macau in 1790 a British ship used the Portuguese flag and its crew had Portuguese names (AN/TT, Manusc. Liv., *State Papers*, liv. 2604, fls. 245–248).

26. G/12/77 (1783), fl. 85. The Senate was aware of the strategy used by the British who bought the drug in Bengal before the arrival of the Macau ships, many of which were rented by the British (*AM*, 3rd series, vol. 17, n. 3, March 1972, pp. 161–165). In 1746, the British finished their business in Madras before the Macau ships arrived to trade (*Records of St. George: Diary and Consultation Book of 1746*, 1931, p. 79), and the crew of the latter informed the British about the current trade situation in China (*Records of St. George: Letters to Fort St. George 1682*, vol. 2, 1916, p. 135).

27. AHU, *Macau*, box 17, doc. 26 (1786), fl. 3: "most of the trade is done by the English [...] and the Macau ships have nowhere else to go because the English are everywhere, and sponsored by the governor of Macau". The Portuguese Law forbade the governors to trade, and Bernardo Aleixo de Lemos e Faria was condemned in Goa (1789: cx. 18, docs. 21, 45).

28. G/12/76 (1782–1783), part 2, fl. 205.

29. G/12/89, fls. 124–125.

30. G/12/103 (1792–1793), fls. 70–71, 74, 80–81, 84–85.

31. According to the EIC records, in 1783 James Henry Cox and John Reid, chief of the "Imperial Company", were the only British residents in Canton, and the EIC had no power over them (G/12/77, fl. 81). In 1786 only two independent traders, John Henry Cox and John M. Intyre, lived in Macau (R/10/15, fl. 14). After helping the supercargoes on a voluntary basis, Intyre was nominated agent of the EIC in that city in 1785, where he assisted the crews of arriving ships and the Canton factory (G/12/79, part 2, fls. 6–7; G/12/89, fl. 9; G/12/98, fl. 2).

32. R/10/15 (1786–1787), fl. 14; G/12/101, fls. 9–10; G/12/103, fl. 10.

33. *AM*, 3rd series, vol. 17, n. 3, March 1972, pp. 133–135.

34. Wen Eang Cheong, *Mandarins and Merchants: Jardine Matheson & Co.*, 1978.

35. P. J. Marshall, "Britain and China in the Late Eighteenth Century", pp. 20–21.

36. In 1777 the Senate accused the British of using their leisure vessels to smuggle opium and seized them (*AM*, 3rd series, vol. 14, n. 4, 1970, pp. 218–219).

37. Jin Guoping and Wu Zhiliang (eds.), *Correspondência Oficial*, vol. 1, doc. 20, p. 409.
38. AHU, *Macau*, box 21, doc. 18.
39. Pierry-Yves Manguin, *Os Nguyen, Macau e Portugal*, 1999, pp. 222–225.
40. AHU, *Macau*, box 24, doc. 13.
41. AHU, *Macau*, box 23, doc. 24.
42. In April 1840, during the Opium War, Charles Elliot came up with a plan to occupy Macau and use it as a strategic British point during the conflicts with China (Montalto Jesus, *Historic Macao*, 1902, pp. 255–260; W. Zhiliang, *Segredos*, pp. 145–147; and A. G. Dias, *Macau e a I Guerra do Ópio*, pp. 17–58).
43. Expression used in a letter sent by the Macau judge to Lisbon, in February 1840 (A. G. Dias, *Macau*, p. 170).

Chapter 10   "Guests and old allies"

1. Expression used by the Senate's procurator in a chop sent to the Mandarinate (1813), mentioning the British presence in Macau [Jin Guoping and Wu Zhiliang (eds.), *Correspondência Oficial*, vol. 5, doc. 109, p. 189].
2. G/12/86, fl. 147; G/12/88, fls. 60, 62, 66; G/12/89, fl. 9; G/12/96, fl. 5; G/12/101, fl. 5; G/12/103, fls. 5, 10; G/12/105, fls. 14, 44; G/12/108, fl. 38.
3. G/12/11, fl. 128; G/12/64, fl. 137.
4. R/10/11, part 2, fls. 30–41, 82–83; G/12/20, fls. 300–309; G/12/72, fl. 5; G/12/73, fls. 3–4; G/12/79, fls. 119–125.
5. G/12/79 (1784–1785), fl. 136. On the final eviction of George Smith and other British independent traders from Macau, see *AM*, 3rd series, vol. 3, n. 5, 1965, pp. 301–306; vol. 10, n. 5, 1968, pp. 241–242; and vol. 17, n. 1–2, pp. 31, 96.
6. R/10/7 (1769–1775), section "1671", fls. 31–33. The EIC forbade opium trade in its vessels in 1771 (fl. 37).
7. G/12/11, fl. 125.
8. G/12/11, fls. 132–134. In 1782 and also six years after, the EIC defined the powers of the supercargoes over the British independent traders and their ships in China (fls. 155–157, and G/12/19, fl. 155).
9. G/12/77, fl. 82.
10. G/12/65, fl. 59.
11. R/10/11, fl. 100.
12. R/10/11, fls. 87–88.
13. R/10/11, fls. 88–90, my emphasis.
14. On the two British failed attempts to occupy Macau in 1802 and 1808, see Joaquim Martins de Carvalho, *A Nossa Alliada!*, 1883, pp. 40–63; AHU,

Macau, box 22, docs. 39, 49, 50, 51; box 27, doc. 54; box 28, docs. 5, 6, 7, 9, 18, 22, 26, 31, 55; box 29, docs. 4, 8, 16, 20, 25, 27, 29, 30, 32, 33; AN/TT, *Ministério do Reino*, sheaf 499, ch. 1; Jin Guoping and Wu Zhiliang (eds.), *Correspondência Oficial*, vol. 2, docs. 221–222, pp. 388–389; vol. 4, docs. 4–5, 71–72, 137, 148, 150, 161, 164; "Official Papers of Sir Samuel Hood, 1st Bt, Vice-Admiral, 1762–1814", section "Miscellaneous Government 1812–1813–1814: Calendar of Correspondence of Rear-Admiral William O'Brien Drury at Macau, 4–12 October 1808", National Maritime Museum, London (MKH/237, *Manuscript*); G/12/93, fls. 425–431; G/12/195, fls. 208–247; and José Inácio Andrade, *Memória dos Feitos Macaenses Contra as Piratarias da China e da Entrada Violenta dos Ingleses na Cidade de Macau*, 1835.
15. R/10/11, fls. 114–115.
16. R/10/11, fls. 116–117.
17. R/10/10, part 2, fl. 193; R/10/11, 1780–1781, part 2, fls. 193–194; R/10/14, fls. 31, 193–194. In 1785 the instructions from London to the Canton Committee forbade the transportation of slaves in EIC vessels (G/12/79, part 2, fls. 59–60).
18. R/10/11, fls. 118–121; G/12/19, fls. 231–252.
19. R/10/11, fls. 106–107, text repeated in other letters (fls. 113–114, 159–160; G/12/73, fls. 58–69, 104). See also G/12/19, fls. 121–150. The letter stated that Macau, although under the power of Goa, really depended on the good will of the Chinese, and so Lisbon, ashamed of the situation, preferred to forget the enclave, ignoring many of its issues (fl. 108). In 1797, Daniel Paine, returning to London from Sydney, visited Macau and criticised the Portuguese, "a despicable set of beings", for obeying the Mandarinate and for making the supercargoes' lives harder ("Diary as Kept in a Voyage to Port Jackson, New South Wales, a Short Residence on that Settlement, and Passage to China", fl. 27).
20. R/10/11, part 2, fls. 39–40.
21. R/10/12, fl. 23; G/12/73, fl. 36.
22. Jacques M. Downs, *The Golden Ghetto*, p. 49.
23. R/10/18, fl. 38.
24. G/12/19, fl. 277.
25. António M. Martins do Vale, *Os Portugueses em Macau*, p. 56.
26. G/12/79, fls. 15–16.
27. R/10/15, fls. 51–53, 173–175, 218, 234–237; G/12/82, part 3, fls. 5, 139–141; and G/12/84, fls. 1, 31–85.
28. R/10/15, fl. 31.
29. R/10/15, fl. 35.
30. R/10/15, fl. 37.
31. R/10/15, fls. 39–40.

32. R/10/15, fls. 34 and 38.
33. R/10/15, fl. 38.
34. G/12/86, fls. 38–41, 109–110, 276.
35. G/12/84, fl. 106.
36. G/12/84, fls. 85–86, 104–107.
37. G/12/84, fl. 60.
38. G/12/86, fl. 41.
39. G/12/86, fl. 15.
40. G/12/86, fls. 15–41, 191–196; G/12/88, fls. 67–71; G/12/89, fls. 167–172, 203–205.
41. Samuel Shaw, *The Journals of Major Samuel Shaw, the First American Consul at Canton*, 1968, p. 239.
42. Samuel Shaw, *The Journals*, p. 240; and G/12/86, fl. 16.
43. Samuel Shaw, *The Journals*, p. 240.
44. Samuel Shaw, *The Journals*, p. 240.
45. G/12/86, fl. 18.
46. G/12/86, fl. 26.
47. G/12/86, fl. 21.
48. G/12/86, fls. 191–192.
49. G/12/88, fl. 67.
50. G/12/89, fls. 114–116.
51. In 1747–1748 a British traveller also described the city as almost deserted and no longer under Portuguese rule, being governed by the Chinese (Anonymous, *A Voyage to the East Indies in 1747 and 1748*, 1762, p. 197), an image that suited the British and that was echoed in English literature, namely in Daniel Defoe's novel *The Farther Adventures of Robinson Crusoe*, 1969, p. 368: "Macau, a town once in possession of the Portuguese, and where still a great many European families resided".
52. G/12/19, fls. 209–211; and Morse, *The Chronicles*, vol. 2, p. 68.
53. AHU, *Macau*, box 11, doc. 25, and box 8, doc. 8 (1775).
54. G/12/86, fl. 11.
55. *AM*, 3rd series, vol. 16, n. 1, 1965, pp. 204–209.
56. *Records of St. George: Letters to Fort St. George, 1762–63*, vol. 43, 1943, p. 53.
57. *Records of St. George: Letters from Fort St. George, 1763*, vol. 37, 1943, pp. 24–25.
58. *Records of St. George: Letters from Fort St. George, 1763*, p. 98.

Chapter 11   The importance of Macau for the British China trade

1.   G/12/77, fl. 88: "We are concerned to observe the differences which have subsisted between the Honourable Company's Supra cargoes and the Portuguese Government at Macau. As a good understanding between you, is so material to the success of the Company's Concerns in China, and so necessary to your own ease, and welfare, we have transmitted copies of the papers which we received from you to our resident in Goa, with directions to lay them before the Governor General of that place for the interposition of his controlling power to secure a proper attention to your privileges and to bring about a perfect reconciliation between you".

2.   Thomas Gilbert, *Voyage from New South Wales to Canton, in the Year 1788*, 1789, p. 81.

3.   Jin Guoping and Wu Zhiliang (eds.), *Correspondência Oficial*, vol. 2, doc. 15.

4.   Jin Guoping and Wu Zhiliang (eds.), *Correspondência Oficial*, vol. 2, doc. 16, p. 31; doc. 17, pp. 32–33.

5.   Jin Guoping and Wu Zhiliang (eds.), *Correspondência Oficial*, vol. 4, doc. 38, p. 69; see also docs. 30, 39, 43.

6.   R/10/6, fls. 163–165v.

7.   AHU, *Macau*, box 7, docs. 17, 27–28.

8.   Jin Guoping and Wu Zhiliang (eds.), *Correspondência Oficial*, vol. 1, doc. 24, p. 75, docs. 27–29, 32; *AM*, 3rd series, vol. 4, n. 1, 1965, pp. 58–59; vol. 10, nn. 1, 3, 4, 1968, pp. 54–56, 128, 286–287; R/10/7, section "1773", fls. 1–4.

9.   *AM*, 3rd series, vol. 10, n. 1, 1968, pp. 54–56.

10.   *AM*, 3rd series, vol. 16, n. 4, 1971, pp. 206–207.

11.   G/12/84, fl. 107 (1787).

12.   G/12/88, fl. 71.

13.   G/12/89, fl. 204.

14.   G/12/105, fls. 74, 116–117, 120; G/12/108, fl. 59; AHU, *Macau*, box 12, doc. 33.

15.   R/10/13, fl. 239; G/12/70, fl. 125.

16.   *AM*, 3rd series, vol. 8, n. 2, August 1967, pp. 105–106; G/12/66, fl. 137; C. Northcote Parkinson, *War in the Eastern Seas, 1793–1815*, 1954, pp. 315–333.

17.   AHU, *Macau*, box 19, doc. 36.

18.   G/12/92, fl. 457, repeated on fls. 499–507.

19.   G/12/8, fls. 1349–1352.

20.   G/12/110, fl. 57.

21.   G/12/92, fl. 458.

Chapter 12   Lord Macartney's embassy to China, 1792–1794

1. Expression used by Lord Macartney in his notebook (P. J. Marshall, "Britain and China in the Late Eighteenth Century", p. 14).
2. On the preparation of the first British embassy to China, the relations with the Portuguese in Beijing, and its stay in Macau, see R/10/20, fls. 63–78, 126–130, 248–265; G/12/11, fls. 8–9; G/12/20, fls. 20–34v, 40–217v; G/12/91; G/12/92; G/12/93, fls. 191–217, 240–252, 264–270, 287–290; G/12/112, fl. 4; Earl H. Pritchard, *Britain and the China Trade*, pp. 199–212; Alain Peyrefitte, *Un Choc de Cultures*; Nigel Cameron, *Barbarians and Mandarins*, 1993, pp. 288–316; and Jin Guoping and Wu Zhiliang (eds.), *Correspondência Oficial*, vol. 2, docs. 36, 41, 51.
3. G/12/18, fls. 93, 95, 105–110, 134–135.
4. G/12/18, fls. 55–79; G/12/20, fls. 17–39, 104–222, 551–569; G/12/90.
5. G/12/18, fls. 2, 108–124. In May of that same year the British trader David Scott informed the EIC that the Portuguese did not take any advantage out of Macau, which would be an important acquisition for the British in case they bought it from their old European allies (cf. Vincent T. Harlow, *The Founding of the Second British Empire 1763–1793*, vol. 2, 1964, p. 535).
6. J. L. Cranmer-Byng, "Introduction", in Lord Macartney, *Britain and China Trade 1635–1842*, vol. 8: *An Embassy to China: Lord Macartney's Journal*, 1793–1794, 2000, pp. 1–7.
7. On the image of China in Great Britain after the embassy, see Shunhong Zhang, "British Views on China during the Time of the Embassies of Lord Macartney and Lord Amherst (1790–1820)", 1990, and Aubrey Singer, *The Lion and the Dragon: Lord Macartney's Embassy to the Emperor Quian Long, 1792–94*, 1992.
8. The EIC wanted the ambassador to convince the emperor to grant them an island in the Pearl River delta where they would establish their factory, "in imitation of the settlement enjoyed by the Portuguese at Macau" (G/12/20, fl. 355).
9. G/12/11, fls. 160–188.
10. G/12/20, fl. 369v.
11. G/12/20, fls. 369v–370.
12. Before the embassy arrived in Macau news about the diplomatic mission reached the enclave through Portuguese ships coming from Bengal (R/10/20, fl. 116).
13. Sir George Staunton, *An Authentic Account of an Embassy from the King of Great Britain to the Emperor of China*, vol. 2, 1798, pp. 384–390, describes the embassy's stay in Macau, the enclave's location, government, defences, religions, and its wealth, once produced by trade and still visible in the architecture. Other descriptions of the embassy, like the ones written by Aeneas Anderson, Samuel Holmes, John Barrow, and Sir Henry Ellis, arouse the curiosity of the British regarding China. The mission is also a scientific exploratory voyage, and many engravings of

China were produced, published and sold by artists such as Thomas Hickey and William Alexander.

14. Expression used by Alain Peyrefitte, *Un Choc de Cultures*, p. ix.

15. See the Chinese documents translated by Alain Peyrefitte, *Un Choc de Cultures*, pp. 149–190, 338–388.

16. On the anti-British action of Beijing's Portuguese bishop, Alexandre de Gouveia, and other priests in that city and in Macau during the embassy, see Lo-shu Fu, *A Documentary Chronicle of Sino-Western Relations*, 1966, vol. 1, pp. 343–344, vol. 2, p. 539; and António Graça de Abreu, "O Insucesso de Macartney e os Padres Portugueses", *Macau*, n. 67, Nov. 1997, pp. 124–131.

17. Aeneas Anderson, *A Narrative*, pp. 389–392, describes the ambassador's arrival, his visit to the governor of Macau's home, his stay at the Casa Garden, Macau's geographical location and the city in general, the EIC buildings, as well as the forts, and the "papists", and Chinese local administration bodies, correcting imprecisions of previous authors, including the fact that Macau is not an island, but a peninsula [see Daniel Paine, "Diary", fl. 25v (1797), and Richard Walter, *A Voyage*, p. 465].

18. James Drummond was born in 1767 and went out to Canton in the EIC's service at an early age. He became president of the Select Committee in 1802.

19. On the failure of the embassy, see AHU, *Macau*, box 20, doc. 2, which describes the voyage from London and states "that the Embassy accomplished nothing" [fl. 2; see box 42, doc. 7, box 43, doc. 27, and BA, *Ms. Av.* 54-XIII-7, n. 4].

20. In 1845, Reverend George Newham Wright, bishop of Cloyne, described Macau in a similar way: "So slight is Portuguese tenure or little at Macau, that the Chinese maintain here, in neighbourship with this despised race of foreigner, one of the most remarkable, most venerated, and really gracefull buildings in the empire, dedicated to the worship of Fo. [...] Macau occupies a position rather of beauty than strength" (*China Illustrated*, 1845, vol. 1, p. 66, and vol. 2, p. 27).

21. Lord Macartney, *An Embassy to China: Lord Macartney's Journal, 1793–1794*, 2000, p. 211.

22. To request a piece of land to trade and afterwards conquer the whole country or kingdom/colony.

23. AHU, *Maço José das Torres*, VI, sheaf 540, fls. 1–3.

24. Souza e Faro governed Macau between 29 July 1790 and July 1793.

25. AHU, *Macau*, box 19, doc. 36, fl. 1 (22-12-1792). The British embassy's aim is to request the emperor to grant the EIC some land on the island of Zhousan and in Canton, as well as the abolition or reduction of taxes paid by the British between Macau and Canton. These requests were denied by the emperor (Cranmer-Byng, "Lord Macartney's Embassy to Peking in 1793. From Official Chinese Documents", *Journal of Oriental Studies*, vol. 4, nn. 1–2, 1957–1958, p. 173).

26. AHU, *Macau*, box 32, doc. 39.
27. John Barrow, *Travels in China*, pp. 18–19. I used this work's second edition, rather than the first edition published in 1804, in order to use the comments about Macau added in 1806 which reveal the attitudes and the intentions (already filtered) of the British regarding their military occupation of Macau in 1802.
28. In 1798 Great Britain, at war with France, planned occupations of strategic locations such as the Cape of Good Hope, Goa, and Macau, but the governor of Goa rejected the military support offered by the British (see A. da Silva Rego, "Os Ingleses em Goa. 1799–1813", *Estudos Políticos e Sociais*, vol. 3, n. 1, 1965, pp. 23–48).
29. AHU, *Macau*, box 22, doc. 39, fl. 1: in January 1802 the governor of Goa, Veiga Cabral, orders Macau to accept the British military help: "as a consequence of the strong Alliance which fortunately subsists between our Majesty and the British one, so it is indispensable to protect all Portuguese possessions in Asia against the French enemy of both nations" (see the letter written by Captain Gerald Osborn, who, in 1802, warned the Macau Government that the French were preparing to take the city and offered military support).
30. See the warning sent by the Portuguese to the Chinese authorities about the British behaviour in India in AHU, *Maço José das Torres*, VI, sheaf n. 540, fls. 1–3.
31. John Barrow, *Travels in China*, p. 20.
32. Document translated into Portuguese by Wu Zhiliang, *Segredos*, p. 141.
33. This accusation was repeated in 1809 by viceroy Han Feng, who praised the peaceful Portuguese and mentioned the despise that the British showed towards the residents and the authorities of Macau ["Memorial de Han Feng", in António Vasconcelos de Saldanha and Jin Guoping (eds.), *Para a Vista do Imperador*, pp. 33–39].
34. António Vasconcelos de Saldanha and Jin Guoping (eds.), *Correspondência Oficial*, p. 30. These ideas are repeated in "Lu Kun's Memorial" (1835) [António Vasconcelos de Saldanha and Jin Guoping (eds.), *Para a Vista do Imperador*, pp. 62–65, 67–68]; which states, on page 58: "The barbarians from several nations who reside there [Macau] are obedient and respect the law. Only the British barbarians are astute and arrogant".
35. Wu Zhiliang, *Segredos*, pp. 132–145.
36. "Lu Kun's Memorial" (1835), p. 68, describes the Chinese strategy regarding the defence of the coast with the help of the Portuguese: "by giving the Macau barbarians what they want, we please them, controlling the British barbarians and demanding respect from them; that is the *yiyizhiyi* policy" [using barbarians against barbarians].

37. The British Ultimatum (11–01–1890) was an ultimatum by the British government delivered to Portugal, forcing the retreat of Portuguese troops in the area between the Portuguese colonies of Mozambique and Angola, a territory claimed by Portugal and included in its *Pink Map*, which clashed with British aspirations to build a Cape to Cairo railway to link its colonies from the North to the South of Africa (see Maria Teresa Pinto Coelho, *Apocalipse e Regeneração. O Ultimatum e a Mitologia da Pátria na Literatura Finissecular*, 1996).

38. José de Arriaga, *A Inglaterra, Portugal e as Suas Colónias*, 1882, p. 69, and Joaquim Martins de Carvalho, *A Nossa Aliada!*, p. 19.

39. José Valentim Fialho de Almeida, *Os Gatos*, vol. 1, 1922, p. 254.

40. Gomes Freire d'Andrade, *A Dominação Inglesa em Portugal: O Que É e de que nos Tem Servido a Aliança da Inglaterra*, 1883, pp. 140–141, 144, 206.

41. Staunton writes "Considerations upon the China Trade" (1813) and meets the viceroy of Canton before the second British embassy to China (G/12/20, fls. 444–488). On the second embassy, see G/12/196; G/12/197; G/12/198; Jin Guoping and Wu Zhiliang (eds.), *Correspondência Oficial*, vol. 5, docs. 158–160, 161, 165–166; AHU, *Macau*, box 40, docs. 20, 38; box 41, doc. 13; box 42, docs. 7, 9–10; and box 43, doc. 27.

42. On Macau's neutral position during the Opium War, see Alfredo Gomes Dias, *Macau e a I Guerra do Ópio*, 1993; and *Sob o Signo da Transição: Macau no Século XIX*, 1998.

43. Alexander Michie, *The English Man in China*, p. 293. On the role of the Macau Portuguese in the foundation of the British colony, see José Maria Braga, *Hong Kong and Macau*, 1951, pp. 47–75; and António M. Pacheco Jorge da Silva, *The Portuguese Community in Hong Kong*, 2007.

44. Vincent T. Harlow, *The Founding of the Second British Empire 1763–1793*, vol. 1, 1952, pp. 1–64.

45. Michael Duffy, "World-Wide War and British Expansion, 1793–1815", pp. 200–201.

46. P. J. Marshall (ed.), *The Oxford History of the British Empire*, pp. 576–595.

Conclusion

1. On the representation of Macau in Anglophone literatures, see Rogério Miguel Puga, "Macau enquanto Cronótopo Exótico na Literatura Inglesa", in *Actas do I Congresso de Estudos Anglo-Portugueses*, 2001, pp. 705–723 (also published in Chinese: *Administração: Revista de Administração Pública de Macau*, vol. 16, n. 59, March 2003, pp. 117–139); Rogério Miguel Puga, "Macau na Poesia Inglesa", in Ana Maria Amaro e Dora Martins (coord.), *Estudos Sobre a China VII*, vol. 2, 2005,

pp. 847–882; and Rogério Miguel Puga, "Macau na Literatura Inglesa", *Review of Culture*, n. 24, October 2007, pp. 90–105.

On the image of China in Great Britain between the sixteenth and the eighteenth centuries, see Thomas H. Lee (ed.), *China and Europe: Images and Influences in Sixteenth to Eighteenth Centuries*, 1991; and Adrian Hsia (ed.), *The Vision of China in the English Literature of the Seventeenth and Eighteenth Centuries*, 1998, pp. 29–68, 69–86, 117–215.

2. On Macau and the China Trade painting, see Patrick Conner, *George Chinnery*, 1992; Patrick Conner, *The China Trade 1600–1860*, 1986, pp. 40–44, *idem*, *George Chinnery 1774–1852*, 1992, pp. 164–268; AA. VV., *Views of the Pearl River Delta: Macau, Canton and Hong Kong*, 1996, pp. 6–7, 16–26, 56–109; Carl Crossman, *The Decorative Arts of the China Trade: Paintings, Furniture and Exotic Curiosities*, 1997, pp. 8–53, 410–437; and AA. VV., *Picturing Cathay: Maritime and Cultural Images of the China Trade*, 2003, pp. 81–83.

3. Guia Lighthouse (1865), the oldest Western lighthouse on the China coast.

4. On the introduction of the Western press in China, via Macau, and on the *Chinese Repository* and other Anglophone periodicals, see Manuel Teixeira, *Imprensa Periódica Portuguesa no Extremo Oriente*, 1999; and Pedro Teixeira Mesquita, "Ensino e Cultura", in A. H. de Oliveira Marques (dir.), *História dos Portugueses no Extremo Oriente*, vol. 3, pp. 539–585.

5. On the founding of the S. Rafael and S. Lázaro (Western) hospitals in Macau (1569), see AHU, *Macau*, box 26, doc. 4; and Padre Manuel Teixeira, *Os Médicos em Macau*, 1967, pp. 39–41.

6. Camões was never in Macau (see Rui Manuel Loureiro, "Camões em Macau. Um Mito Historiográfico", *Review of Culture*, n. 7, July 2003, pp. 108–125; and Padre Manuel Teixeira, *A Gruta de Camões em Macau*, 1999, pp. 7–27).

7. Alexander Michie, *The English Man in China during the Victorian Era*, 1900, pp. 296–298.

8. Expression used by Michie, *The English Man in China during the Victorian Era*, p. 291, referring to Macau, which he also describes as "the quiet old city" (pp. 295, 291–92) when presenting the strategic importance of the city for the British: "Other competitors also began to appear and to assert their right to participate in the trade of the Far East, and Macau became the hostelry for merchants of all nations [...]. Chief among these guests were the Dutch and English East India Companies, both of which maintained establishments at Macau for some two hundred years. The English Company had made use of Macau anchorage first under a treaty with the viceroy of Goa, and subsequently under Cromwell's treaty with the Portuguese Government in 1654, which permitted English ships to enter all the

ports in the Portugueses Indies. Before the close of the seventeenth century ships were despatched direct from England to Macau."

9. Expression used by John Keay, *Lost Post: The End of the Empire in the Far East*, 1997, p. 61.

10. Several Histories of Hong Kong (E. J. Eitel, *Europe in China*, pp. 1–8) deal with the British use of Macau until 1841, a period that has been seen as the "prelude" to the British colony (Austin Coates, *Prelude to Hong Kong: Macau and the British*, 1966).

11. Several Chinese sources mention the exodus of many Anglophone traders and firms from Macau to Hong Kong, a phenomenon that impoverished the economical and international status of the Sino-Portuguese enclave ["Qi Ying's Memorial" (18450, "Yi Xin's Memorial" (1868), and "Zhang Zhidong's Memorial" (1887), in António Vasconcelos de Saldanha and Jin Guoping (eds.), *Para a Vista do Imperador*, pp. 96–97, 130 and 142, respectively].

12. Expression used by the Macau Senate in the chop sent to the Mandarinate in 1809 [Jin Guoping and Wu Zhiliang (eds.), *Correspondência Oficial*, vol. 4, doc. 122, p. 247].

Bibliography

Presentation criteria

Expanding on the points made in the general introduction, the following criteria were used when drafting and presenting the bibliography:

1. All works referred to in the text and in the footnotes are included in the final bibliography, which representatively reflects the ongoing academic debate on the many different topics that this work deals with.

2. Regarding historical sources, the first year of publication or writing of the original manuscript is given in non-curved parentheses when not explicitly stated in the title of the text.

3. Texts by anonymous authors are provided at the beginning of the each section and by alphabetic order of their titles.

4. Various works by the same author are given by year of publication with works published in the same year listed alphabetically.

5. The publisher and publishing location of periodicals are not provided. The date of publication is provided in the simplest possible fashion (for example, 21–05–1994). Whenever a magazine/journal series or volume number is not provided, this lapse is due to its omission in the respective publications.

6. For a better understanding of the themes comprising the bibliography, a list is provided below:

    Sources

    Manuscript sources
    Printed sources
    - Portuguese and translated Chinese sources
    - British and international sources

Studies
- Macau: Sino-Portuguese relations
- Japan: the *Namban* century (1543–1639) and the British factory at Hirado (1613–1623)
- British expansion, the East India Company, Anglo-Portuguese relations in the Far East, and the founding of Hong Kong
- Portuguese History

Manuscript sources

The Family Records Centre/Public Record Office (London)
Calendar of P. C. C. [Prerogative Court of Canterbury] Registered Copy Wills 1795: PROB 11/1267, 56 RH–59 RH [unpublished will of Thomas Kuyck van Mierop].

Public Record Office (London)
Chancery
C 12/1006/35.

Foreign Office
FO 233/189
FO 1048/12, 16, 19, 20, 21.

State Papers
SP 46/151
SP 89/3–4, 9–10, 12, 17, 28, 31, 50, 67, 80.

E 140/9/4:
Parker, Robert, "Journals of Robert Parker, Agent of the English East India Company, Trading in Miscellaneous Commodities at Its Factory in Bantam (Banten), Java, with Details of Trading Ventures to Siam (Thailand), Amoy (Hsia-men), Macau, Surat, Manila and Elsewhere. 1678–1682", 3 vols.

British Library—*India Office Records* (London)
East India Company/China Records/China and Japan Factories:
G/12 (*Factory Records, China and Japan, 1596–1840*): G/12/1–112, 195–198; G/40/1.
R/10 (*China: Canton Factory Records, 1623–1833*): R/10/5–8, 10–21.

National Maritime Museum—*Caird Library* (London)
"Official Papers of Sir Samuel Hood, 1st Bt, Vice-Admiral, 1762–1814", section "Miscellaneous Government 1812–1813–1814: *Calendar of Correspondence of Rear-Admiral William O'Brien Drury at Macau*, 4–12 October 1808" [MKH/237, *Manuscript*].

Paine, Daniel, "Diary as Kept in a Voyage to Port Jackson, New South Wales, a Short Residence on that Settlement, and Passage to China, with Return by the Way of Manilla, Batavia, and Sta Helena, Interspersed with Remarks and Observations in the Years 1794, 5, 6, 7 and 8 by Daniel Paine" [JOD/172, *Manuscript*].

New York Historical Society (New York)

Butler, Caroline Hyde (Laing), "Journal on a Trip to China 1836–1837", New York Historical Society, New York, 1836–1837.

Arquivo Histórico Ultramarino (AHU, Overseas Historical Archive, Lisbon)

Macau, boxes: 1–2, 4–8, 11–15, 17–24, 26–29, 31–32, 37, 39–46, 48–49, 55–56, 60, 62–64;

Macau, Maço José das Torres, VI, sheaf 540.

Biblioteca da Ajuda (Ajuda Library, Lisbon)

Manuscritos Avulsos (Ms. Av.): 54–X–19, no. 19; 54–XIII–7, n. 4.

Jesuítas na Ásia: cod. 49–IV–56; 49–V–22, 24; 51–VII–31, 34.

Biblioteca Nacional de Portugal (Portuguese National Library, Lisbon)

Fundo Geral, cod. 7640.

Jesuítas na Ásia, cod. 49–V–29.

Filmoteca Ultramarina Portuguesa [Portuguese Overseas Film Library (Goa Historical Archives microfilms), Lisbon]

Livros das Monções, 19–D.

Livros dos Segredos, cod. 1.

Arquivo Nacional da Torre do Tombo (Portuguese National Archives, Torre do Tombo, Lisbon)

Colecção de São Vicente: vol. 12.

Ministério do Reino: sheaf 499.

Livro das Monções: books 27, 29, 31, 33–35, 38, 41, 43–45, 48, 50, 57.

Manuscritos da Livraria: *State Papers*, book 2604.

Printed sources

Portuguese and translated Chinese sources

Anonymous, "Descrição da Cidade de Macau ou a Cidade de Macau Reivindicada" [*c*.1693], in Artur Teodoro de Matos, "Uma Memória Seiscentista", *Macau*, n. 92, December 1999, pp. 194–204.

——, "Treslado da ordem que se fez em caza do capitão geral António Barboza Lobro [*sic*.] sobre o conteudo nelle" [1673], in Acácio Fernando de Sousa, "Do Japão a Macau: O Comércio em Tempo de Proibições", *Revista de Cultura*, n. 17, October–December 1993, pp. 38–39.

A Abelha da China. 1822–1823. Edição do Exemplar Original do Instituto da Biblioteca Nacional e do Livro, Centro de Publicações da Universidade de Macau-Fundação Macau, Macau, 1994.

Arquivo das Colónias: Publicação Oficial Trimestral, vol. 5, nn. 25–27, 33–38, Imprensa Nacional, Lisbon, 1922–1931.

Arquivos de Macau, Arquivo Histórico de Macau—Imprensa Nacional, Macau: 1st series, vol. 1; 3rd series, vols. 1, 3, 4, 6–10, 14–19; 4th series, vol. 8:1.

Biker, Júlio Firmino (ed.), *Colecção de Tratados e Concertos de Pazes que o Estado da Índia Portugesa Fez com os Reis e Senhores com quem Teve Relações nas Partes da Ásia e África Oriental desde o Princípio da Conquista até ao Fim do Século XVIII*, vols. 1, 2, 3, facsimile edition, Asian Educational Services, Madras, 1995 [1881].

Bocarro, António, *Década 13 da História da Índia Composta por António Bocarro Cronista daquele Estado*, introduction and notes by Bulhão Pato, edited by Rodrigo José da Lima Felner, Tipografia da Academia Real das Ciências de Lisboa, Lisbon, 1876 [*c*.1635].

Castro, José Ferreira Borges de (org.), *Colecção dos Tratados, Convenções, Contratos e Actos Públicos Celebrados ente a Coroa de Portugal e as Mais Potências desde 1640 até ao Presente*, 8 vols., Imprensa Nacional, Lisbon, 1856–1858.

Couto, Diogo de, *Cinco Livros da Decada Doze da Historia da India*, n.p., Paris, 1645 [1596–1600].

Dias, Alfredo Gomes, *Macau e a I Guerra do Ópio*, Instituto Português do Oriente, Macau, 1993.

Jin, Guoping and Wu Zhiliang (eds.), *Correspondência Oficial Trocada entre as Autoridades de Cantão e os Procuradores do Senado: Fundo das Chapas Sínicas em Português (1749–1847)*, 8 vols., Fundação Macau, Macau, 2000.

Lâm, Tcheong-Ü-e Ian-Kuong-Iâm, *Ou-Mun Kei-Leok: Monografia de Macau (Monograph of Macau)*, translation by Luís Gonzaga Gomes, Quinzena de Macau, Lisbon, 1979 [*c*.1751].

Laval, François Pyrard de, *Viagem de Francisco Pyrard de Laval*, translation by Joaquim H. da Cunha Rivara, revised and updated by Artur de Magalhães Basto, vol. 2, Livraria Civilização, Porto, 1944 [1611].

Linhares, Conde de, *Diário do 3.º Conde de Linhares, Vice-Rei da Índia*, 2 vols., Biblioteca Nacional, Lisbon, 1937–1943 [1631–1634].

Manrique, Frei Sebastião, *Itinerário de Sebastião Manrique*, 2 vols., introduction and notes by Luís Silveira, Agência Nacional das Colónias, Lisbon, 1946 [1649].

Matos, Artur Teodoro de (dir.), *Documentos Remetidos da Índia ou Livro das Monções (1625–1736)*, CNCDP, Lisbon, 2001.

Pissurlencar, Panduronga Sacarama Sinai (ed.), *Assentos do Conselho do Estado*, vols. 1–5, Tipografia Rangel, Goa, 1953–1957.

Rosário, Frei Álvaro, "Ataque dos Holandeses a Macau em 1622, Relação Inédita do P. Frei Álvaro do Rosário", published by Charles R. Boxer, *Boletim da Agência Geral das Colónias*, n. 38, 1928, pp. 17–30.

Saldanha, António Vasconcelos de and Jin Guoping (eds.), *Para a Vista do Imperador: Memoriais da Dinastia Qing. Sobre o Estabelecimento dos Portugueses em Macau (1808–1887)*, Instituto Português do Oriente, Macau, 2000.

Santarém, Visconde de (ed.), *Quadro Elementar das Relações Políticas e Diplomáticas de Portugal com as Diversas Potências do Mundo desde o Princípio da Monarquia Portuguesa até aos nossos Dias*, vols. 14–18, Tipografia da Academia Real das Ciências, Lisbon, 1858–1865.

Sarzedas, Conde de, *Diário do Conde de Sarzedas, Vice-Rei do Estado da Índia (1655–1656)*, edited by Artur Teodoro de Matos, Comissão Nacional para a Comemoração dos Descobrimentos Portugueses, Lisbon, 2001.

British and international sources

Anonymous, *A Voyage to the East Indies in 1747 and 1748*, Tully's Head, London, 1762.

——, *A List of Company's Covenant Servants, at Their Settlements, in the East Indies, and Island of St. Helena, and China*, East India Company, London, 1780, 1782, 1790, 1795.

Anderson, Aeneas, *A Narrative of the British Embassy to China, in the Years 1792, 1793, and 1794*, J. Debrett, London, 1795.

Askari, Syed Hasan (ed.), *Fort William-India House Correspondence and Other Contemporary Papers Relating Thereto (Foreign, Secret and Political)*, vol. 16: *1787–1791*, National Archives of India, Delhi, 1976.

Ball, B. L., *Rambles in Eastern Asia, Including China and Manilla, during Several Years' Residence. with Notes of the Voyage to China, Excursions in Manilla, Hong-Kong,*

Canton, Shangai, Ningpoo, Amoy, Fouchow, and Macao, 2nd edition, James French and Company, Boston, 1856.

Banerjee, I. B. (ed.), *Fort William-India House Correspondences and Other Contemporary Papers Relating Thereto*, vol. 11: *1789–92*, National Archives of India, Delhi, 1974.

Barrow, John, *Travels in China*, T. Cadell and W. Davis, London, 1806 [1804].

Bennet, George, *Wanderings in New South Wales, Batavia, Pedir Coast, Singapore, and China; Being the Journal of a Naturalist in those Countries, during 1832, 1833, and 1834*, 2 vols., Richard Bentley, London, 1834.

Birdwood, Sir George and William Foster (eds.), *The First Letter Book of the East India Company: 1600–1619*, Bernard Quaritich, London, 1893.

Campbell, John (ed.), *Navigantium atque Itinerantium Bibliotecha: or, a Compleat Collection of Voyages and Travels*, vol. 1, n.p., London, 1744.

Canton Register, 02–03-1830.

Careri, John Francis [Giovanni Francesco] Gemelli, *A Voyage Round the World in Six Parts*, anonymously translated from Italian, in *Collection of Voyages and Travels, Some Now First Printed from Original Manuscripts, Other Now First Published in English*, vol. 4, Thomas Osborne, London, 1752 [1726].

Cocks, Richard, *Diary of Richard Cocks: Cape-Merchant in the English Factory in Japan 1615–1622 with Correspondence*, introduction and notes by Edward Maunde Thompson, 2 vols., The Hakluyt Society, London, 1883 [1615–1622].

Davis, Sir John Francis, *The Chinese*, 2 vols., Charles Knight, London, 1836.

Entick, John, *A New Naval History: Or, Compleat View of the British Marine*, n.p., London, 1757.

Farrington, Anthony, *The English Factory in Japan, 1613–1623*, 2 vols., The British Library, London, 1991.

Forbes, Robert Bennet, *Letters from China: The Canton-Boston Correspondence of Robert Bennet Forbes, 1838–1840*, compiled by Phyllis Forbes Kerr, Mystic Seaport Museum, Mystic-Connecticut, 1996.

Foster, Sir William (ed.), *The English Factories in India: 1618–1669*, 13 vols., Clarendon Press, Oxford, 1906–1927.

Ghirardini, Gio, *Relation du Voyage Fait à la Chine sur le Vaisseau l'Amphitrite, en l'Année 1689*, Nicolas Pepie, Paris, 1700.

Gilbert, Thomas, *Voyage from New South Wales to Canton, in the Year 1788, with Views of the Islands Discovered*, George Stafford and J. Debrett, London, 1789.

Gupta, P. C. (ed.), *Fort William-India House Correspondence*, vol. 13: *1796–1800*, National Archives of India, Delhi, 1959.

Hakluyt, Richard, *Voyages in Eight Volumes*, introduction and notes by John Masefield, 8 vols., Dent, London, 1962 [1598–1600].

Hamilton, Alexander, *A New Account of the East Indies by Alexander Hamilton with Numerous Maps and Illustrations*, 2 vols., notes and introduction by Sir William Foster, The Argonaut Press, London, 1930 [1727].

Hanway, Jonas, *A Review of the Proposed Naturalization of the Jews*, n.p., London, 1753.

Hickey, William, *Memoirs of William Hickey (1749–1775)*, vol. 1, notes and introduction by Alfred Spencer, Hurst & Blackett, London, 1913.

Kingsford, C. L. (ed.), "The Taking of the *Madre de Dios*, anno 1592", in C. L. Laughton (ed.), *The Naval Miscellany II*, vol. 40, Navy Records Society, London, 1912, pp. 85–121.

Kinsman, Rebecca Chase, "Life in Macau in the 1840's: Letters of Rebecca Chase Kinsman to Her Family in Salem. From the Collection of Mrs. Rebecca Kinsman Munroe", *The Essex Institute Historical Collection*, selected by Mrs Frederick C. Munroe, vol. 86: January 1950, and October 1950, vol. 87: October 1951 [1843–1844], pp. 15–40, 311–330 and 388–409.

Lapérouse, Jean-François, *Voyage de Lapérouse autour du Monde pendant les Annéss 1785, 1786, 1787 et 1788*, Club des Libraires de France-Edito-Service, Geneva, 1970 [1791].

Ljungstedt, Anders, *An Historical Sketch of the Portuguese Settlement in China and of the Roman Catholic Church and Mission in China & Description of the City of Canton*, Viking Hong Kong Publications, Hong Kong, 1992 [1835].

Lockyer, Charles, *An Account of the Trade in India: Containing Rules for Good Government in Trade, Price Courants, and Tables*, Samuel Crouch, London, 1711.

Low, Harriett, *Lights and Shadows of a Macau Life: The Journal of Harriett Low, Travelling Spinster, Part One: 1829–1832/ Part Two: 1832–1834*, 2 vols., introduction, transcription and notes by Nan P. Hodges and Arthur W. Hummel, The History Bank, Woodinville, 2002.

Macartney, Lord, *An Embassy to China: Lord Macartney's Journal, 1793–1794*, Routledge, London, 2000.

Michie, Alexander, *The English Man in China during the Victorian Era as Illustrated by the Career of Sir Rutherford Alcock*, William Blackwood and Sons, London, 1900.

Morrison, Eliza (ed.), *Memoirs of the Life and Labours of Robert Morrison; Compiled by his Widow*, II, Longman, Orme, Brown, Green, and Longmans, London, 1839.

Mortimer, George [*Lieutenant of the Marines*], *Observations and Remarks Made during a Voyage to the Islands of Teneriffe, Amsterdam, Maria's Islands near Van Dieman's Land: Othaheite, Sandwich Islands; Owhyhee, the Fox Islands on the North West Coast of America, Tinian, and from Thence to Canton, in the Brig Mercury*, author's edition, London, 1791.

Mundy, Peter, *The Travels of Peter Mundy (1608–1667)*, edited by Sir Richard Carnac Temple and L. Anstey, 5 vols., Hakluyt Society, London, 1907–1936.

Paske-Smith, M., *Western Barbarians in Japan and Formosa in Tokugawa Days 1603–1868*, J. L. Thompson, Kobe, 1930.

Pratt, Peter (ed.), *History of Japan Compiled from the Records of the English East India Company*, 2 vols., edited by M. Paske-Smith, Curzon Press, London, 1972 [1882].

Purchas, Samuel, *Hakluytus Posthumus or Purchas His Pilgrimes*, 20 vols., James MacLehose, Glasgow, 1905 [1625].

Records of St. George: Despatches from England 1681–1747, 2 vols., Superintendent-Government Press, Madras, 1916–1931.

Records of St. George: Diary and Consultation Book of 1686–1713, 17 vols., Superintendent-Government Press, Madras, 1913–1929.

Records of St. George: Diary and Consultation Book of 1746, Superintendent-Government Press, Madras, 1931.

Records of St. George: Letters to Fort St. David 1748–49, vol. 3, Superintendent-Government Press, Madras, 1935.

Records of St. George: Letters to Fort St. George 1682–1763, 5 vols., Superintendent-Government Press, Madras, 1916–1943.

Records of St. George: Letters from Fort St. George for 1689, 1689, 1763, 3 vols., Superintendent-Government Press, Madras, 1916, 1953.

Records of St. George: Public Despatches to England 1719–1740, 5 vols., Superintendent-Government Press, Madras, 1929–1931.

Sainsbury, Ethel Bruce (ed.), *A Calendar of the Court Minutes etc. of the East India Company 1671–1673*, introduction and notes by W. T. Ottewill, Oxford at the Clarendon Press, London, 1932.

Sainsbury, Ethel Bruce and William Foster (eds.), *A Calendar of the Court Minutes etc. of the East India Company 1635–1670*, 7 vols., Oxford at the Clarendon Press, London, 1907–1929.

Sainsbury, W. Nöel (ed.), *Calendar of State Papers, Colonial Series, East Indies, China and Japan, 1513–1624*, 3 vols., Longman, London, 1862–1878.

———, *Calendar of State Papers, Colonial Series, East Indies, China and Persia, 1625–1629*, Longman-Trübner, London, 1884.

———, *Calendar of State Papers, Colonial Series, East Indies and Persia, 1630–1634*, Her Majesty's Stationery Office, London, 1892.

Saletore, B. A. (ed.), *Fort William-India House Correspondences and Other Contemporary Papers Relating Thereto*, vol. 9: *1782–85*, National Archives of India, Delhi, 1959.

Shaw, Samuel, *The Journals of Major Samuel Shaw, the First American Consul at Canton. With a Life of the Author*, introduction and notes by Josiah Quincy, Che'eng-wen Publishing Company, Taipei, 1968 [1784–1790].

Staunton, Sir George, *An Authentic Account of an Embassy from the King of Great Britain to the Emperor of China*, 2 vols., P. Wogan, R. Cross, P. Byrne, J. Rice, J. Haplin and N. Kelly, Dublin, 1798 [1796].

Sumarez, Philip, *Log of the Centurion Based on the Original Papers of Captain Philip Sumarez on Board HMS Centurion, Lord Anson's Flagship during his Circumnavigation 1740–44*, transcription and notes by Leo Heaps, Hart-Davis, MacGibbon, London, 1973.

Walter, Richard, *A Voyage Round the World in the Years MDCCXL, I, II, III, IV, by George Anson, Esq., Commander in Chief of a Squadron of His Majesty's Ships, Sent upon an Expedition to the South-Seas*, John and Paul Knapton, London, 1748.

Williams, Glyndwr (ed.), *Documents Relating to Anson's Voyage Round the World 1740–1744*, Navy Records Society, London, 1967.

——, *The Prize of All Oceans: The Triumph and Tragedy of Anson's Voyage Round the World*, Harper Collins, London, 1999.

Studies

Macau: Sino-Portuguese relations

Blussé, Leonard, "Brief Encounter at Macau", *Modern Asian Studies*, vol. 22, n. 3, 1988, pp. 647–664.

Boxer, Charles Ralph, *South China in the Sixteenth Century*, Hakluyt Society, London, 1953.

——, *Fidalgos no Extremo Oriente. 1550–1770*, Fundação Oriente-Museu and Centro de Estudos Marítimos de Macau, Macau-Lisbon, 1990.

——, *Macau na Época da Restauração/Macau Three Hundred Years Ago*, Fundação Oriente, Lisbon, 1993.

Cabral, João de Pina e Nelson Lourenço, *Em Terra de Tufões: Dinâmicas da Etnicidade Macaense*, Instituto Cultural de Macau, Macau, 1993.

Caldeira, Carlos José, *Macau em 1850: Crónica de Viagem*, preface by Susan J. Henders, Instituto de Ciências Sociais da Universidade de Lisboa-Quetzal Editores, Lisbon, 1999.

Coelho, Rogério Beltrão, *Casa Garden: The Casa Garden*, Fundação Oriente, Macau, 1991.

Collis, Maurice, *Foreign Mud: Being an Account of the Opium Imbroglio at Canton in the 1830's and the Anglo-Chinese War that Followed*, Faber and Faber, London, 1956.

Cranmer-Byng, J. L. (ed.), *Britain and the China Trade, 1635–1842*, selected by Patrick Tuck, vol. 8: *An Embassy to China: Lord Macartney's Journal, 1793–1794*, Routledge, London, 2000.

Dias, Alfredo Gomes, *Macau e a I Guerra do Ópio*, Instituto Português do Oriente, Macau, 1993.

———, *Sob o Signo da Transição: Macau no Século XIX*, Instituto Português do Oriente, Macau, 1998.

———, *Portugal, Macau e a Internacionalização da Questão do Ópio (1909–1925)*, Livros do Oriente, Macau, 2004.

Downs, Jacques M., *The Golden Ghetto: The American Commercial Community at Canton and the Shaping of American China Policy, 1784–1844*, Lahig University Press, Bethlehem, 1997.

Figueiredo, Fernando, "Os Vectores da Economia", in A. H. de Oliveira Marques (dir.), *História dos Portugueses no Extremo Oriente*, vol. 3: *Macau e Timor. Do Antigo Regime à República*, Fundação Oriente, Lisbon, 2001, pp. 95–296.

Flores, Jorge Manuel, "Macau e o Comércio da Baía de Canton (Séculos XVI e XVII)", in Artur Teodoro de Matos and Luís Filipe F. Reis Thomaz (dir.), *As Relações entre a Índia Portuguesa, a Ásia do Sueste e o Extremo Oriente: Actas do VI Seminário Internacional de História Indo-Portuguesa*, n.p., Macau-Lisbon, 1993, pp. 21–48.

———, "Macau: O Tempo da Euforia", in A. H. de Oliveira Marques (dir.), *História dos Portugueses no Extremo Oriente*, vol. 1, tomo 2: *De Macau à Periferia*, Fundação Oriente, Lisbon, 2000, pp. 179–213.

França, Bento da, *Subsídios para a História de Macau*, Imprensa Nacional, Lisbon, 1888.

Fu, Lo-Sho (ed.), *A Documentary Chronicle of Sino-Western Relations (1644–1820)*, 2 vols., The University of Arizona Press, Tucson, 1966.

Gomes, Artur Levy, *Esboço da História de Macau 1511–1849*, Tipografia Soi Sang, Macau, 1957.

Greenberg, Michael, *British Trade and the Opening of China 1800–42*, Cambridge University Press, London, 1951.

Guimarães, Ângela, "A Conjuntura Política: Antes de Hong Kong", in A. H. de Oliveira Marques (dir.), *História dos Portugueses no Extremo Oriente*, vol. 3: *Macau e Timor. Do Antigo Regime à República*, Fundação Oriente, Lisbon, 2000, pp. 13–33.

———, *Uma Relação Especial: Macau e as Relações Luso-Chinesas (1780–1844)*, Centro de Investigação e Estudos de Sociologia, Lisbon, 2000.

Hao, Yen-Ping, *The Comprador in Nineteenth Century China: Bridge between East and West*, Harvard University Press, Cambridge-Massachusetts, 1979.

Jesus, Montalto C. A., *Historic Macau*, Kelly & Walsh, Hong Kong, 1902 (republished 1926).

Lehan, Richard, *The City in Literature: An Intercultural and Cultural History*, University of California Press, Los Angeles, 1998.

Loureiro, Rui Manuel, "Camões em Macau. Um Mito Historiográfico", *Review of Culture*, n. 7, July 2003, pp. 108–125.

Manguin, Pierre-Yves, *Os Nguyen, Macau e Portugal: Aspectos Políticos e Comerciais de uma Relação Privilegiada no Mar da China (1773–1802)*, Comissão Territorial de Macau para a Comemoração dos Descobrimentos Portugueses, Macau, 1999.

Maria, Frei José de Jesus, *Ásia Sínica e Japónica*, 2 vols., preface and notes by Charles Ralph Boxer, Instituto Cultural de Macau-Centro de Estudos Marítimos de Macau, Macau, 1988.

Mesquita, Pedro Teixeira, "Ensino e Cultura", in A. H. de Oliveira Marques (dir.), *História dos Portugueses no Extremo Oriente*, vol. 3: *Macau e Timor. Do Antigo Regime à República*, Fundação Oriente, Lisbon, 2000, pp. 485–692.

Miranda, Susana Münch, "Os Circuitos Económicos", in A. H. de Oliveira Marques (dir.), *História dos Portugueses no Extremo Oriente*, vol. 2: *Macau e Timor. O Declínio do Império*, Fundação Oriente, Lisbon, 2001, pp. 261–288.

Múrias, Manuel (ed.), *Instrução para o Bispo de Pequim e outros Documentos para a História de Macau*, reedição fac-similada, Instituto Cultural de Macau, Macau, 1988.

Paddison, Ronan (ed.), *Handbook of Urban Studies*, Sage, London, 2001.

Pereira, António F. Marques, *As Alfândegas Chinesas de Macau*, Tipografia de José da Silva, Macau, 1870.

Pires, Benjamim Videira, S.J., "O "Foro do Chão" de Macau", *Boletim do Instituto Luís de Camões*, vol. 1, no. 4, March 1967, pp. 319–334.

Ptak, Roderich, "Early Sino-Portuguese Relations up to the Foundation of Macau", *Mare Liberum*, n. 4, December 1992, pp. 289–297.

———, "A China Meridional e o Comércio Marítimo no Este e no Sudeste da Ásia entre 1600 e 1750", *Povos e Culturas*, n. 5, 1996, pp. 199–217.

Puga, Rogério Miguel, "Macau na Poesia Inglesa: Sir John Francis Davis, Sir John Bowring, W. H. Auden, Gerald H. Jollie e Alexandre Pinheiro Torres", in Ana Maria Amaro and Dora Martins (coord.), *Estudos Sobre a ChinaVII*, vol. 2, Instituto Superior de Ciências Sociais e Políticas, Lisbon, 2005, pp. 847–882.

———, *s.v.* "Hunter, William C.", in Yuwu Song (ed.), *Encyclopedia of Chinese-American Relations*, McFarland & Company Publishers, Jefferson (North Carolina) and London, 2006, p. 142.

———, "O Primeiro Olhar Norte-Americano sobre Macau: Os Diários de Samuel Shaw (1754–1794)", in Ana Gabriela Macedo *et alii* (org.), *Intertextual Dialogues, Travel & Routes*, Actas do "*XXVI Encontro da APEAA 21 to 23 April 2005*, Universidade do Minho, Braga, 2007, pp. 227–251.

———, "A Vida e o Legado de Marta da Silva van Mierop", *Review of Culture*, n. 22, April 2007, pp. 40–51.

———, "Macau na Literatura Inglesa", *Review of Culture*, n. 24, October 2007, pp. 90–105.

———, "Macau in Samuel Purchas's *Hakuytus Posthumus, or Purchas His Pilgrimes* (1625)", *Review of Culture*, n. 28, October 2008, pp. 16–41.

Rego, Silva, *A Presença Portuguesa em Macau*, Agência Geral das Colónias, Lisbon, 1947.

Saldanha, António Vasconcelos de, *A "Memória sobre o Estabelecimento dos Portugueses em Macau" do Visconde de Santarém (1845): Os Primórdios da Discussão da Legitimidade da Presença dos Portugueses em Macau*, Instituto Português do Oriente, Macau, 1995.

Serafim, Cristina Seuanes, "Organização Política e Administrativa", in A. H. de Oliveira Marques (dir.), *História dos Portugueses no Extremo Oriente*, vol. 2: *Macau e Timor. O Declínio do Império*, Fundação Oriente, Lisbon, 2001, pp. 293–341.

Silva, António M. Pacheco Jorge da, *The Portuguese Community in Hong Kong*, Instituto Internacional de Macau, Macau, 2007.

Smith, Carl T., "Parsee Merchants in the Pearl River Delta", *Review of Culture*, n. 10, April 2004, pp. 36–49.

Smith, Carl T. and Paul A. Van Dyke, "Armenian Footprints in Macau", *Review of Culture*, n. 8, October 2003, pp. 20–39.

———, "Four Armenian Families", *Review of Culture*, n. 8, October 2003, pp. 40–50.

Sousa, Acácio Fernando de, "Do Japão a Macau: O Comércio em Tempos de Proibições", *Revista de Cultura*, 2nd series, no. 17, October–December 1993, pp. 35–39.

Sousa, George Bryan de, *A Sobrevivência do Império: Os Portugueses na China (1630–1754)*, translation by Luísa Arrais, Publicações Dom Quixote, Lisbon, 1991.

———, "Commerce and Capital: Portuguese Maritime Losses in the South China Sea, 1600–1754", in Artur Teodoro de Matos and Luís Filipe Thomaz (eds.), *As Relações entre a Índia Portuguesa, a Ásia do Sueste e o Extremo Oriente: Actas do VI Seminário Internacional de História Indo-Portuguesa*, n.p., Macau-Lisbon, 1993, pp. 321–348.

Teixeira, Padre Manuel, *Macau e a sua Diocese*, 16 vols., Imprensa Nacional, Macau, 1940–1961.

———, *Os Médicos em Macau*, Imprensa Nacional, Macau, 1967.

———, *Macau no Século XVIII*, Imprensa Nacional de Macau, Macau, 1984.

———, *A Gruta de Camões em Macau*, Fundação Macau-Instituto Internacional de Macau, Macau, 1999.

———, *Imprensa Periódica Portuguesa no Extremo Oriente*, Instituto Cultural de Macau, Macau, 1999.

Thampi, Madhavi, "Parsis in the China Trade", *Review of Culture*, n. 10, April 2004, pp. 16–25.

Vale, António M. Martins do, *Os Portugueses em Macau (1750–1800): Degredados, Ignorantes e Ambiciosos ou Fiéis Vassalos d'El Rei?*, Instituto Português do Oriente, Macau, 1997.

———, "Macau: Os Eventos Políticos. 2", in A. H. de Oliveira Marques (dir.), *História dos Portugueses no Extremo Oriente*, vol. 2: *Macau e Timor. O Declínio do Império*, Fundação Oriente, Lisbon, 2001, pp. 159–227.

Wills Jr., John E., "The Survival of Macau, 1640–1729", in Jorge M. dos Santos Alves (coord.), *Portugal e a China: Conferências do II Curso Livre de História das Relações entre Portugal e a China (séculos XVI–XIX)*, Fundação Oriente, Lisbon, 1999, pp. 111–124.

Wu, Zhiliang, *Segredos da Sobrevivência: História Política de Macau*, Associação de Educação de Adultos de Macau, Macau, 1999.

Japan: The Namban century (1543–1639) and the British factory at Hirado (1613–1623)

Costa, João Paulo Oliveira e, *Portugal and the Japan: The Namban Century*, Imprensa Nacional-Casa da Moeda, Lisbon, 1993.

———, "A Rivalidade Luso-Espanhola no Extremo Oriente e a Querela Missionológica no Japão", in Artur Teodoro de Matos and Roberto Carneiro (dir.), *O Século Cristão do Japão: Actas do Colóquio Internacional Comemorativo dos 450 Anos de Amizade Portugal-Japão (1543–1993)*, 1994, Mosteiro dos Jerónimos, Lisbon, pp. 477–524.

———, "O Cristianismo no Japão e o Episcopado de D. Luís Cerqueira", 2 vols., PhD Thesis, Universidade Nova de Lisboa, Lisbon, 1998.

———, "Japão", in A. H. de Oliveira Marques (dir.), *História dos Portugueses no Extremo Oriente*, vol. 1, tomb 2: *De Macau à Periferia*, Fundação Oriente, Lisbon, 2000, pp. 379–471.

Coutinho, Valdemar, *O Fim da Presença Portuguesa no Japão*, Sociedade Histórica da Independência de Portugal, Lisbon, 1999.

Massarella, Derek, *A World Elsewhere: Europe's Encounter with Japan in the Sixteenth and Seventeenth Centuries*, Yale University Press, London, 1990.

Milton, Giles, *Samurai William: The Adventurer Who Unlocked Japan*, Sceptre, London, 2003.

Paske-Smith, M., *Western Barbarians in Japan and Formosa in Tokugawa Days 1603–1868*, J. L. Thompson, Kobe, 1930.

Riess, Ludwig, "History of the English Factory at Hirado (1613–1622)", *Transactions of the Asiatic Society of Japan*, vol. 26, 1898, pp. 1–114.

British expansion, the East India Company, Anglo-Portuguese relations in the Far East and the founding of Hong Kong

AA. VV., *Views of the Pearl River Delta: Macau, Canton and Hong Kong: Catalogue of Exhibition Presented at the Hong Kong Museum of Art (November 1996–February 1997) and the Peabody Essex Museum (June–September 1997)*, Urban Council of Hong Kong, Hong Kong, 1996.

———, *Picturing Cathay: Maritime and Cultural Images of the China Trade*, University Museum and Art Gallery—The University of Hong Kong, Hong Kong, 2003.

Abreu, António Graça de, "O Insucesso de Macartney e os Padres Portugueses", *Macau*, 2nd series, n. 67, November 1997, pp. 124–131.

Andrade, Gomes Freire d', *A Dominação Inglesa em Portugal: O que É e de que nos Tem Servido a Aliança da Inglaterra*, João António Rodrigues Fernandes, Lisbon, 1883.

Andrade, José Inácio de, *Memória dos Feitos Macaenses Contra as Piratarias da China e da Entrada Violenta dos Ingleses na Cidade de Macau*, Tipografia Lisbonense, Lisbon, 1835.

Bassett, D. K., "Early English Trade and Settlement in Asia, 1602–1690", in Anthony Disney (ed.), *An Expanding World*, vol. 4: *Historiography of Europeans in Africa and Asia, 1450–1800*, Variorum-Ashgate, Aldershot, 1995, pp. 128–153.

———, "The Trade of the English East India Company in the Far East, 1623–84", in Om Prakash (ed.), *An Expanding World—The European Impact on World Economy 1450–1800*, vol. 10: *European Commercial Expansion in Early Modern Asia*, Variorum-Ashgate, Aldershot, 1997, pp. 208–236 [article originally published in *Journal of the Royal Asiatic Society*, vol. 104, 1960, pp. 32–47 and 145–157].

Blussé, Leonard and Femme Gaastra (eds.), *Companies and Trade: Essays on Overseas Trading Companies during the Ancien Régime*, Leiden University Press, Leiden, 1981.

Bolton, Kingsley, *Chinese Englishes: A Sociolinguistic History*, Cambridge University Press, Cambridge, 2003.

Boxer, Charles Ralph, "Vicissitudes das Relações Anglo-Portuguesas no Século XVII", in AA. VV., *600 Anos de Aliança Anglo-Portuguesa: 600 Years of Anglo-Portuguese Alliance*, Her Majesty's Government-British Broadcasting Corporation, London, n.d., pp. 26–30.

Braga, José Maria, *Hong Kong and Macau*, Notícias de Macau, Hong Kong, 1951.

———, "A Seller of 'Sing-Songs': A Chapter in the Foreign Trade of China and Macau", *Journal of Oriental Studies*, vol. 6, n. 1–2, 1961–1964, pp. 61–108.

Bruce, John, *Annals of the Honorable East-India Company, from Their Establishment by the Charter of Queen Elizabeth 1600, to the Union of the London and English East-India Companies, 1707–8*, 3 vols., Black, Parry, and Kingsbury, London, 1810.

Caledonian Mercury, n. 12312, 21–08–1800.

Cameron, Nigel, *Barbarians and Mandarins: Thirteen Centuries of Western Travellers in China*, Oxford University Press, Oxford, 1993.

Carvalho, Joaquim Martins de, *A Nossa Aliada!*, Tipografia de António Henriques Morgado, Porto, 1883.

Ch'en, Anthony Kuo-tung, The *Insolvency of the Chinese Hong Merchants, 1760–1834*, Academia Sinica, Taipei, 1990.

Cheong, Wen Eang, *Mandarins and Merchants: Jardine Matheson & Co., A China Agency of the Early Nineteenth Century*, Curzon Press, London, 1978.

———, *The Hong Merchants of Canton: Chinese Merchants in Sino-Western Trade*, Curzon Press, Richmond, 1997.

Conner, Patrick, *The China Trade 1600–1860*, The Royal Pavilion, Art Gallery and Museum, Brighton, 1986.

———, *George Chinnery 1774–1852: Artist of India and the China Coast*, Antique Collectors' Club, Woodbridge, 1992.

Cordier, Henri, *Histoire Générale de la Chine et des ses Relations avec les Pays Étrangers depuis les plus Anciens jusqu'à la Chine de la Dynastie Mandchoque*, 2 vols., Librairie Paul Genthner, Paris, 1920.

Cranmer-Byng, J. L., "Lord Macartney's Embassy to Peking in 1793. From Official Chinese Documents", *Journal of Oriental Studies*, vol. 4, nn. 1–2, 1957–1958, pp. 117–187.

———, "The First English Sinologists: Sir George Staunton and the Reverend Robert Morrison", in F. S. Drake (ed.), *Symposium on Historical, Archaeological and Linguistic Studies on Southern China, South-East Asia and the Hong Kong Region*, Hong Kong University Press, Hong Kong, 1967, pp. 247–260.

———, "Introduction", in *Britain and China Trade 1635–184*, vol. 8: *Lord Macartney, An Embassy to China: Lord Macartney's Journal, 1793–1794*, Routledge, London, 2000, pp. 1–17.

Crone, G. R., *The Discovery of the East*, Hamish Hamilton, London, 1972.

Crossman, Carl, *The Decorative Arts of the China Trade*: *Paintings, Furniture and Exotic Curiosities*, Antique Collector's Club, Woodbridge, 1997.

Deyan, Guo, "The Study of Parsee Merchants in Canton, Hong Kong and Macau", *Review of Culture*, n. 8, pp. 51–69.

Disney, A. R., *Twilight of the Pepper Empire: Portuguese Trade in Southwest India in the Early Seventeenth Century*, Harvard University Press, Cambridge-Massachusetts, 1978.

Duffy, Michael, "World-Wide War and British Expansion, 1793–1815", in P. J. Marshall (ed.), *The Oxford History of the British Empire*, vol. 2: *The Eighteenth Century*, Oxford University Press, Oxford, 2001, pp. 184–207.

Dyke, Paul A. Van, *The Canton Trade: Life and Enterprise on the China Coast, 1700–1845*, Hong Kong University Press, Hong Kong, 2005.

Eames, James Bromley, *The English in China Being an Account of the Intercourse and Relations between England and China from the Year 1600 to the Year 1843 and a Summary of Later Developments*, Curzon Press, London, 1974.

Eitel, E. J., *Europe in China: The History of Hong Kong from the Beginning to the Year 1882*, Luzac & Company, London, 1895.

Ernesto, Adriano José, "A Cessão de Bombaim à Inglaterra", BA Dissertation, University of Lisbon, Lisbon, 1952.

Eyles, D., "The Abolition of the East India Company's Monopoly 1833", PhD Thesis, University of Edinburgh, Edinburgh, 1955.

Farrington, Anthony, *East India Company Ships, 1600–1833: Based on a Catalogue of the East India Company Ships' Journals and Logs 1600–1834*, The British Library, London, 1999.

Ferreira, Patrícia Drumond Borges, *As Relações Luso-Britânicas na China Meridional (Século XVII)*, Centro de Estudos de História do Atlântico-Secretaria Regional do Turismo e Cultura, Funchal, 2002.

Foster, Sir William, The *English Factories in India: 1634–1636*, Clarendon Press, Oxford, 1911.

———, *England's Quest for Eastern Trade*, A & C Black, London, 1933.

Gaastra, Femme S., "War, Competition and Collaboration: Relations between the English and Dutch East India Company in the Seventeenth and Eighteenth Centuries", in H. V. Bowen *et al.* (eds.), *The Worlds of the East India Company*, The Boydell Press-National Maritime Museum–University of Leicester, Suffolk, 2004, pp. 50–68.

Harlow, Vincent T., *The Founding of the Second British Empire 1763–1793*, 2 vols., Longman, London, 1952–1964.

Howard, Paul Wilson, "Opium Suppression in Qing China: Responses to a Social Problem, 1729–1906", PhD Thesis, University of Pennsylvania, Philadelphia, 1998.

Hsia, Adrian (ed.), *The Vision of China in the English Literature of the Seventeenth and Eighteenth Centuries*, The Chinese University Press, Hong Kong, 1998.

Janin, Hunt, *The India-China Opium Trade in the Nineteenth Century*, McFarland & Company, Jefferson, 1999.

Keay, John, *The Honourable Company: A History of the English East India Company*, Harper Collins, London, 1993.

———, *Lost Post: The End of the Empire in the Far East*, John Murray, London, 1997.

Kilpatrick, Jane, *Gifts from the Gardens of China*, Frances Lincoln, London, 2007.

Lach, Donald, *Asia in the Making of Europe*, vol. 1, Chicago University Press, Chicago, 1994.

Lawson, Philip, *The East India Company: A History*, Longman, London, 1998.

Loyd, Christopher, "Introduction", in Philip Sumarez, *Log of the Centurion. Based on the Original Papers of Captain Philip Saumarez on Board HMS Centurion, Lord Anson's Flagship during His Circumnavigation 1740–1744*, Hart-Davis/MacGibbon, London, 1973, pp. 10–13.

Madrolle, Claudius, *Les Premiers Voyages Français à la Chine. La Compagnie de Chine (1698–1719)*, Augustin Challamel, Paris, 1901.

Manning, Catherine, *Fortunes a Faire: The French in Asian Trade, 1719–48*, Variorum-Ashgate, Aldershot, 1996.

Marshall, P. J. (ed.), "Britain and China in the Late Eighteenth Century", in Robert A. Bickers (ed.), *Ritual & Diplomacy: The Macartney Mission to China (1792–1794): Papers Presented at the 1992 Conference of the British Association for Chinese Studies Marking the Bicentenary of the Macartney Mission to China*, Wellsweep-British Association for Chinese Studies, London, 1993, pp. 11–29.

———, "Private British Trade in the Indian Ocean before 1800", in Om Prakash (ed.), *An Expanding World—The European Impact on World Economy 1450–1800*, vol. 10: *European Commercial Expansion in Early Modern Asia*, Variorum-Ashgate, Aldershot, 1997, pp. 237–262.

———, "The English in Asia to 1700", in P. J. Marshall (ed.), *The Oxford History of the British Empire*, vol. 2: *The Eighteenth Century*, Oxford University Press, Oxford, 2001, pp. 264–285.

Mathew, K. M., "The Dutch Threat and the Security of the Carreira in India Waters 1595–1664", in Artur Teodoro de Matos and Luís Filipe Thomaz (dir.), *A Carreira da Índia e as Rotas dos Estreitos: Actas do VIII Seminário Internacional de História Indo-Portuguesa*, n.p., Angra do Heroísmo, 1998, pp. 779–783.

Milburn, William, *Oriental Commerce*, 2 vols., Black, Parry, London, 1813.

Morse, Hosea Ballou, *The International Relations of the Chinese Empire*, vol. 1: *The Period of the Conflict 1834–1869*, Longmans, Green, London, 1910.

———, *The Chronicles of the East India Company Trading to China 1635–1834*, vols. 1–4, Clarendon Press, Oxford, 1926.

Owen, David Edward, *British Opium Policy in China and India*, Yale University Press, New Haven, 1934.

Parkinson, Cyril Northcote, *War in the Eastern Seas, 1793–1815*, George Allen & Unwin, London, 1954.

Parry, J. H., *Trade & Dominion: The European Overseas Empires in the Eighteenth Century*, Phoenix Press, London, 2000.

Peyrefitte, Alain, *Un Choc de Cultures. La Vision des Chinois*, Fayard, Paris, 1991.

———, *O Império Imóvel*, Gradiva, Lisbon, 1995.

Prestage, Edgar, *The Diplomatic Relations of Portugal with France, England, and Holland from 1640 to 1668*, Voss & Michael, Watford, 1925.

———, "The Anglo-Portuguese Alliance", *Transactions of the Historical Society*, 4th series, vol. 17, 1934, pp. 69–100.

Pritchard, Earl H., *Anglo-Chinese Relations during the Seventeenth and Eighteenth Centuries*, published in *University of Illinois Studies in the Social Sciences*, vol. 17, nn. 1–2, March–June 1929, University of Illinois, Urbana, 1929.

——, *Britain and the China Trade 1635–1842*, vol. 6: *The Crucial Years of Early Relations: 1750–1800*, Routledge, London, 2000.

Puga, Rogério Miguel, "Images and Representations of Japan and Macau in Peter Mundy's *Travels* (1637)", *Bulletin of Portuguese/Japanese Studies*, vol. 1, December 2000, pp. 97–109.

——, "A Dimensão da Alteridade em *The Travels* de Peter Mundy (1637): Contribuição para o Estudo das Relações Anglo-Portuguesas no Extremo Oriente", *Review of Culture*, n. 3, July 2002, pp. 136–152.

——, "The 'Lusiads' at Sea and the Spaniards at War in Elizabethan Drama: Shakespeare and the Portuguese Discoveries", in Holger Klein and José Manuel González (eds.), *Shakespeare Yearbook*, vol. 13: *Shakespeare and Spain*, The Edwin Mellen Press, Lewiston, Queenston and Lampeter, 2002, pp. 90–114.

——, "The Presence of the 'Portugals' in Macau and Japan in Richard Hakluyt's *Navigations*", *Bulletin of Portuguese/Japanese Studies*, vol. 5, December 2002, pp. 81–115.

——, "Os Descobrimentos Portugueses em *The Principal Navigations* de Richard Hakluyt", *Anais de História de Além Mar*, n. 3, 2003, pp. 63–131.

——, "Macau enquanto Cronótopo Exótico na Literatura Inglesa", in *Actas do I Congresso de Estudos Anglo-Portugueses*, Centro de Estudos Anglo-Portugueses-Universidade Nova de Lisboa, 2001, pp. 705–723 (also published in Chinese: *Revista de Administração Pública de Macau*, vol. 16, n. 59, March 2003, pp. 117–139).

——, "Chinese Pidgin English as a Narrative Strategy in Austin Coates' *City of Broken Promises* (1967) and Timothy Mo's *An Insular Possession* (1986)", *BELL: Belgian Journal of English Language and Literatures*, n. 2, 2004, pp. 103–112.

——, "'A gem of a place': Macau após a Guerra do Ópio: O Diário de Rebecca Chase Kinsman", in Ana Maria Amaro *et al.* (coord.), *Estudos Sobre a China VI*, vol. 2, Centro de Estudos Chineses-Instituto Superior de Ciências Sociais e Políticas, Lisbon, 2004, pp. 903–955.

——, "'Scramble for Africa': As Viagens Inglesas à África Ocidental no Reinado de D. João III", in Roberto Carneiro and Artur Teodoro de Matos (ed.), *D. João III e o Império: Actas do Congresso Internacional Comemorativo do seu Nascimento*, Centro de História de Além-Mar, Universidade Nova/Centro de Estudos dos Povos e Culturas de Expressão Portuguesa da Universidade Católica, Lisbon, 2004, pp. 717–752.

——, "A Convenção de Goa (1635) e a Primeira Viagem (Luso-)inglesa a Macau", *Revista de Estudos Anglo-Portugueses*, n. 14, 2005, pp. 71–108.

——, "As Primeiras Viagens Inglesas a Macau (1635–1699)", *Anais de História de Além-Mar*, n. 6, 2005, pp. 159–214.

——, "Macau e o *China Trade*: O Estabelecimento Regular da East India Company na China", *DAXIYANGGUO: Revista Portuguesa de Estudos Asiáticos*, n. 8, 2005, pp. 127–154.

——, *s.v.* "Hunter, William C.", in Yuwu Song (ed.), *Encyclopedia of Chinese-American Relations*, McFarland & Company Publishers, Jefferson (North Carolina) and London, 2006, p. 142.

——, "The Image of Macau in Tudor England: Richard's Hakluyt's *Navigations* (1589–1600)", *Journal of Sino-Western Cultural Studies*, vol. 2, n. 12, December 2006, pp. 18–32.

——, "Macau na Literatura Inglesa", *Review of Culture*, n. 24, October 2007, pp. 90–105.

——, "Macau nos Anos (18)30: O Diário de Caroline Hyde Butler Laing (1837)", *Revista Portuguesa de Estudos Chineses (Zhongguo Yanjiu)*, vol. 1:2, 2007, pp. 71–112.

——, "O Primeiro Olhar Norte-Americano sobre Macau: Os Diários de Samuel Shaw (1754–1794)", in Ana Gabriela Macedo et alii (org.), *Intertextual Dialogues, Travel & Routes*", *Actas do "XXVI Encontro da APEAA 21 to 23 April 2005*, University of Minho, Braga, 2007, pp. 227–251.

——, "*City of Broken Promises* enquanto Romance Histórico", *Review of Culture*, n. 25, 2008, pp. 62–80.

——, "Macau in Samuel Purchas' *Hakluytus Posthumus, or Purchas His Pilgrimes* (1625)", *Review of Culture*, n. 28, October 2008, pp. 16–41.

——, "O Início do Comércio na China da East India Company e as Relações Anglo-Sino-Portuguesas em Macau na Primeira Metade do Século XVIII", *Revista de Estudos Anglo-Portugueses*, n. 17, 2008, pp. 35–69.

——, "A Importância de Macau para o Comércio da East India Company na China e as Relações Anglo-Portuguesas no Enclave na Segunda Metade do Século XVIII", *Review of Culture*, n. 30, April 2009, pp. 6–7.

——, "The First Museum in China: The British Museum of Macao (1829–1834) and its Contribution to Nineteenth-Century British Natural Science", *Journal of the Royal Asiatic Society*, series 3, vol. 22, nn. 3–4, 2012, pp. 1–12.

Rego, A. da Silva, "Os Ingleses em Goa. 1799–1813", *Estudos Políticos e Sociais*, vol. 3, n. 1, 1965, pp. 23–48.

Santarém, Visconde de, *Quadro Elementar das Relações Políticas e Diplomáticas de Portugal com as Diversas Potências do Mundo desde o Princípio da Monarquia Portuguesa até aos nossos Dias*, vols. 14–18, Tipografia da Academia Real das Ciências, Lisbon, 1858–1865.

Sargent, A. J., *Anglo-Chinese Commerce and Diplomacy (Mainly in the Nineteenth Century)*, Clarendon Press, London, 1907.

Sawers, Larry, "The Navigation Acts Revisited", *Economic History Review*, 2nd series, vol. 40, 1992, pp. 262–284.

Scammell, G. V., "England, Portugal and the *Estado da Índia c.*1500–1635", *Modern Asian Studies*, vol. 16, part 2, April 1982, pp. 177–192.

Singer, Aubrey, *The Lion and the Dragon: Lord Macartney's Embassy to the Emperor Quian Long, 1792–94*, Barrie & Jenkins, London, 1992.

Sirr, Henry Charles, *China and the Chinese*, vol. 1, Wm. S. Orr, London, 1849.

Somerville, Boyle, *Commodore Anson's Voyage into the South Seas and around the World*, William Heinemann, London, 1934.

Soothill, W. E., *China and England*, Oxford University Press, London, 1928.

Stifler, Susan Reed, "The Language Students of the East India Company Canton Factory", *Journal of the North China Branch of the Royal Asiatic Society*, vol. 69, 1938, pp. 46–82.

Stone, Lawrence (ed.), *An Imperial State at War: Britain from 1689 to 1815*, Routledge, London, 1993.

Trewman's Exeter Flying Post, n. 1923, 21-08-1800.

Tuck, Patrick, "Introduction: Sir George Thomas Staunton and the Failure of the Amherst Embassy of 1816", in Patrick Tuck (ed.), *Britain and the China Trade 1635–1842*, vol. 10: *Sir George Thomas Staunton. Notes of Proceedings and Occurrences during the British Embassy to Pekin in 1816: George Thomas Staunton*, Routledge, London, 2000, pp. vii–xlii.

Vink, Marcus P. M., "The *Entente Cordiale*: The Dutch East India Company and the Portuguese Shipping through the Straits of Malacca, 1641–1663", *Revista de Cultura*, year 5, vol. 1, nn. 13–14, January–June 1991, pp. 289–309.

White, Ann Bolbach, "The Hong Merchants of Canton", Doctoral Thesis in History, University of Pennsylvania, Philadelphia, 1967.

Wild, Anthony, *The East India Company: Trade and Conquest from 1600*, Harper Collins, London, 2000.

Wiltshire, Trea, *Encounters with Asia: Merchants, Missionaries and Mandarins*, FormAsia, Hong Kong, 1995.

Wright, Rev. G. N., *China Illustrated. Its Scenery, Architecture, Social Habits, & c. Drawn from Original and Authentic Sketches, by Thomas Allom*, 4 vols., Fisher, London, 1845.

Zhang, Shunhong, "British Views on China during the Time of the Embassies of Lord Macartney and Lord Amherst (1790–1820)", PhD Thesis, University of London, London, 1990.

Portuguese history

Blanco, Maria Manuela Sobral, "O Estado Português da Índia: Da Rendição de Ormuz à Perda de Cochim (1622–1663)", vol. 1, PhD Thesis, University of Lisbon, Lisbon, 1992.

Brasão, Eduardo, *A Diplomacia Portuguesa nos Séculos XVII e XVIII*, 2 vols., Resistência, Lisbon, 1979–1980.

Coelho, Maria Teresa Pinto, *Apocalipse e Regeneração. O Ultimatum e a Mitologia da Pátria na Literatura Finissecular*, Lisboa, Cosmos, 1996.

Danvers, Frederick Charles, *The Portuguese in India: Being a History of the Rise and Decline of Their Eastern Empire*, 2 vols., Frank Cass, London, 1966.

Godinho, Vitorino Magalhães, *Ensaios sobre História de Portugal II*, Livraria Sá da Costa, Lisbon, 1978.

Gonçalves, Luís da Cunha, "A Restauração de 1640 no Oriente", *Boletim da Segunda Classe da Academia das Ciências*, vol. 9, 1915, pp. 396–404.

Marques, A. H. de Oliveira, *História de Portugal*, 2 vols., Editorial Presença, Lisbon, 1997.

Nobre, Pedro, "A Entrega de Bombaim à Grã-Bretanha e as suas Consequências Políticas e Sociais no Estado da Índia (1661–1668)", Master's Degree Thesis, FCSH-New University of Lisbon, Lisbon, 2008.

Serrão, Joaquim Veríssimo, *História de Portugal*, vols. 4–6, Editorial Verbo, Lisbon, 1996–2000.

Index